THE BEST OF
RACING POST

Edited by
JOHN LOVESEY
Designed by
NEIL RANDON
Copy: **Sadie Evans, Michael Church**
Systems: **Ian Gray, Alan White**
Production: **Tim Beeke**
Picture research: **Sue Connolly, Orla McGeough**

THE BEST OF
RACING POST

First published in Great Britain by
H. F. & G. Witherby Ltd,
14 Henrietta Street, London WC2E 8QJ

This compilation © Racing Post 1992

A CIP catalogue record for this book is
available from the British Library

ISBN 0-85493-222-4

Photoset in Great Britain by
Racing Post

Printed and bound in Great Britain by
Butler and Tanner Ltd, Frome, Somerset

CONTENTS

INTRODUCTION

by BROUGH SCOTT

FOR me it's been like going into the dug-out. It was January 1988 that I took up the pompous-sounding title of editorial director at *Racing Post* with a view to establishing a new rhythm within the paper. What a team they have been. Here's some of the best stuff they have played.

Of course most of our output is missing and unrepeatable – but not for the usual reasons! At the absolute heart of a daily racing paper is the service of cards and form and statistics and analysis which by its very nature is over, win or lose, once the day has past. Such ultra-professional *Racing Post* purists as Adrian Cook and Graham Dench would be horrified if I stooped to the word 'tip', but you get the gist.

The squad that Graham Rock with Francis Kelly assembled put the whole process of making selections on to a different plane. "I am going to make him famous," said Graham, our founding editor, of Adrian Cook, and 'Diomed' has made the prophecy come true. Not just with individual hits like Tony Bin's 25-1 Arc triumph in 1988 but the runaway win in the 1991 National Press Challenge based on selections on every race every day. That's tipping for grown-ups.

But the idea has been to give reasons, provide facts and above all search for value. Emily Weber went through the Brighton card at 6,210-1. Andrew Barr landed a £11,243.50 perm on the Sandown jackpot. Derek McGovern's Sports Betting team had a sickeningly good run in '91 tipping Michael Stich at 40-1 for Wimbledon and Ian Baker-Finch at 50-1 for the Open golf championship, whilst Mike Palmer's greyhound experts kept up their well-won reputation by going for outsider Ballinderry Ash against the favourite in the 1991 Derby Final.

That's the sort of 'feel good' factor that we all need to make up for the 70 per cent or more of the time when the wretched beasts or humans don't run to tune. But just because of that statistic it is essential that a racing paper be judged on its overall service as much as for its selection box. That's why we are so proud of the 'Pricewise' grid we show for all big races, and that's why I am so thrilled with the writing that makes up this book.

In the end it's all we could keep for you. The rest, all those acres of lists and charts and tables and reports and results, have to pack out the massive red-backed volumes that contain every paper we have ever published. What's in this book is a pot-pourri of the ideas and designs and pictures and profiles that we feel live on beyond the daily page.

My abiding belief has been that racing's central dynamic is its ability to appeal across the spectrum, and that a racing paper should reflect this. You have to be academic as well as anecdotal, earthy as well as ethereal, and before anyone starts suggesting we are getting a bit fancy for a 'betting rag', let's say why the hell not? Why shouldn't a racing and betting paper be written and presented to a style and to a standard that any publication would envy?

Looking out from that original dug-out on to a team that had struggled gallantly to overcome the usual problems of an over-hasty start-up 18 months earlier, it was obvious I needed a couple of allies and one or two signings to get us to play some football. Michael Harris, an award-winner at *Pacemaker*, was already on his way to the editor's chair. We then lured John Lovesey across from *The Sunday Times* to help us take stock, whilst the galloping pens of John Oaksey and Marcus Armytage were brought in to add a touch of horsiness to the mix.

But as we settled in, it became more and more obvious how blessed we were with the players already in position. The best testament to that is how the few who have moved have invariably gone to much larger, more lucrative operations. Colin Mackenzie went to the *Daily Mail*, Jim McGrath to the *Telegraph*, Martin Trew to the *Daily Express*, Ron Cox to the *Guardian*, Lawrence Wadey to unmentionable millions in Hong Kong.

And of course there was Paul Hayward, promoted from junior data shoveller to chief reporter in 18 months, only to be swiftly head-hunted to set the world alight for *The Independent*.

Paul is in these pages but so too is as richly diverse a set of writers ever corralled into a racing team. The astonishing scholarship of Tony Morris, the odd-ball shock waves of John McCririck, the saddle-room perceptions of Tom O'Ryan, the tireless solidity of Tim Richards, the wide-ranging wisdom of Howard Wright, and through it all the maverick, multi-faceted genius of the inimitable Paul Haigh.

There are many others. Old colleagues like Norman Harris and the late Roger Mortimer whose cryptic wit no doubt plays hell with all those prigs in heaven. New specialists like Sue Montgomery, young tyros like Richard Griffiths, chameleon-like entertainers like Henry Kelly, all of them united in their fascination with the many-sided, magnficent absurdity of the racing and betting games.

These pieces are reprinted as written with only occasional amendments for space reasons. They carry their date at the end but we do not believe they have dated. They are a subjective, reflective mix of some of the enthusiasms of the past five years.

If this book works it should be like a prism. You should be able to pick it up and from any angle it should surprise you with the light and shimmer coming through.

In that way it should be like the best of racing. Like *The Best of Racing Post.*

Raynes Park, June 1992

THE HERO

Racing's heroes do not always fit a classic mould. One person's hero is, after all, often another's anathema. Apart from the horses, jockeys and trainers many others are heroes too; the stable staff, for example, fulfilling gruelling early-morning roles. Moreover, television today helps create heroes quite unexpectedly and instantaneously. Whereas once a place in the hearts of thousands was won perhaps slowly, today millions can warm to a new figure in a twinkling. Notwithstanding, the quintessential hero remains unchanged. Racing was created for heroes. It was always so

In 1989 at Wincanton, when Desert Orchid made a winning seasonal debut a new word appeared in racing's lexicon – 'Dessiemania'. For the racegoers, his win hardly mattered; they were already enslaved.

Lester returns with the old magic

In October 1990 a fairy-tale was enacted in racing. Lester Piggott, at 54, made a sensational return as a professional jockey. His first outing was at Leicester

by TIM RICHARDS

GREAT to be back. And great to have him back. Lester Piggott was mobbed on his return to the saddle at Leicester yesterday when the old magic only just failed to make it a winning comeback.

Racegoers, fans and autograph-hunters followed their legendary pale-faced idol's every stride on every occasion he stepped out of the weighing room. He was swamped in a sea of photographers the moment he set foot on the racecourse. To Lester, who retired five years ago and will be 55 in three weeks' time, it was like a homecoming. He loved it all.

After failing by a short head on Lupescu, his comeback ride in the first, Piggott stood surrounded by a mass of media men in the winner's enclosure. He summed up his feelings when he said: "It's great to see you all."

He had come back a winner even though his three mounts failed to produce the goods. Lupescu went under a short head to the Gary Carter-ridden Sumonda in the first. Balasani was seventh to Gilt Preference, and Patricia beat only four home. Now Piggott and his legion of followers head for Chepstow today, where his four mounts are Ruddy Cheek, Nicholas, Shining Jewel and Lost City.

He admitted of his narrow defeat in the first: "I'd love to have won and I thought for a second I was going to. Gary came to beat me and then I nearly got back at him. It was great to get so close; I was frightened I might be last."

Piggott, his hair slightly greyer than when he hung up his saddle at Nottingham in 1985, looked drawn and it was hardly surprising when he admitted: "I can do 8st 5lb. I just missed my lunch yesterday. I'm pretty fit, though I'm bound to need a race or two to get race-fit."

When asked if his technique had changed due to his five-year absence Piggott, who has ridden more than 5,200 winners world-wide, said: "I haven't changed it. It's always there."

Piggott's mount Lupescu bumped Sumonda and wandered about due to greenness and Piggott had to make an early visit to the stewards' room to explain what happened. Before the inquiry Lord Gainsborough, senior steward at the meeting, shook Piggott's hand and welcomed him back on such an historic occasion.

Piggott was back on his patch and no-one enjoyed it more than the man himself. As he walked into the course in dark glasses, tweed jacket, grey trousers, a mackintosh on his arm and carrying a white plastic bag he became centre stage again.

Photographers surrounded him all the way to the weighing room, only to find to their surprise they were barred from entry.

Leicester's racecourse manager David Henson, who reckons Piggott put 1,000 on the gate making the attendance around 3,000, said: "From where Lester was sitting on the scales they looked like a bunch of monkeys outside as they scrambled to get their cameras against the glass to snap Lester."

Piggott arrived on the course at 1.15 and at 1.50 the police were called to the weighing room. When Piggott emerged he was flanked by a policeman and a policewoman. But still racegoers reached out to slap him on the back and cheer him to the parade ring. Piggott smiled all the way.

Even when they knew he had just been beaten as he returned on Lupescu, they refused to believe it. One punter roared: "You're still the champion of the world. You're back." Another said: "I just wanted Lester to go out there and prove he could do it. I knew he wouldn't let us down. He's come back to prove his point, and done just that. It was great. He's the main man."

Piggott received a bigger cheer than Gary Carter on Geoff Wragg-trained Sumonda, the odds-on winner. Carter, 29 years Piggott's junior, spoiled the Long Fellow's 'homecoming' and said: "When you're in a photo it doesn't matter who you're against. You just want to win. If Lester thinks he can come back and step out of the shadows, good luck to him. It's great that he's back."

16 October 1990

At Leicester, Piggott was back where he belonged. As he made his way to the parade ring racegoers cheered and reached out to slap him on the back.

Private man but a major talent

In December 1984 Dick Hern suffered a crippling hunting accident in Leicestershire. It was a savage blow but it failed to lay him low as a successful trainer

by PAUL HAIGH

THERE'S a line which 'Jakie' Astor often quotes to Dick Hern and which Dick Hern likes a lot: "Most things don't matter at all – and nothing matters very much."

It was said originally by either H. A. Balfour or Lord Salisbury – Astor isn't sure which, and isn't, to be honest, all that bothered, but after 25 years of friendship he is sure of Hern's fondness for it.

Most people who know anything about racing know that Hern – quite possibly the greatest horseman in the world – had a fall from his hunter three years ago which left him unable to walk and, maybe just as importantly, unable to ride, either.

But hardly anybody except his friends has much idea what he's like, or any idea of the side of his character which is illuminated a little by his liking for such a flippant remark.

In an age during which most of us are slaves to the media, Hern is one of the few who really do not give a damn. As a result he's one of the least-known celebrities in the sport: "The Howard Hughes of racing," someone called him once, probably to his mild amusement.

Having decided at the beginning of his training career, like some of the great trainers of the past, that his only real duty was to his horses and their owners, he has never seen the point in publicity, either to improve his business or to gratify his ego.

In the absence of any offers of information about Hern from Hern we have just had to make up our own minds and guess about him from what we see and what those who know him can tell us.

The actual story of his life tells us a bit about him.

We know that he was born to be a horseman: "I cannot remember being unable to ride," he said once. "I think my father probably sat me on a pony before I could walk."

We know that during their progress from North Africa into Germany with a horse regiment, he and Michael Pope, to whom he later became assistant trainer, found time and the inclination to clear a minefield off the local trotting track and organise race meetings at Ravenna in North Italy. It's almost as well known that after the war he became an Army riding instructor and that among his pupils were the members of the British Equestrian team that won the gold medal at the Helsinki Olympics. That tells us something about his talents, but only a bit about his other qualities.

It's difficult to imagine 'The Major' troubled by anything so mundane as a shortage of cash. But that was something he had to overcome when, without capital and having spent five years with Pope, he applied for the job of private trainer to Lionel Holliday, another old soldier and one who, by all accounts, was a seriously difficult man to deal with.

Holliday went through private trainers like Marciano went through sparring partners and was not, apparently, a man possessed of any great charm: "Heil Holliday" was one man's way of greeting him at the racecourse.

Hern won Holliday over, though, as he's won over all his owners since. He scored with his first runner and ended the season with 40 winners and fifth place in the trainers' table, which must have had something to do with it, but his character must have helped too.

He was with Holliday for five years before going to West Ilsley, and in the last of them, 1962, he won the first of his four trainers' titles. He might also have had the first of his Derby winners that year if the favourite, Hethersett, who later proved himself clearly the best horse in the race, hadn't tripped over the fallen Romulus and become one of seven fallers.

It was at West Ilsley, though, that Hern developed his skills as a trainer to the full and became a sort of hero figure to other trainers. They include Michael Stoute, who, when asked after his own record-breaking season of 1986 about his rivalry with Henry Cecil and Guy Harwood, pointed out almost indignantly that "the Major's got a better record than any of us".

And that's still true. Cecil may be catching him, but still no British trainer can match Hern's total of 41 Group 1 wins. He's won the Derby twice (with Troy and Henbit), the Oaks three times and the St Leger six times. For a lot of people, if the Major had never done anything else but train the Brigadier he'd have done enough.

Success hasn't been completely unbroken. But there's never been a setback to come anywhere near what happened three years ago.

When things started to go wrong a year after his fall, quite a few of us assumed mistakenly that this was the beginning of the end for Hern as a trainer; that he'd somehow lost his knack and that the extraordinary determination he was showing in trying to go on as if nothing had happened just wasn't going to be enough.

But oddly the accident and its aftermath seem somehow to have made him more accessible. He hasn't changed his policy – far from it. If he didn't have time for interviews before, he certainly doesn't have time for them now. But Dick Hern stories seem to have filtered out in the past few years as they never really did before, when people seemed con-

tent to let his horses' achievements do the talking and allow the man the privacy he demanded.

It's only since the accident that people have pointed out that he doesn't always take himself as seriously as his media silence might imply. People who don't know him have also paid more attention to him because of their admiration for the way in which he's coped with his injury. Even those who haven't backed his horses ante-post have been excited by the strength of his attack on this year's Derby, and it's not excessively sentimental to suggest that hardly anyone would mind at all if one of his horses won.

28 May 1988

PS. Major Hern did not win the Derby in 1988, but he did the following year with Nashwan.

Inimitable voice of a a National institution

On the eve of the drama of the 1991 Grand National, to profile the man and the voice a whole nation associates totally with racing was irresistible

by TONY O'HEHIR

THE voice of English racing first attended the Grand National as a 16-year-old in 1934 when he witnessed Golden Miller gallop into steeplechasing history. Fifty-seven years later, Peter O'Sullevan will again slip into Liverpool as the countdown begins to quicken for horseracing's greatest spectacular.

For the man whose name and unmistakable tones are as much part of National day as Becher's, The Chair and Red Rum, the 1991 renewal will mark his 44th commentary involvement in an event he regards as the most emotional of the racing year. His accurate claim that, in some way, the National invariably produces a fairy-tale underplays his own role as the principal story-teller in the televised history of the race which began with Merryman's win in 1960.

O'Sullevan's first job at the National came 13 years earlier. "I started on radio as a race reader in 1947. The following year I broadcast from the 12th fence. And after that I was involved on radio, at one pitch or another around the track, until 1959. The only exception was 1952 when Mirabel Topham, in her wisdom, decided to use her own commentary team."

In 1953 he became the first regular BBC TV and horseracing commentator to operate without a race-reader. He commentated on the first television Grand National in 1960 and has a number of other commentating milestones to his name, including the first horse race transmitted live via satellite.

O'Sullevan has worn many hats in racing – superb journalist, owner of Be Friendly and Attivo, animal welfare campaigner, company director and punter.

But it is as the man behind the microphone on racing's big days that O'Sullevan has become a legend, with Liverpool the stage for many of his most memorable commentaries. Calling The Horses (the title of his hugely successful autobiography) is an immensely satisfying experience when things go right and a desperately lonely one when they don't. Nowhere is that more applicable than at Liverpool where it is extremely difficult to be blasé about the sheer scale of the Grand National, its volume of runners, countless hazards and frighteningly high audience.

Tales of jockeys having to pay frequent visits to the toilet on National morning are part of the Liverpool legend. For commentators, too, the race is the stomach churner of every year. There is no fear of broken bones, only broken reputations, on the day when everyone is watching and listening. At Liverpool even the most experienced 'callers' become box-walkers.

Make no mistake, O'Sullevan, for whom preparations for the National exclude any "convivial involvement", suffers over the days leading up to the big event, from a mixture of heightening excitement and apprehension. Thinking of what might go wrong and realising that even the most painstaking preparation is no guarantee of complete accuracy, O'Sullevan also happens to be one of the sport's most famous faces and that, too, presents its problems as the National nears.

Virtually everyone recognises him and many want to engage him in conversation. "It is difficult to accommodate one's natural wish to be courteous," is O'Sullevan's polite way of saying he appreciates being left alone until it is all over.

For him the National has always been different from the other great racing occasions he has described so memorably. "I start thinking, and worrying, about the National longer in advance than any other race. I have the colours done but not learnt a week in advance," he said.

O'Sullevan is always among the early arrivals in the Liverpool press room. When the initial pleasantries are over it will be straight down to detail. Studying the colours, gathering background information, getting everyone's first name right, number of winners ridden, "so and so rides X in the National on Saturday" and so on.

Day one of the three-day meeting and a chance to see the National course live in the John Hughes Memorial Chase. The same fences will be jumped in the Fox Hunters Chase on Friday. In the broadcasting game both are regarded as dummy runs for the big day. Technically that may be true, but for a commentator those races can lull one into a false sense of security.

O'Sullevan's claim that Liverpool is a totally different place on National day is spot-on. A bit like a Cup Final compared with a kick-around on the local park pitch. When the 40 National contestants are milling around at the start jockeys do not have exclusive rights to butterflies. When the maestro says "this looks like *it*", he is not kidding. As a relative novice of five Nationals for BBC Radio, at Becher's Brook, I know no other race where the 'off' prompts an instant, but mercifully brief, attack of self-inflicted strangulation.

Once O'Sullevan has dispatched the cavalry into John Hanmer country at the first fence, the moment he describes as "the most fraught" part of his National commentary is less than a circuit away.

"The approach to The Chair is always a difficult time. That part of the race is not a monitor job. I concentrate on the live action and it is a question of how long to dwell on the fence looking for fallers. By the time some of them have jumped it the leaders have got to the water [jump]," he explained.

When *they* cross the Melling Road for the second time, the unique O'Sullevan climax is fast approaching. So, too, is another annual National problem for the race commentator. "Once they have jumped the second-last they are coming towards you. The angle of the camera completely exaggerates how far the horse on the far side is in front of the horse on the near side. And trying to interpret what the monitor shows and what the track is telling me is hazardous. Get it right and nobody notices. Get it wrong and you are 'that blind ******".

O'Sullevan believes that some of the BBC's outside broadcast equipment has not kept pace with modern technology. "It has to be said that, like this commentator, some of the BBC's monitors are getting very old," he said. "It would make life a lot easier if someone devised a way of properly screening monitors from the effects of natural light."

But anyone suspecting that O'Sullevan is *racing into the closing stages* of an outstanding commentating career might need to think again. When we spoke on Sunday there was a definite hint from the great stayer that he intends finding another few lengths. "1997 would be my 50th National. By all normal statistics it would appear totally unattainable and I suppose I'd be mad to take 1,000-1 about it," he laughed.

Imagine the occasion. Grand National day 1997, Red Rum still at the head of the pre-race parade and "as they cross the Melling Road it's over to 79-year-old Peter O'Sullevan".

Hanmer wouldn't dare . . . or would he?

3 April 1991

As much a part of the National as Becher's, Peter O'Sullevan says: "I start thinking, and worrying, about the race longer in advance than any other."

A Princess who calls no quarter in a race

The Princess Royal first rode in a race as an extension of her work for charity. She has since earned genuine respect for her performances on the Flat and over fences

by HOWARD WRIGHT

CHARITY work takes many different forms. In the Princess Royal's case it has included forging a race-riding career which in the first place she never sought, and then never imagined would progress beyond her first attempt.

"It had not crossed my mind before, and I honestly thought that the race was going to be a one-off," she says, recalling how a series of coincidences led her to ride Against The Grain at Epsom in April 1985.

It came about through the Worshipful Company of Farriers who, in the year the Princess was its Master, decided to stage a celebrity amateur riders' race as part of a major fund-raising effort on behalf of Riding for the Disabled, with which she is also closely connected.

"Curiously enough, nobody in the Company thought to ask if I would like to ride in the race," she says. "In fact it was me, thinking it might be marginally helpful to them to get the thing going, who offered my services. I have to admit that I didn't think it would happen, but I got caught up in it and, having said I would do it, I was jolly well going to have to do it."

David Nicholson, whom the Princess already knew and who was the closest trainer to her Gloucestershire home, was called in to help. He had another advantage. "David's reputation as a trainer of idiotic amateurs was already quite high," she says, with self-deprecation which hides her reputation as an equestrian competitor of Olympic and international class.

Three-day eventing and horse trials had taught her several disciplines, but race-riding was a different matter. "The learning process involved a shift in balance," she explains, "because when you pull up your stirrups, your centre of gravity is in a different place.

"To some degree it's an attitude of mind whether event-riding helps or hinders in adapting to racing. Because three-day eventing is about all aspects of horsemanship, it shouldn't hinder you too much. The attitude is to speed, as much as anything else, and lack of control.

"In three-day eventing you expect to be 50 to 75 per cent in control. The main thing I've discovered about race-riding, particularly in National Hunt, is that to be successful you need to be 99 per cent out of control and go with it.

"On the whole three-day event riders have a much broader outlook towards their riding than those in other disciplines. So it's not quite such a shock to the system to change from one to the other. But you compete in three-day events on your own, so the other adaptation you have to make is to the fact you are surrounded by other people in head-to-head competition.

"I had to learn to live with it."

There were 16 runners at Epsom, over a course which some would say was hardly ideal for an amateur in her first race. That aspect held no terrors for her.

"For an event rider, cross-country courses cover the most horrendous bits of ground, so Epsom doesn't look that bad to people like us. It was much more difficult to imagine what it would be like to ride about three times faster than you would normally go.

"In that sense, it was an advantage riding a horse that was already in National Hunt racing. He was used to running on courses which were perhaps more difficult and trappy than Epsom, and was a good, sensible older horse who knew what he was doing. I wouldn't fancy riding a two-year-old round there!"

Against The Grain finished fourth, beaten three-and-a-half lengths behind No-U-Turn, ridden by Elain Mellor. The winner proved to be well named; for the Princess, despite her early reservations, there was no going back. Reflecting on her subsequent, and continuing, riding career, she says: "I have to admit I don't think there's been hardly a race when things have gone totally according to plan!

"As an event rider you might think that there aren't really too many things that can go wrong in a race. It's a fairly straightforward business of getting from one end to the other faster than anybody else. But the short answer is that when you've got a lot of other horses around you, any number of circumstances can change the picture.

"Positioning has been the interesting part of race-riding, particularly on the Flat, where things happen more quickly. National Hunt Flat races gave me a bit more experience, but they were rougher, partly because the fields were very big and they were ridden by more experienced amateurs.

"The trainer used to say, 'Follow so-and-so', which was a very interesting comment because all I could see was a pair of white breeches. To be honest, if you're in the middle of the pack, you haven't a clue who anybody is, unless you recognise the back-end of a horse. 'Follow that one' became 'where's it gone'!"

One occasion on which things did go right in the perfect place was at Ascot in July 1987, when the Princess won the season's richest race for women amateurs on Ten No Trumps, who went on to win a Listed race next time out.

"Sometimes things work out as they're supposed to, and they did that day," she recalls, "though I had to make a decision about the horse that went on. I had to think about how soon it was going to blow up and when to get out of its way.

"It is possible to be mounted on the best horse in a Flat race and in theory you should win, as long as you hang on. It doesn't always work out like that, because the others can get in the way and upset things.

"And horses don't know the form. Perhaps that's

always been their attraction; they're not judging me on the same basis as anybody else might. As far as they're concerned, I'm just another body."

The Princess is alive to criticism of amateurs' races, and admits to some sympathy for the view. "Competitiveness tends to make people do things that perhaps they wouldn't do if left to their own devices," she says. "And to some extent the pressure of the betting public, on a rider at the end of the race, is also quite considerable.

"That's why I never pick up my whip if I can possibly help it. It needs a hell of a lot of practice and strength to be able to swing a whip competently and make any amount of difference to the animal. I'm quite surprised I haven't been had up before the stewards, yet, for not doing enough.

"It strikes me that, on the whole, horses run better without a huge degree of interference from the jockey, though there are some who patently need more encouragement than others to indicate that the moment has come to be serious, and would they kindly get on with it.

"Having said that, the dividing point between getting too carried away and losing all sense of rhythm and balance, and doing any good in terms of driving like professional jockeys, is pretty fine. I probably err on the side certainly of doing less rather than more."

An enthusiastic member of the Lady Jockeys Association, the Princess is a fervent supporter of girls in racing.

"It's certainly true in eventing that for a girl to be successful, the partnership needs to be very strong.

"Physically she can't boss the beast around and has to come to an understanding, whereas a man is much more likely to make a horse go without having taken the trouble to understand it, because of his physical strength.

"That's probably not as true in racing, and race-riding, where it's the degree of strength which, at the end of the day, is going to make a difference. And this will probably always keep girls back.

"But the more sympathetic approach can help with some horses, particularly one who maybe has had a hard time, shown some signs of success but has gone off a bit. That sort needs confidence being given back to them, and a quieter approach may help.

"That's why I don't believe it's silly to say a girl could ride, say, a Derby winner. It's simply a question of the trainers and owners having faith in the individual."

16 October 1991

The Princess Royal, riding Ten No Trumps, won the season's richest race for women amateurs at Ascot in July 1987.

The free and very unafraid spirit

From the humblest of beginnings, Jenny Pitman has struggled to the top in racing and today is Britain's most formidable and forthright lady trainer

by MARCUS ARMYTAGE

JENNY PITMAN stands in the winner's enclosure, a Napoleonic figure. The British racing press hangs on her every word. This is the love side of what has, on occasions, been a love-hate relationship. She jokes and they collectively laugh, but they are careful not to push racing's first lady too far.

The sight is now a common one, Mrs P in the winner's enclosure eulogising about the future of yet another budding star. From an inauspicious start in life she has progressed to the top of the training tree against the odds. She made it when she became the first woman to train a Grand National winner with Corbiere in 1983, a race that has not always done its winning trainers too many other favours. And then, the following year, she won the Gold Cup with Burrough Hill Lad.

Now she has one of the most powerful jumping strings in the country. She has earned respect for herself and her horses. She has not stood still, always building for the future.

Jenny Harvey was born on a small leased farm in Leicester, one of seven children. She could ride before she learned to walk. "I don't know," says Jenny self-mockingly, "if that meant I was just plain bloody lazy!"

It was a tough upbringing but one that set her up for the future. "I was never assistant to anyone other than my father," she reflects. "He was a proper stockman – cows, sheep, pigs and horses, the lot. Training horses is about being a stockman – feeding, looking after them mentally, knowing when you're doing too much with them, not just galloping them. He was my greatest tutor."

Aged 15, Jenny went to work for local trainer Chris Taylor at weekends. "I was always going to work with horses. I was a stable girl for a good many years and enjoyed doing my two."

When Taylor moved to Cheltenham she went too. That is where she met Richard Pitman. When he went to Fred Winter's in Lambourn she went too and worked for the late Major Champney, the old school of trainer. "He wanted a fair day's work for a fair day's pay. I loved the thrill of riding at speed and never dreamed you could break your neck doing it, but girls weren't allowed to ride under Rules then."

Being a housewife did not suit Jenny's free spirit. "I hated being cooped up like a budgie in a cage," she says. Within a year of marriage she had produced Mark. "It was a shock to my system and I wasn't even riding out. Fourteen months on and I had Paul, so I was well and truly handcuffed and shackled!"

Things began to look up when they bought a plot of land, stables and a caravan with planning for a bungalow at Hinton Parva. Jenny recalls: "We moved in on 1 April and everyone thought it was a joke! It had snowed the night before and we all slept the first night in overcoats.

"People thought we were crackers but I went into the yard the next morning and felt 10 years younger."

It was the beginning of Jenny Pitman the trainer.

She started by taking liveries for Lambourn trainers, Fulke and Peter Walwyn, Fred Winter and Barry Hills; horses that needed breaking, a rest or had been injured. She soon progressed to the point-to-point field. Her first runner was a winner at Tweseldown. "Everyone said 'Well done Richard' afterwards. They all thought because he was a well-known jockey that he had trained the horse! He hardly ever went in the yard at Hinton Parva and when he did anything with the horses, it was usually to hunt them too hard," she recalls with some amusement.

The next stage in this evolution came when the late Tony Stratton-Smith asked her to be his private trainer. A combination of circumstances led her to accept but only to train his horses, not as private trainer. She says: "It had never occurred to me to train professionally. At the time I was a big fish in a little pond. Now I'd be a little one in a big pond."

Due to her impending separation with Pitman she had to look elsewhere to earn her living. She bought Weathercock House, although at the time it was a complimentary term for what was a ruin.

Of all the horses she has trained since, Corbiere holds a special place in her heart. "He did most for us and my biggest regret is not having him buried here. He was so brave and I felt that was the differ-

ence between him winning and losing the National. Then Burrough Hill Lad put the icing on the cake. He proved we could train other good horses."

Detractors will comment that Jenny Pitman is now turning out the winners of good races with expensive horses. It is little more than jealousy. True, she has some well-off owners to pay some handsome prices for Irish-bred potential. However, her critics seem to forget that many of her best horses still cost less than £10,000, including Royal Athlete and Willsford. "When I started £4,500 was a big order," she says.

It is, however, knowing that some people would like to see her go down the tubes that gives Jenny her greatest spur. "I don't want to give them that pleasure. Corbiere settled a lot of ghosts in that respect but when you think about it those people don't matter."

Jenny is not a raving feminist, far from it, but she has had to struggle in a man's world for the recognition she and other women deserve. She recalls with amusement a BBC National preview in which they wanted to feature Corbiere. "Just before what I thought would be my greatest hour they sent a bloody football reporter to do the piece. In fact, it was Hugh McIlvanney. We always laugh about it now and he's a great friend, but it was the sort of thing I was up against. Women are tolerated in this game, rather than accepted."

Her image with the press has not always been rosy. "I've never been a fence-sitter. In my opinion, if you believe in something you've got to say it. It's tough if it ruffles a few feathers. It can be frustrating at times, a lot of people in positions of authority in racing have never trained or ridden."

However, since Corbiere won the National she has had letters every day from her supporters, many of them divorced women themselves, who have picked her out as a champion of their cause.

So can she put her finger on what makes her a good trainer? "No, I think it's down to knowing your horses. You're as good as your last record, you never feel secure in this job and it's that which keeps you on your toes. I have to take a pill to get to sleep at night."

And the future? Weathercock House is now a veritable palace but it is an old house and does not suit the dust allergy for which Jenny has had two operations this winter. "I'll swap residences with Mark in 10 to 15 year's time. It will suit me to take a back seat then. Besides, I prefer being at home. You notice the little things then."

14 March 1990

Jenny Pitman, trainer of one of the most powerful strings in the country, says training horses is "about being a stockman, not just galloping them".

Newcomer joins the exclusive 200 club

When Peter Scudamore rode 200 winners in a season, it was time to compare him with Sir Gordon Richards, one of the famous double-centurions of the Flat

by ROGER MORTIMER

THE remarkable flow of successes this jumping season achieved by Peter Scudamore has reminded some of the more elderly followers of racing of the hey-day of the late Sir Gordon Richards on the Flat.

Of course, comparisons between the two are not really fair to Scudamore, jumping and the Flat being two entirely different ball-games.

A rider can, however, be badly hurt in an accident on the Flat. Manny Mercer was killed going down to the start at Ascot, while Richards had his leg broken by a kick at Salisbury in 1941 and his career came to an end in 1954 at Sandown in the race after the Eclipse Stakes. Abergeldie, in the royal colours, reared over backwards leaving the paddock and rolled on Richards, breaking his pelvis and dislocating four of his ribs.

Healthwise, the real crisis in Richard's career came early in 1926 when an X-ray revealed a tubercular patch on one lung and he spent the rest of that year in a sanatorium in Norfolk. Happily he had fully recovered by the start of the 1927 season.

In World War II an account of the tuberculosis in his medical history caused him to be turned down when he tried to join the RAF and then the Army.

There are, of course, far greater risks involved in riding over fences and hurdles. Most jumping jockeys suffer from broken limbs or worse at one time or another. It follows that a top jockey on the Flat sometimes continues to race-ride until he is over 50, whereas top jump jockeys are apt to see the red light in their thirties.

Richards was born in 1904 and finished riding in 1954. Peter Scudamore is rising 31 and it is on the cards that he has no more than five years' riding ahead of him. He has yet to win the Grand National or the Cheltenham Gold Cup.

It will be remembered that Richards won the Derby only once and that was on Pinza in 1953 in what was his 28th and final attempt. Year after year on Derby Day the newspaper headlines shouted: "Can Gordon break his Epsom hoodoo?"

Shortly before Pinza's victory, the Queen conferred a knighthood on Richards for his services to horse-riding. It was generally agreed that the honour was well deserved, as he had been a marvellous friend to racing through both his professional skill and his impeccable integrity.

In a career that began in 1920, Richards rode 4,870 winners from 21,815 mounts. It must be remembered that his total of winners would have been considerably larger but for the interruption caused to racing by World War II. He was champion jockey 26 times and won 14 Classics. His best seasons were 1947, 1949 and 1933, when his total of winners were 269, 261 and 259 respectively. At Chepstow he once rode 11 of the 12 winners at the meeting.

Modern jockeys have more opportunities than Richards enjoyed. There are now a large number of evening meetings during the summer and modern transport, including aircraft and helicopters, to enable a jockey to ride at two meetings in one day.

The son of a Shropshire miner, Richards was one of a family of 12 children. The basis of his success was his single-minded determination to ride as many winners as possible, no matter how much work was involved. It was a golden age of English jockeyship and he was up against stiffer competition than Piggott ever was, or than Eddery faces today.

It was a great advantage to Richards that he never had weight problems and, at the age of 50, he could go to scale at 8st 3lb. Richards was tremendously popular with the racing public, who trusted him implicitly. The 6th Earl of Rosebery summed him up by saying that no man had ever lost fewer races he ought to have won.

Richards was naturally intelligent, an excellent speaker, and could have made his mark in professions other than racing. He had a happy and simple home life and seemed a very lonely man when his wife Margery died. The jaunty way he walked gave the impression of serene self-confidence but in fact he tended to be highly-strung.

The racing world of Richards in his riding days was entirely different to that of today. The British thoroughbred was then supreme (the supremacy was not invariably acknowledged in the United States), but world racing today is dominated by American-bred horses. The backbone of English racing was still supplied by the great owner-breeders, but now they have almost entirely disappeared. The top figures today are oil tycoons who can afford to buy the best yearlings in the American market.

Sixty horses was reckoned a big stable between the wars, whereas today there are jumbo-sized establishments containing up to 200 horses. A modern owner would be lucky to get away with £150 a week for keeping a horse in a smart Newmarket stable.

The famous Alec Taylor of Manton charged his wealthy owners £4.10s a week and sent his bills out once a year, the week before Christmas. He was not robbing himself, as he left over £500,000. Preparation for the Manton Cup horses began the previous autumn and candidates for those prestigious events were out both morning and afternoon, a regime impossible with modern labour.

The aristocracy has opted out of racing and familiar names and colours have vanished, probably never to return. In general racing has lost its social status and in my view it is now roughly on a par with dog racing at Catford or Slough!

For most of Richards' riding days there were no starting stalls, photo-finishes, patrol cameras, sponsored races or evening meetings. There was a different system for declaring runners, no racecourse commentaries, no TV, no campaign against overzealous use of the whip. Anti-doping measures were primitive and the rules with regard to doping were not a good advertisement for British justice.

The Tote had disappointed and was struggling to stay solvent. Jumping was run by the National Hunt Committee and the paladins of the Flat used to refer to the jumping world as "the needy and greedy". A lot of courses, Newmarket in particular, did not

fancy writing 'Welcome' on the mat and were proud of their snobbish exclusiveness. The Betting and Gaming Act and the Levy Board were still a long way off. Racing is undoubtedly more democratic today; whether it is more enjoyable is a matter of opinion.

Michael Scudamore, Peter Scudamore's father, never rose to the heights in the saddle that his son has achieved but he was a good, bold horseman and in one respect he is one up on his son as he won the Grand National on Oxo and the Gold Cup on Linwell. Today he runs a small jumping stable in Herefordshire.

Peter Scudamore rode his first winner in 1978 at Devon and Exeter. No doubt he learnt plenty when riding for David Nicholson and in 1981/82 he had 120 winners, sharing the championship with John Francome. Of course this has been his *annus mirabilis* and to achieve what he has achieved he needed luck on his side.

First, he has been helped by a marvellously mild winter, which means there have been far fewer stoppages in racing than is usually the case. Second, there has been the truly astonishing success of the trainer Martin Pipe who, only a few years ago, had hardly been heard of. Pipe is the son of a West Country bookmaker and the regularity with which he has been churning out winners has naturally led to a certain amount of jealousy. Hence the absurd and unfounded stories about his methods.

Certainly the Pipe–Scudamore combination has been a truly formidable one. At one time it was being said that Pipe specialised in maiden hurdle races at minor meetings in the West and that there were dozens of jockeys who could have equalled Scudamore's record if given the opportunity.

However, the stable began to be regarded with increased respect following victories in the Hennessy Cognac Gold Cup and Welsh National. Recently the Pipe stable carried off a valuable Flat race at Ascot.

Scudamore is essentially a family man. He is not a glamorous figure and he lacks the cheek so frequently displayed by John Francome, often to the displeasure of the Establishment. Scudamore is respected for his horsemanship and his high-quality professional skill.

Like Sir Gordon, he is the consummate professional.

29 April 1989

PS. Roger Mortimer, racing correspondent of The Sunday Times for almost 30 years, died in 1991, aged 82.

Sir Gordon Richards and Peter Scudamore – models of qualities that have made their names bywords for integrity and skill in Flat and jump racing.

An unsung worker in a stable's backroom

The life of a stable lad is a form of heroism in its routine devotion to the thoroughbred. A typical day for one lad at Ian Balding's yard was minutely examined

by EMILY WEBER

7.30am

CHRIS picks up his kit from the tack room. He's seen the list showing which horses he is down to ride today. Then he's off to his first mount, Stormy Reef, a three-year-old filly owned by the Queen. The filly has been mucked out so Chris just has to prepare her for exercise. He takes a damp cloth or stable rubber out of his bucket, and a body brush. Using the brush in one hand and the rubber in the other, he quickly cleans her coat. Stormy Reef hates being groomed but Chris nimbly evades her attempts to maim him: "Sweet, isn't she?" he says cheerfully. The other lads are bustling around with their kit as we watch Chris's routine: "Fame at last, Chris," says one girl. "Not on a racecourse, unfortunately," comes the answer. By 7.45 Chris has tacked up and is leading Stormy Reef out of her stable into the yard.

7.45am

First lot pulls out at 7.50. Forty horses go to the covered school next to the yard. They warm up by walking and trotting for 10 minutes. Some 'spook' as they trot past the entrance. Soon the horses are on the gallops 400 yards away. The sun is not yet over the horizon: the lads say it's the coldest morning of the winter. The horses trot and canter on the oval Dormit track, plunging excitedly in the mist. The lads sit tight and soon they are steadily cantering round the track. Ian Balding stands in the middle, watching quietly, his dogs sitting beside him. By 9.00 it's all over. The horses are back in their stables, being groomed or 'dressed over' again before being rugged up and having a feed.

9.20am

Chris tucks into a boiled egg and several slices of toast. There's a choice of seven different cereals, boiled, poached or fried eggs, sausages and bacon, as well as tea or coffee. Several lads are reading papers. There's plenty of banter of the "Have to do some work today, Chris" and "No smoking in the toilets, then" variety. Chris retaliates in kind but keeps smiling. There's general chat about the lads' weekly Spot The Ball competition.

9.50am

Mucking out must be finished before second lot pulls out. Chris says it takes about 10 minutes a horse "although when I first started I was always late. I had to get to the yard early so I finished in time." The dry straw or paper (shredded newspaper is used for one bed) is piled up round the side. Chris separates the wet straw and droppings and puts them on a square of sacking. He tops up the beds with about half a bale of clean straw or paper for each horse. Now the beds are finished, he joins the other lads in sweeping the yard. Second and third lots are for the two-year-olds and are much shorter than the first lot. Second lot is at 10.25 and third lot at 11.30.

12.15pm

Tack cleaning. Chris washes and oils his saddle and bridle. The yard shuts down for the afternoon. Lunch is a choice of cold meats, baked beans, hot sausage rolls and buttered bread rolls. Options for the afternoon include a trip to Newbury, a drive to Tadley, watching television in his room or having a snooze.

4.00pm

Chris starts back to the yard for evening stables. The morning stables routine is repeated. Each horse is mucked out, given hay and water, and groomed. Ian Balding starts his evening rounds at 5.00. He spends about three minutes with each horse, going over the coat and legs, and feeding titbits of nuts. Once Chris has shown all his three horses he is finished for the day. Then it's back to the canteen for supper. Some of the lads are going for a drink but Chris isn't interested: "I'm not a drinking person. Sometimes I'll play pool but really I like to do something sporty like play squash or badminton. I go to an aerobics class once a week, which the others think is poofy, but I like to be fit."

7.00pm

Chris has settled down to a video. He used to do Forest Flower and bought a recorder on the proceeds. There are several mementoes of the filly round his room. Chris is happy to spend a quiet evening in his room: "It doesn't bother me if I stay in. Whatever I do, I'm usually in bed by 10.00."

25 January 1989

Coffee and a few home truths

Over coffee in 1990, Steve Cauthen, an ambassador par excellence for racing, talked about his life, his problems with making the weight and much else

by TOM O'RYAN

RED PIPE was the horse that started it all off for Steve Cauthen, at River Downs on 17 May 1976, little more than a fortnight after his 16th birthday. The following year he was champion jockey with 487 winners, including a record 23 in one week, and in 1978, on Affirmed, he became the youngest rider to carry off the American Triple Crown. Thus Cauthen was already a legend when he crossed the Atlantic and is now firmly established as one of the all-time greats. Here's how he reacted to questions as he entered his 12th Flat season on British soil.

☐ **QUESTION: How have you spent the winter months and how important is it to you to have a complete break after a hectic season?**

■ ANSWER: I did quite a bit of shooting, some skiing and I spent quite a lot of time on my farm in Kentucky with my family. And I also went for a week to Barbados. Every year is different, but I think you definitely need a certain amount of time to totally switch off. By the end of the season, you've literally lived horses 24 hours a day, seven days a week for eight months. And no matter how much you enjoy it, too much of a good thing can be bad for you.

☐ **This must be a very special time with the whole season ahead and so many good horses to look forward to. How do you monitor the ability of the horses you ride work on at Warren Place? And because there are so many, do you need to keep notes?**

■ This time of year is exciting for everybody. All your geese are swans. They haven't let you down

yet. So if you're not optimistic now, you never will be. I do keep some notes, but I've got a very good memory, with horses particularly. Tell me a joke and I'll probably forget it in five minutes, but most things about horses I remember. It's the same with races. I can remember what happened at every stage of certain races 10 years ago. If you have made notes, it's always interesting to look back, say five months later, and see whether you were right, wrong or way off target. But the thing is, with two-year-olds, your opinions change as the year goes on, simply because they change so much. It's like kids. All of a sudden they spurt up two feet seemingly overnight, and you don't even recognise them.

☐ **What do you do to ensure your own personal fitness at this time of the year and how much of a problem is your weight?**

■ I keep pretty active and I never let myself get unfit. But the only gateway to get race-riding fit is in races, basically to get your wind right. There's no doubt that most jockeys, not only me, won't be at their 110 per cent peak fitness for the first few races, but that's the way it is, just like a horse. As for my weight, the fact of the matter is I'm 5ft 6in and should be about 9st 6lb, and yet I try to ride at 8st 6lb or 8st 7lb. Although I can get down to 9st without too much difficulty, everything after that is a real struggle because I'm going under my natural weight. I prefer to diet, rather than to sweat, because sweating is just a temporary thing; all you're doing is jerking the fluid out of your body, dehydrating yourself.

☐ **Do you feel, then, that it's easier for a jockey to enjoy a longer career in Britain than in America?**

■ That's totally what I feel and partly why I'm here. Obviously, I came here and fell in love with the country and felt accepted, but part of the reason I'm still riding today is that I don't have to do it full-time. I think if I hadn't come over, I probably wouldn't be riding today. I'd probably be fed up with it by now. In the States, it's non-stop. There's no let-up at all.

☐ **Do you feel that coming to Britain at the age of 18 was more beneficial to you as a jockey than if you'd ridden in the States for, say, five years before making the transition?**

■ I think it's been proven, both by myself and Cash Asmussen. Obviously, I think we were both above-average riders when we came, but guys like Jorge Velasquez and Darrel McHargue came over and had a go at riding in Europe and they were above-average riders, too; top-class guys. But they were more set in their ways. It's like trying to teach an old dog new tricks, whereas we were very open-minded and able to adapt much more readily. I was

intrigued by what European racing had to offer and, as it's turned out, it suits me very well.

☐ **A lot of Mr Cecil's horses are laid-back types. Do you feel that is a reflection of his training methods, and what qualities do you think make him such a talented trainer?**

■ There's no doubt that Henry was born with an innate talent, a God-given talent. He's a very intelligent man, who is very aware of all his horses and gives a lot of thought to which races suit them best. He tries to give his horses confidence, just like he tries to give everyone around the stable confidence that they're doing a good job. But above and beyond all that, he grafts his balls off, like most people who are successful. You see a lot of gifted people who don't use their talent, and eventually they fall by the wayside. If you don't work at it, you're going to end up hitting a brick wall.

☐ **You are now 29. How long do you see yourself riding, and would you consider a training career when you finally quit the saddle?**

■ As long as I'm enjoying myself, healthy and have the desire to keep my weight down, which is always going to be a struggle, I'll carry on riding. One day I'll know that I've had enough, that it's not giving me the same thrill or whatever. But that day hasn't come yet. I don't think I'd be a public trainer. I've been very fortunate to have been around a lot of good trainers and I haven't stood around like a bump on a log. I've tried to learn as much as I can. I feel I've got an interest and an ability to help bring horses on, but at the same time when you set up a public racing stable, you're taking an awful lot on and I'm not sure I want all that. There's too many other ways I can be involved without being a trainer. In the States I've got a farm and all my family are involved with horses and with breeding. I'm also interested in TV work and a lot of other things. I suppose I haven't given it much thought, but as I gradually get nearer the day, I'll know which direction I'll want to go.

☐ **You always project a very good image. Do you feel that is a very important aspect of a professional sportsman's career?**

■ Not only is it important for a sportsman, it's even more important from a human being's point of view. My family brought me up to be a decent, respectable person and I owe it to them, as well as to myself, to be nice to people. As far as racing goes, it's a great sport, with beautiful animals involved, and there's lots of really nice people associated with it, right from the stable-lads to the Queen and the Queen Mother. Racing has given me a good life, and I think everybody in the game needs to promote it and put forward a good image. I feel I've got an awful lot out of European racing, British racing, and anything I can do to make it better, I'd like to do. It's like the prize-money here. I'm all for trying to make it better. Although this is a great racing country, I feel it has slacked way behind in a lot of ways, not only in the prize-money, but in the state of some of the racecourses; they're dilapidated, quite frankly. And if, as you say, I'm a good ambassador, well that's basically because I am what I am. I'd like to think I'm a nice person, who wants good things put forward for racing, rather than bad. It's as simple as that.

24 March 1990

At home with one of the sport's ambassadors. Jockey Steve Cauthen is a man concerned that the "good things" are put forward for racing.

Being here to meet Red Rum for me is like a trip to Mecca

Meet The King ...and I

RED RUM

Red Rum stays the star of the show

Not even Big Mac can outshine Red Rum or draw more attention. Indeed, when the famous horse comes on stage, everyone else has only a walk-on part

by JOHN McCRIRICK

SNOOKER veteran Rex Williams jokes that whenever he plays Alex 'The Leprechaun on Heat' Higgins "crowds flock to see me!"

It's much the same with At Large and Red Rum.

Appearances at packed betting shops playing straight man to the triple Grand National legend are personally stimulating though not, I fear, for Rummy.

On Thursday, we were drawn together again at

Brightest jewel from a golden era

In 1989 Brigadier Gerard, perhaps the greatest miler of modern times, was found dead in Newmarket. It was time to honour in words a quite extraordinary horse

by TONY MORRIS

BRIGADIER GERARD'S place in the pantheon of the Turf is assured. That much is certain, while his exact ranking among its hierarchy can never be known and will for ever be a subject of lively debate.

But for many who lived through that golden era of privilege for racegoers, when Nijinsky, Mill Reef and the Brigadier provided countless delights, the one home-grown talent among that great triumvirate shone brightest of all – and not just because he was home-grown.

For three full seasons he starred, equal to every task (bar one), dependable to a degree unknown in ordinary athletes, virtually unknown among the extraordinary. When speed was needed, he had it – sufficient to run away from specialist sprinters like Mummy's Pet and Swing Easy in the Middle Park. At the mile, his own true métier, he attained a pinnacle previously achieved only by Tudor Minstrel, never since approached, and it was over a mile, in the 1971 Guineas, that he set the standard, cutting down Mill Reef and My Swallow and leaving them for dead.

The level of that performance, scarcely credible at

Mecca's new shop in Brierley Hill, near Birmingham, on the day when SIS finally came to Britain's second city. In a travesty of reality, TV screens proclaimed: "John McCririck and Red Rum". Only the superstar, as everyone knew, merited a billing.

And as the star of the show, winner of the Grand National a record three times, in 1973, 1974 and 1977, came down the ramp of his horsebox, I swear, at the moment he caught sight of me, his top lip curled as though to say: "Oh, no, not him again!"

Me fawning over the hero must be oppressive to the recipient – other unwilling victims include the greatest jockey, J. Francome, and the Noble Lord. And phlegmatic old Rummy, after half a dozen pairings with me, including that ill-fated relaunch of Uttoxeter last year, has to be fed up by now with all the accompanying adulatory ranting.

At 24, with up to four such appearances a week around Grand National time and a steady stream of engagements throughout the year, he is recognised everywhere. Leading Red Rum down the street, the wintry sun gleaming on his flanks, it was delightful to look up to office windows full of joyful, smiling faces. The pleasure at just seeing Rummy, proudly wearing a red sash spelling out those far-off Aintree deeds, is universal. And Ginger McCain's head lad, Ken Critchley, 31, who has done the old boy for five years, avows he is "a complete gent – you could never find a horse to behave like him".

As the crowd, some of them actual punters, milled around in the increasingly hothouse atmosphere to touch and stroke the still sleek body,

Rummy was imperturbable, voraciously accepting beloved Polo mints and the plaudits of awestruck humans, aged from two to over 80, as his due.

Looking like an NH jockey, which he never was, Critchley, with no sense of doing down a rival, told casually of how Aldaniti "scattered the place" in a similar confining situation. He also explained why he believed Rummy remains in the pink: "If he was put out in a field he'd soon get a big drop belly."

At that, he nodded unfairly in my direction before adding: "He's looked upon at home in Southport, where he's been in the same box for nearly 20 years, as just one of the horses. Except for work and being ridden, his routine and feed are the same as ever."

Critchley, married with two daughters, acknowledged his debt to Red Rum both in their reciprocal compatibility and also financially. "Wages for lads, especially in the North," he stated quietly, "are very poor. Most lads, especially married ones, somehow just fiddle through. Being associated with Rummy makes all the difference. The reflected glory is great. So is meeting all sorts of people – you (he stared at me hard) are one of the hazards of the job!"

Another was the dramatic moment he recounted when some prankster tried to do a Shergar and kidnap Red Rum at a function. "I'd left the keys in the horse-box and suddenly there it was trundling off down the field with Red Rum inside! They didn't get out of the gate but it was a shock all right and I've been very careful ever since."

4 February 1989

---

the time, was confirmed, time and again, first over a mile in all-aged company, then against all-comers at a mile and a quarter.

When conditions favoured his rivals, on heavy ground or out of his distance, he had the quality of raw courage to add to his class, and only on that still-mystifying afternoon at York, against Roberto, did he meet his match.

In time, the Brigadier's trainer would imagine he had found one better, but the form-book could never confirm it and their respective ratings would refute the notion.

There was only one Brigadier, who for three seasons regularly defied his contemporaries, his elders and his juniors, and rejoiced in the unanimous affection of racegoers.

At stud he had his moments, with winners of the St Leger (Light Cavalry) and Champion Stakes (Vayrann) among his progeny. But in a way it was no sadness that his status was never shared, nor yet compared, with any of his sons. His was a unique talent, and its memory a unique legacy.

30 October 1989

Racing Record of Brigadier Gerard

b c 1968 by Queen's Hussar-La Paiva. Won 17 races

1970

24 June	Newbury	Berkshire Stakes	WON
2 July	Salisbury	Champagne Stakes	WON
15 Aug	Newbury	Washington Singer Stakes	WON
1 Oct	Newmarket	Middle Park Stakes	WON

1971

1 May	Newmarket	2,000 Guineas Stakes	WON
15 June	Ascot	St James's Palace Stakes	WON
28 July	Goodwood	Sussex Stakes	WON
28 Aug	Goodwood	Goodwood Mile	WON
25 Sep	Ascot	Queen Elizabeth II Stakes	WON
16 Oct	Newmarket	Champion Stakes	WON

1972

20 May	Newbury	Lockinge Stakes	WON
29 May	Sandown	Westbury Stakes	WON
20 June	Ascot	Prince of Wales's Stakes	WON
8 July	Sandown	Eclipse Stakes	WON
22 July	Ascot	King George VI and Queen Elizabeth Stakes	WON
15 Aug	York	Benson & Hedges Gold Cup	2nd
23 Sep	Ascot	Queen Elizabeth II Stakes	WON
14 Oct	Newmarket	Champion Stakes	WON

The day the Arkle legend was born

Etched firmly in the memory of all followers of jump racing is the day Arkle floored the mighty Mill House, as one writer discovered on the 25th anniversary

by PAUL HAIGH

ANYONE who was then alive and conscious is supposed to be able to remember where they were when the news came through that John Kennedy had been shot.

Racing, on its own smaller and happier scale, had an event like that in the early 1960s too. Anyone who then took any interest at all in National Hunt racing knows where he or she was when Arkle beat Mill House in the Cheltenham Gold Cup 25 years ago next week.

Ask them and see. They'll remember because it was the race in which Arkle announced himself.

An enthusiastic, but on his own admission very incompetent, 19-year-old point-to-point rider called Martin Pipe "was in Taunton managing a big credit office" for his bookmaker father. He remembers: "A very good race, but Arkle being just different class, a giant, unbeatable. He was always the loser in our books after that, but it was still always exciting to see him race, always good to see him win."

David Nicholson, then a leading jump jockey who was going to ride against the phenomenon a few times in the future, was in the stands at Cheltenham. "He was very, very good," remembers Nicholson. "People talk about horses having another gear. He really did have it."

Jim Dreaper, son of the great Tom Dreaper, who trained Arkle, was at prep school in County Meath. "I was aware of the build-up to the race," he says, "and a lot of people in the school were taking an interest. We watched it in the library on an old black-and-white TV set that was normally only turned on for The Brains Trust and something called Dixon of Dock Green. Anything else was supposed to be going to corrupt our young minds; but this time, thanks to the intervention of the geography master, we were allowed to see the race. I have a memory of delight when the horse won.

"I also remember this upstairs phone, which no-one was allowed to use and which normally only rang when there was a bereavement, going off at 9.30 at night and me being whisked out of bed by the matron to talk to my mother about Arkle and what he'd done."

Desert Orchid's owner Richard Burridge was at prep school too: "I bunked off a hockey game and listened to it in the school dormitory. I remember being terribly upset. I was such a Mill House fan. Of course I became an Arkle fan later – we all did – but I wasn't then."

Fortunately there was no intrusion into his private grief by Quelch or any other beak. That would have been too much for an emotional 12-year-old to have had to bear.

The inventory of reminiscences could go on a long time. Ask anyone who's old enough and they'll remember. The fact that Arkle really began a quarter of a century ago means that there is now a whole generation of racing people who haven't quite got the idea of what he was like.

Quite understandably there are now a lot of them about who think he must have been a great champion, but still just a horse to be compared with other champions. Just a few years ago, for example, Willie Mullins, a level-headed and realistic man but one too young to remember, said, after seeing Dawn Run add a French Champion Hurdle to all her other accomplishments: "Well, she must be as good as Arkle was now."

There was no point in telling him that Arkle might well have left Dawn Run, great as she was, a fence behind at the end of three and a quarter miles. It was the wrong moment to say such a thing – and he wouldn't have believed it anyway.

Some background is needed to that 1964 Gold Cup in which Arkle made his messianic arrival. Most of the background is Mill House. 'The Big Horse', as Mill House was frequently called by sentimentalists, had been bought in Ireland a couple of years earlier by Jack Doyle for Bill Gollings, and had been brought to England where he was trained eventually by Fulke Walwyn, and had then absolutely slaughtered everything in sight.

He ran up a string of successes over hurdles and fences which culminated in victory as a six-year-old in the 1963 Gold Cup. He was already being compared with Golden Miller. He was hero-worshipped to such an extent that his fans could hardly imagine how he might be defeated.

Even more importantly, he had a victory to his

credit over Arkle, who had established much the same reputation by staying at home in Ireland. The two had met in the 1963 Hennessy Gold Cup. Mill House had won by eight lengths after Arkle had made a mistake at a crucial stage. "Mill House nearly had him on the floor," claimed the hero-worshippers. The Irish just refused to accept the form. The Gold Cup was the rematch.

Interest in the confrontation spilled out of racing into the public at large. In those days the Radio Times was *the* magazine everyone had in their homes and some indication of what had been generated can be gleaned from the fact that the Radio Times had the two of them on the front page. "At about 3.30 this Saturday afternoon," said the blurb inside, "two big brown horses will come out for a race at Cheltenham to decide which of them is the best steeplechaser in the world."

It was decided. Mill House did absolutely nothing wrong. He jumped for Willie Robinson as only he could – with the same huge, fast, accurate leaps that had until then seen off all opposition; and he galloped so powerfully between fences that he left Pas Seul, a previous Gold Cup winner, a distance behind.

Everyone looked at Arkle and Pat Taaffe, waiting for the moment when they could say that Mill House had got them at it – and it never came. At the second last Taaffe asked Arkle, and Arkle went. There are no sectional times in steeplechasing, but if you see that bit of film you will see that he went very quickly from there on in – even more quickly than the two of them had been going before.

"This is it," said Peter O'Sullevan. "This is the best we've seen." He was right then. But Arkle got better.

Poor Mill House, who looked like a bull with a sword in him that day, was pitted against him in three more races and was beaten further each time: the last of them being in the Gallaher Gold Cup at Sandown, a race which David Nicholson, then riding Mill House, remembers more vividly than any other. Mill House was getting more than a stone and was in tremendous form: "But Arkle went past us as though we were dead." The Sandown record went down by 17 seconds in that race.

Mill House was broken for a while, then came back, after Arkle had gone, to carry top weight to victory in the 1967 Whitbread, a race which had hard men blubbing with joy at the beauty of his rehabilitation. Arkle went on to win more or less what he liked and by about as far as he liked. He made them change the system and make two handicaps: one "if he runs", one "if he doesn't". When with 12st 7lb he was once narrowly beaten on his first run of the season in the Hennessy by Stalbridge Colonist, a horse who later nearly won a Gold Cup himself, who was carrying only 10 stone, and who was brilliantly ridden by Stan Mellor, people were absolutely astonished.

Arkle was different. And that truth was first revealed to us 25 years ago. Ask people if they can remember where they were when they saw it. They'll be able to tell you.

10 March 1989

Arkle comes to the last clear of Mill House in the 1964 Gold Cup. Twenty-five years on, the aficionado knew where he was when it happened.

A holiday haven for a jumping legend

Away from the battlefield Desert Orchid gained sustenance during his summer breaks deep in the remote and beautiful countryside of the North Yorkshire moors

by TOM O'RYAN

FIVE Swaledale sheep nervously stand their ground as the white giant approaches at a leisurely walk. The inquisitive look on their black faces suddenly turns to fright and, at the last second, they scurry away, tails bobbing, into the heather, to avoid a confrontation with a living legend.

Desert Orchid, ears pricked as usual, doesn't bat an eyelid at the silly antics of his woolly-backed friends and continues to stroll along, as sure-footed over the occasionally rough terrain as he is at Ascot when negotiating that tricky downhill run to Swinley Bottom. Here, at his holiday hideaway the steeplechaser is at peace with the world.

"This is a special place," says his part-owner Richard Burridge, who has chosen it as his home. "It has a unique feeling, there are no pressures, and it gives Des a complete psychological break."

While the energetic Burridge is, it seems, game for almost anything he never rides the horse whom he claims has changed his life. "I might have a sit on him in the yard, but I enjoy watching him as much as anything else. And anyway," he adds with a wry smile and a poorly-disguised hint of superstition, "why spoil a winning team?"

The team comprises two local girls, Carol Milburn and Clare Pears, with Lambourn-based Trevor Lowe who, this year and last, devoted his holidays to playing a major part in Dessie's moorland preparation. "I'm terribly lucky, they all do such a fantastic job," says Burridge, genuinely concerned that Lowe, having returned to work the previous day, is not around to gain more fulsome recognition. It's an ill wind, however, even in this remote corner of the country,

that does nobody any good and Lowe's absence did, at least, offer me the golden opportunity of making up the team. Not that the ride on Desert Orchid was going begging.

"Carol can take Des, Clare can ride his sister, Irish Orchid, by Free State, and you can take another of his sisters, Tudor Orchid, a four-year-old by Tudor Rhythm. Only problem is," grins Burridge, "Tudor is a bit bossy, tends to think the world revolves around her and has been known to kick things. You'll probably find that we'll give you a fairly wide berth – just don't take it personally."

Says Carol: "You'll know if she's going to kick. She tends to bend sideways like a banana first." Fortunately for all concerned, not least yours truly, Tudor Orchid is on her very best behaviour. A rich bay with a white blaze, she bears not the slightest resemblance to her snowy-coloured brother, who stands in the yard, ready for the off, like a police horse on public duty. Burridge, complete with full-length leather chaps and lizard-skin boots, mounts his seven-year-old point-to-pointer, Made For Life, and within minutes the four of us are out on the moor.

Dessie is in his usual place, at the head of affairs. Relaxed, but alert, he doesn't miss a single sight or sound. "He's so intelligent," enthuses Richard, "it's a great pleasure and a great blessing to have anything

to do with him." On the silent moor time stands still and looking around from horseback at the vast acres of rugged territory, emblazoned with its autumnal purple overcoat, it's the nearest thing to heaven on earth.

From the heady heights of Glaisdale Rigg, the fields below, divided up by drystone walls, resemble a giant patchwork quilt, and the farms dotted about are no more than specks in the distance. Burridge trots on to open a gate and after another mile or so we reach civilisation. Dessie grudgingly allows Made For Life to give him a lead as we descend the steep winding hill through Glaisdale, a cluster of houses that seem to belong to a bygone age.

Two women approach in a blue Rover. Apparently oblivious to the fact that there are four horses in the string, they have eyes for only one; they slow down, point, and drive on. Bobby Ford, the local butcher, comes out of his shop to cast an admiring glance and ask after Dessie's welfare, and across the road, a housewife, up to her elbows doing the washing-up in the kitchen sink, pauses for a moment and almost presses her nose against the window to get a closer look at the nation's favourite horse.

"The great thing about Des," says Richard Burridge, "is that everybody loves him so much and he loves all the attention. Some people think he's the most wonderful thing in the world and they just don't know how to react when they do meet him. We're in the middle of an extraordinary thing, really. Just the other day, the blacksmith's wife, Mary Hawkin, was telling somebody that her husband had been shoeing Desert Orchid, only to be asked: 'What, not the *real* Desert Orchid?' It's as if they half-expected a dummy version. He's such a legend, some people can't believe this is where he actually is. He's like a myth – too big to be tied down to one place."

As we make our way out of the village, Dessie suddenly breaks into a trot and regains the lead. "When he sees anything that resembles a winning post, he wants to get to it first," laughs Burridge, acknowledging the red-and-white school sign on the grass verge. But Carol Milburn is enjoying an armchair ride on the charismatic 10-year-old, who is not so much a racehorse as a national institution, with his own commercial manager and a large fan club.

"To tell you the truth," confides Carol, "he's the best ride out of the four. He might have a kick and a buck sometimes, but it would only be because something had set him off; he wouldn't mean it."

Carol has seen him run only once – at Liverpool last April when Dessie hit the deck for the first time in 34 races over fences. You can almost sense her feelings of guilt, but it is a common enough complaint. Many other superstitious fans also shouldered the blame. Some felt so upset that they actually put pen to paper and apologised because they "didn't do this" or "didn't do that" on the ill-fated day.

Burridge recalls a particularly amusing letter he received from one devotee, who pointed out that although she wasn't able to be at the Gold Cup, she dressed up just the same and watched the race on television at home with her binoculars around her neck. "I can imagine sometime in the future, saying to the jockey in the paddock, 'Oh, we'll win today – Mrs Simpkins has got her lucky blue gloves on'."

We have been walking for two hours and are almost home when Tudor Orchid boldly decides to challenge her celebrated brother for the lead. Ears flat back, he scowls menacingly and side-steps like a ballet dancer across the road, causing me to snatch up. "Dessie doesn't like being headed, especially by one of his sisters," shouts Richard.

Back in his box, Desert Orchid looks magnificent. His legs are as clean as a whistle, and the muscles across his powerful quarters are toned firm. Burridge considers he is in better shape this time than he was last year. "Everyone who's ridden him says he's more forward."

6 September 1989

On holiday, Desert Orchid (Carol Milburn) leads Irish Orchid (Clare Pears), Made For Life (Richard Burridge) and Tudor Orchid (Tom O'Ryan).

Fond farewell to the Tinman

When Fred Archer took his own life with a revolver, the homage was unparalleled and 100 years on a review was compiled in the tone of the earlier time

by JOHN RANDALL

LAST Monday afternoon, on 8 November 1886, Fred Archer shot himself. As the news sped across the wires to all corners of the Empire, this thunderbolt was the main topic of conversation among men of every rank and class. Even a week later the shock has scarcely begun to abate.

It was known that poor Fred was ill – he had uncharacteristically given up some rides the previous week – but nobody was prepared for the brightest star in the racing firmament to be extinguished so abruptly. It is a mark of his stature that he, a mere jockey, received the ultimate accolade – a leader in The Times:

Hardly anything that could befall an individual would cause a more widespread and painful sensation throughout England than the news which came from Newmarket yesterday afternoon. A great soldier, a great statesman, a great poet, even a Royal Prince, might die suddenly without giving half so general a shock as has been given by the news of the tragical death of Fred Archer . . .

To the populace his skill, his daring, and his prodigious good fortune had endeared him, as the same gifts used to endear a successful gladiator to the populace of Rome. Consequently the news of his death has come with a sense of shock and almost personal loss literally to millions.

The sense of sorrow which encompassed the whole country is conveyed by the Sporting Chronicle's London correspondent in a description of the normally gay district of Covent Garden three days later:

One would have expected to see bright and smiling faces, instead of which general gloom prevailed. Even the streaming crowd that perennially passes through this well-known thoroughfare of luxury and plenty had caught the melancholy contagion. Every face wore a look of sadness.

Writers in the weekly papers, having more time to digest the news than their daily counterparts, were better able to strike the right note. John Corlett, owner and editor of the Sporting Times, and perhaps the scribe who was closest to Archer, wrote an impressive eulogy:

Carlyle defined genius as being the capacity for taking infinite pains. In that sense Archer was most certainly a genius, and he never left anything to chance. If there was an advantage to be gained by being first at the post, be sure that he would be the first man there. If there was anything to be gained by reducing his weight, that weight would be reduced . . .

His insight into a race was extraordinary, and he noted all that was going on. Fordham never knew anything except about his own horse. Archer, in expressing a positive opinion, spoke the simple language of confidence, and his character was totally devoid of conceit and swagger. He had a countenance that lit up wonderfully, the best feature of it being the eyes, with which he always looked you straight in the face.

Was Archer really the greatest of all reinsmen? The Daily Telegraph, like 'the Thunderer', devoted a leader to him and was in little doubt on the issue:

Archer was in all probability the cleverest, the most diplomatic, most resolute, and accomplished jockey that ever sat down in the pigskin . . .

During the last seven or eight years, he was so conspicuous and influential that . . . he overshadowed every other man, gentle or simple, that our great national sport numbered among its votaries.

One or two other observers remarked that Fordham was probably superior, if only at Newmarket. Nevertheless, in Horse and Hound, Audax asserted:

As an all-round jockey Fred Archer has had no equal, in my opinion. One main secret of his success was his undeviating attention to business, always seeing that his weight was right, his horse properly saddled, and that he reached the post in good time . . .

So skilful was he, and so keenly did he watch the starter's movements, that he knew when to go, and won scores of races by his judgment at the starting-post. In the actual race, too, how different was his riding to that of the many headless horsemen that call themselves jockeys, and I pause to think how many races I have seen him snatch out of the fire, and drop a tear of unfeigned sorrow to think I shall never see his brilliant horsemanship again.

It took more than ability to make Archer a non-

pareil, and a hero to millions who had never seen him. Audax referred to:

The brightest ornament of his profession, and one who made many real friends by his undeviating truthfulness, his modesty under adulation which might have turned weaker heads, and his gentlemanly bearing in every relation of life . . .

From the first gentleman in the land to the mildest punter at the street corner, his name was respected as the emblem of manliness and integrity.

His universal popularity was underlined by The Sporting Life, who described him as:

One who by his probity and perseverance, by his great talent and unswerving devotion to his "masters", as well as by his geniality and kindness in private life, had raised himself to a pinnacle in his profession and in public estimation never before achieved by one in his calling.

It was Archer's integrity which particularly drew the attention of the non-sporting Press, which seems usually to believe that only rogues and vagabonds frequent the Turf. The Manchester Guardian wrote, as if in surprise:

In a career which is peculiarly exposed to temptation Archer won and maintained a character for incorruptible honesty.

The Morning Advertiser added:

In his private life few men connected with the Turf possessed so unimpeachable a record. No breath of suspicion ever attached to him; and this in a profession in which suspicion is only too easily aroused speaks volumes for his integrity.

It is nevertheless well known that 'the Tinman'

was an appropriate sobriquet for one who had an eye to the main chance and never complained about large additions to his exchequer. The Sporting Times remarked:

For a time he owned a few racehorses of his own, but he soon gave them up, for, as he laughingly observed to us, "When I ride one of my own there is no one to pay me a fee."

The Pink 'Un also quoted his colleague and friend Fred Webb as saying:

The reason why Archer is so thin is fretting because he can't ride two winners in one race.

The jury's verdict at the inquest was that the great man had shot himself during temporary insanity. The Press did not mention that, had he survived the fatal bullet, he might have stood trial for the crime of attempted suicide. Instead they discussed the underlying reasons for the calamity.

The Sporting Clipper said:

Surely, if an argument were wanted in favour of raising the scale of weights in handicaps, Archer's awful fate supplies it as there can scarcely be any doubt that the delirium was primarily occasioned by excessive wasting.

The Sporting Chronicle concurred:

The scale of weights . . . confines the profession of a jockey chiefly to boys and mannikins, by rendering it impossible for a full-grown and fairly well-developed man to make his living by it.

'Vigilant' of The Sportsman argued:

That Archer's health was suffering from the privations to which he subjected himself in order to ride at certain weights can hardly fail to have struck many people during the present year.

Even stronger language was used by the Sporting Times:

For the appalling tragedy of this great jockey we hold our infernal system of lightweight racing to be indirectly responsible – that wretched system which drives from the saddle, and often into the grave, the most able of our horsemen.

The Daily Telegraph added:

Many a jockey lies now in the churchyard of All Saints', at Newmarket, and in the cemetery at the top of the town, who fell a victim to the necessity of reducing his constantly increasing weight.

Despite the force of these words, hopes for reform are doomed to frustration. The Jockey Club is so slow to remedy ills which are plain to the veriest simpleton, that even in a century's time it is likely that the champion jockey will be forced to starve himself in order to pursue his career.

☐ *Continued overleaf*

Fred Archer was prodigiously gifted but his life ended tragically when he shot himself with a revolver. His grave, appropriately, is in Newmarket.

A genius: the first folk hero of racing

by TONY MORRIS

THE tributes paid to Fred Archer at the time of his death leave us in no doubt as to the immense reputation enjoyed by a prodigiously gifted young man. But his contemporaries were too close to him to place his contribution to the Turf in its proper historical perspective.

His incomparable strength, his immaculate balance, his impeccable judgment of pace, his shrewd tactical brain, his unrivalled nerve, his all-consuming dedication and his ideal temperament made him the complete jockey, the master craftsman of his era. But he was much more than the sum total of his many talents.

Archer was the first folk hero of racing, whose rise to fame and riches effectively elevated the status of his profession to new heights. His career, lovingly chronicled by a press who *made* celebrities the way television does today, was largely instrumental in turning the focus of public attention from the nobility and gentry who ran racing to their hired servants, the horsemen whose expertise had long lacked proper recognition.

Moreover, because his later achievements were realised against a tide of trauma and tragedy which would inexorably engulf him, he became larger in death than in life, a romantic figure of epic-heroic proportions. The legend grew and endured, beyond the time when his riding belonged in human memory, and now our only reference to his once-vivid skills lies in the cold statistical evidence.

That, 100 years on, tends to suggest that he remains the supreme master of his profession, the Bradman, the Pele, the Bach or the Shakespeare of the saddle. He won a record 13 consecutive championships, from the age of 17 until his untimely death.

The first jockey to exceed 200 winners in a season, he went on to accomplish the feat eight times,

twice winning on more than 41 per cent of his mounts. His career ratio of 34.0 per cent winners to rides compares with figures of 22.3 per cent for Richards and 22.0 per cent for Piggott. And Archer's record in the Classics, winning on more than a third of his mounts, remains unrivalled.

Of all his wondrous deeds, none better exemplified all Archer's exceptional qualities than the episode which began on Newmarket Heath on 1 May 1880. There he was savaged by a colt called Muley Edris, who lifted him from the ground and embedded his teeth in the jockey's right arm. In the struggle to release himself, the jockey suffered torn muscles, and medical aid was immediately summoned. The injury would not respond to treatment and, for the time being at least, riding was out of the question. For more than two weeks Archer's arm was in a sling, but he returned to the saddle on 18 May and rode a couple of winners on the following day.

In fact he was still desperately weak, but he had done enough to convince his employers that he was sufficiently fit to take fancied mounts in both the Prix du Jockey-Club and the Derby. And he repaid their trust by winning at Chantilly by a short head on Beauminet and at Epsom by a head on Bend Or. That Derby, won with one hand on a colt who seemed beaten until four strides from the post, ranks as Archer's supreme achievement. His mission accomplished, the jockey then admitted the full extent of his injury, taking two months off to recover.

The Archer Record

Year	Mounts	Wins	%	Year	Mounts	Wins	%
1870	15	2	13.3	1879	568	197	34.7
1871	40	3	7.5	1880	362	120	33.1
1872	180	27	15.0	1881	532	220	41.4
1873	422	107	25.4	1882	560	210	37.5
1874	530	147	27.7	1883	631	232	36.8
1875	605	172	28.4	1884	577	241	41.8
1876	662	207	31.3	1885	667	246	36.9
1877	602	218	36.2	1886	512	170	33.2
1878	619	229	37.0	**TOTAL**	**8,084**	**2,748**	**34.0**

Archer's Classic winners

2,000 Guineas (13 mounts): won on Atlantic (1874), Charibert (1879), Galliard (1883), Paradox (1885)

1,000 Guineas (13 mounts): won on Spinaway (1875), Wheel of Fortune (1879)

Derby (13 mounts): won on Silvio (1877), Bend Or (1880), Iroquois (1881), Melton (1885), Ormonde (1886)

Oaks (11 mounts): won on Spinaway (1875), Jannette (1878), Wheel of Fortune (1879), Lonely (1885)

St Leger (12 mounts): won on Silvio (1877), Jannette (1878), Iroquois (1881), Dutch Oven (1882), Melton (1885), Ormonde (1886)

Total: 21 wins from 62 mounts

7 November 1986

Julie: a power packed jockey

Breaking into the hard world of American jockeys is not easy, particularly if you are a woman, but one lady who made it insisted she be judged purely on ability

by PAUL HAIGH

JULIE KRONE, the most successful woman jockey in the world, is very likeable but definitely not a person to mess about with. In 1986 the second of these truths was revealed at Monmouth Park, New Jersey, to fellow jockey Miguel Rujano.

Rujano, in order to persuade her to give him and his mount more room in a race one day, slashed her across the face with his whip. As Rujano was waiting to weigh in afterwards, Krone, who stands 4ft 10½in and weighs 100 pounds exactly, threw a punch at him which knocked him flat. Later at the swimming pool next to the jockeys' room Rujano tried to get his own back by throwing her in. They struggled for a bit, then both fell into the water. Rujano tried to duck her. Krone eluded his grasp, got out of the pool, equipped herself with a deckchair, and hit him over the head with it.

They were both fined $100. In conversation Krone is as direct as you would expect. "Look," she says after you've spent only half a minute mumbling a question about the difficulties and/or advantages of being a woman in what has so far been a man's world. "Let's not bother with all this sexist stuff. Did you see me ride today?" (Pause for a nod.) "And could you pick me out in a race?" (Pause for a headshake.) "Okay. That's all. I'm a jockey."

When D. Wayne Lukas, a man who is not renowned for the sentimentality of his decisions where his horses are concerned, heard that she was going to be riding at Churchill Downs, he snapped her up for Darby Shuffle, one of his five entries in the Breeders' Cup Juvenile Fillies.

When Bernard S. Flint, a trainer of slightly less ce-

lebrity than the other but just as intensely ambitious about the Breeders' Cup, put her up on the apple of his eye, Dr Bizzare, in the Juvenile, he thought he was doing his horse a favour.

Moreover, Krone recently won a highly-publicised match with 'The Shoe'. She is clearly getting her own way about being judged by the same criteria as any other American rider – male or female.

There is a contradiction about her position nevertheless. All the attention, all the media coverage, all the hype has not been directed at her *only* because she's a good jockey. Racecourse managements wouldn't be running around organising matches with Bill Shoemaker if she were an up-and-coming male rider at the same stage. She is highly intelligent, immensely confident, and never in any circumstances at a loss for words.

She was recently invited to appear on the networked show of David Letterman, a smart-talking, mickey-taking chat-show host, and her friends wondered whether for once in her life she might be even slightly intimidated.

Not at all. She marched across the studio, shook him by the hand and, adapting a good line of Mae West's, asked in her squeaky-cheeky voice that sounds funny even to her fellow Americans: "Is that a burrito in your pocket or are you just pleased to see me?"

A burrito, apparently, is a large Mexican hot dog. And if anyone was off-balance after that, it was Letterman.

She became a jockey not by accident but by design. Her mother was "a self-taught rider" who passed on what she had learnt to her daughter. Julie herself knows the exact day she decided she was going to be a jockey: "I saw Steve Cauthen on TV riding Affirmed – it was after they'd won the Triple Crown – and they were showing the races. I just looked at that and I said 'That's what I want to do'."

The move up a gear came when she went down to Florida in 1980 to live at her grandmother's place, while trying to get some rides at Tampa Bay Downs. There she met Julie Snellings, who had herself been a promising young jockey until she was paralysed by a fall. They liked each other. Snellings, only a few years older, saw the talent too and used her experience to help develop it.

The take-off point for her career came when she moved to New York and began, with the help of her highly-efficient agent Larry Cooper, to impose herself on Monmouth Park and The Meadowlands.

How good is she?

"She's easily the best woman rider in the world," said Shoemaker after their match, "and from what I've seen of her, here and in other races, she can ride with any jockey in the country."

12 November 1988

Thanks a million times, Willie!

In the week Willie Carson brought home his 3,000th winner, the moment had come to assess the man who was tailor-made to be a Flat-race jockey

by JOHN OAKSEY

THE crowd which welcomed Willie Carson's 3,000th English winner at Salisbury on Tuesday was saying "Thank you" for us all. For at least 20 years the appearance of 'W. Carson' beside a horse's name in the morning papers has been a guarantee to anyone backing that horse of, at least, a fair run for their money. Far more often than not it has meant that, if the horse is good enough, it will win.

From the moment Willie started riding, and falling off Mrs McFarland's Shetland pony Wings, it was clear little things like pain and failure were not going to deter him. Newspapers had not then begun to resemble telephone directories in size and weight quite as closely as they do now but, for 'Stirling's smallest paper boy' they must already have taken a bit of carrying. The price of those first rides on Wings was earned the hard way and, who knows, perhaps the strength, fitness and tireless energy which have long been Willie Carson's trademarks had their foundations laid on those early morning paper rounds.

But apart from the inspiration of a film about racing (opinions differ: it may have been Rainbow Jacket or Elizabeth Taylor in National Velvet, maybe both) there were no other obvious 'foundations'. Unlike Fred Archer and Lester Piggott, Willie had no racing blood in his veins. His father packed bananas for Fyffes and, except that he stood knee high to a grasshopper and quite liked the idea, there was no obvious reason why Willie should ever make it as a jockey. Nor, for quite a while, did any such reason become apparent to his first employers. The enforced transfer from Gerald Armstrong to his appren-

tice-conscious brother Sam certainly looked an improvement, but then a short head went the wrong way at Catterick and the rides dried up.

Willie was 23 before he lost the allowance and, for several seasons, neither he nor anyone else could be sure his career was going much further. A run-of-the-mill 30-winners-a-year sort of life looked the best he could hope for and any mention, at that time, of a jockeys' championship would almost certainly have produced the now famous barnyard cackle of derision!

It was from an unexpected quarter that the all-important leg-up materialised. Bernard van Cutsem was a slightly aloof and aristocratic Fairy Godmother with a pirate's face, a good poker player's nerve and well above average skill when it came to training horses. He was, I believe, the first trainer who, when asked, after a valuable and well-backed handicap success, "What is the plan now?" replied simply, "That *was* the plan!"

He was also the first but by no means the last trainer to recognise how invaluable Willie Carson's sheer consistent reliability could be to any stable. Willie's first championship soon followed the van Cutsem–Lord Derby retainer but it would be an exaggeration to say his arrival at the top was greeted with universal enthusiasm in the world of professional race-watchers. "Brute force and ignorance" was the mournful comment of Raceform's chief race-reader John 'Hawkeye' Sharratt and you could, at that stage, see what he meant about Willie's still comparatively primitive *modus operandi*. In 1977, when Dick Hern was compelled by Lord Weinstock to retain Willie Carson as stable jockey in place of that great stylist Joe Mercer, I remember attacking the change on grounds of taste as well as loyalty.

How wrong can you be? As a direct result of that unsentimental but undeniably businesslike decision, Joe Mercer went happily on to be champion jockey with Henry Cecil, while, at West Ilsley, a bond of friendship and loyalty was forged between Willie Carson and Dick Hern which remains unbroken to this day. Nothing in the five-times-champion's long career has done him more credit than his unflinching and outspoken support for the Major.

So where does Willie Carson stand in the Hall of Fame he has now joined? Only Sir Gordon Richards (4,870) Lester Piggott (4,349) and Doug Smith (3,111) have ridden more winners in this country. Pat Eddery (who this month equalled Fred Archer's 2,748) is the only imminent challenger while, from the past, Fred Archer's unique record of 2,748 winners *and* 13 championships in only 16 seasons will never be approached, let alone surpassed.

Over Archer, Lester Piggott and, among his contemporaries, Steve Cauthen, Willie has, of course, one huge advantage. If nature had drawn up a blueprint for a Flat-race jockey, it would, I imagine have fitted him like a glove. The grinding routine of diets, purges and sauna baths has never been his lot and, a superbly fit 47, there seems no reason, barring accidents, why Willie should not go on as long as his still evident enthusiasm lasts. I have never, personally, found it easy to imagine a much more enjoyable way of life . . .

But "barring accidents"? You cannot bar them, that's the snag and, with one or two jumping exceptions, I never saw anything much closer to a graveyard than Willie's fall at York from Silken Knot. A keen hunting man, he is no stranger to hitting the ground at speed, and bounced back from that York horror with cackle, toothy grin and energy all intact.

Nor would "Brute force and ignorance" any longer be an even half-accurate description of Willie Carson's method. He never stops trying and as a result has developed a wonderfully simple, consistent style which, unlike those of Lester Piggott, Pat Eddery and Yves Saint-Martin, could and should be copied by anyone lucky enough to have Willie's build and strength. It is, among other things, a particularly satisfactory style if you happen to have backed the horse Willie is riding. None of that motionless, poker-faced, still-as-a-marble-statue stuff for him. Nine times out of 10, Willie is the first to move. But, as that familiar, tireless, rhythmic punch and drive builds up, it is the others you feel sorry for.

Having, at first, objected to the new whip guidelines, Willie now agrees with Peter Scudamore that they "have, at least, made people think". His own whip, though a vital part of his method, is more often waved than used – and *never* wielded either with excessive violence or out of rhythm.

Rightly or wrongly, Willie believes that Lester and Pat Eddery have a degree of 'natural' talent which he lacks. But even if that is right, I repeat my conviction that no-one will ever harm their jockeyship by copying Willie Carson. Like Lester, Pat Eddery can, at full stretch, get his body into positions so contorted it seems a miracle he stays on at all. By some magic of their own, Lester and he both manage to transmit so much of their own will to win that nothing else matters. But when lesser mortals try to imitate them the result is almost always a clumsy and undignified disaster.

By contrast Willie Carson's legacy to the sport will be a sound, practical, all-purpose method which loses very, very few races anyone else could have won.

25 May 1990

That Willie Carson is a splendid pilot is not in doubt. And, in 1990, he won a flight in a Spitfire for winning the Leslie & Godwin Spitfire Stakes at Goodwood.

How fate played dirty with poor Glynn

Some of racing's heroes and aspiring champions end up in dire straits. Fortunately, there are those who are prepared to do something to help

by BROUGH SCOTT

LET'S get bad luck into perspective. To Cardiff on Saturday to watch Wales routed by the Aussies, a nation mourns. To Staines on Monday to see Glynn Wilkinson. No, you don't remember him. Does anybody care?

Wilkinson was a wagon-driver's son from Teesside who was apprenticed to Sam Hall in the late 1970s.

Energetic and naturally enthusiastic, he had ridden 24 jumping winners when his knee was smashed in a schooling accident at Middleham in 1983. Fate had decided to play dirty and ever since has kept toying with poor Glynn like some monstrously sadistic cat.

On Monday night he was an unhappy sight. He's 34 but, despite thick glasses, thinning hair and a stomach that's beginning to push against the waistband, he has a quiet, deferring manner that makes him seem younger than his years.

He was sitting very upright at a table in his mother's terraced house just round the back of Englefield Green cemetery. You tend to sit a bit stiffly when you have a double fracture of the skull. It was his daughter Beverley Jane's second birthday. He hasn't seen her for three months. But that's only part of the story.

The first battle was to try to ride again and it took him three long years to lose it. Time after time he would visit the Rehabilitation Centre at Camden. He was the star pupil, the most optimistic in the class. We would watch him doing all sorts of amazing exercises with the knee. But in the end the flesh was too weak.

Unlike some wounded heroes, he wasn't big on self-pity. He got on to a training course for the brewing trade. He passed his exams in Shrewsbury and got a job at The Wensleydale Heifer, in West Witton, and then at the Blue Dolphin Holiday Camp at the North Sea resort of Filey.

No hard feelings about Dessie

When in 1991 a race, named in honour of a famous rider, adopted a new moniker – the name of a horse – a call Down Under was undertaken immediately

by JONNY BEARDSALL

From the outside he had graduated successfully from the racing game; he had learnt a trade and was about to marry one of his colleagues. But the knee wasn't made for lifting and the wedding was to bring neither party happiness.

For physical and family reasons he turned down a position in the South and started work at the Hytex rubber factory in Rotherham. Gareth and Beverley Jane had appeared but home affairs were not flourishing.

As a fresh start he began selling milk in Teesside but after three months of enforced separation, the marriage was clearly over.

We are into the start of this year and a stay with his sister at Egham got him a job but ended in hospital with pneumonia. The cat's paw had grabbed anew but once again released him. Whilst in care the doctors had another look at his knee and with modern microsurgery were able to clear much of the old debris out. A month ago at the St Leger meeting Glynn looked much better than he had in years.

He was due to visit his children next day. He had a job at the Schweppes plant in Ashford, and he had just survived a car smash three days before. "I think my luck is on the turn," he said. So it was. Back again.

Next morning the family visit was disallowed in acrimony. Next week he was rushed to intensive care, the car crash (he had fallen asleep at the wheel after late-night overtime) had split his skull and blood had seeped out of the brain. Now there will be no work before Christmas. "We were terribly worried," said his mother on Monday.

But she is not the only one. At a time when racing's external image is besmirched by an unprecedented amount of internal wrangling, we ought to be very proud of what we have been able to do for Glynn Wilkinson.

For it was the Injured Jockeys Fund who supported him through Camden and through his brewery trade course. It is the IJF and its heroic northern almoner Hilary Kerr who are involved with Glynn's latest help. And the IJF only exists because of racing's goodwill. Over 500 cases have gone through our books, from paraplegics to multiple sclerosis to simple victims of misfortune. Last year's Christmas card and calendar made £120,000 but we had payments to beneficiaries of over £300,000. Let no-one get charity fatigue.

Especially not today when Newmarket sees the unveiling of its newest visible evidence of what's possible when charities, local council and racing community work together – the Racing Welfare flats at Phantom and Moreton. Twenty-four old people's apartments are now in the pipeline.

It will never be easy. You remember the aching disbelief as the Wilkinson tale unfolded. "I just can't get over my luck," said Glynn, his eyes watering only slightly. "But at least it can only get better." It will do. If we bother enough.

17 October 1991

LATE last night as Terry Biddlecombe slipped into his kangaroo pyjamas 9,000 miles away in Perth, Western Australia, the 3.45 at Wincanton came under starter's orders. This race, the first running of the Desert Orchid South Western Pattern Chase, was until this year run in his honour as the Terry Biddlecombe Chase.

Far away but not playing possum, the rambunctious champion jump jockey of yesteryear was far from ruffled.

Biddlecombe left England over three years ago to sprout new roots Down Under. But doubtless Wincanton will always be special to him as the scene of his first and last winner. As an unknown amateur, he had just turned 17 when he won a novice hurdle at the track in 1958. "I got up to beat Fred Winter by a short head on a mare called Burnella and I also rode my last winner there for Fulke Walwyn."

Delighted for Desert Orchid to be recognised by the racecourse, he was full of praise for the grey horse. "It's marvellous for his connections. He's a superb horse and I think it's a wonderful gesture. I wish them all the luck."

Soaking up seasonal temperatures of 32 degrees, he lives some 45 minutes' drive south of Perth. His 30-acre cattle ranch, Ross Court, is also home to his thoroughbred breeding-and-breaking operation and he has 19 horses in his stable at present.

"I've a big 'Pommie' house with an upstairs," he says, so-called because most of his neighbours live in Ramsey Street-style bungalows.

"We're into hard times in Western Australia at the moment. There's not much money about but it's really magic out here."

So with Biddlecombe's name erased from the Racing Calendar, the devoted legions of forty-somethings who followed his colourful career, without the Nineties' commercialised trappings of pens, T-shirts, mugs or videos, will now have scarcely anything to remember him by. They might just be having second thoughts about Wincanton's decision.

After all, Dessie is only a horse . . . isn't he?

25 October 1991

Terry Biddlecombe, the colourful hero of thousands, was not put out when his name was erased from the Racing Calendar in favour of a horse.

Arthur lets his horses do all the running

In the midst of triumph or misfortune Arthur Stephenson remains a bulwark against hype. For him the performance of a horse is the beginning and end of it all

by COLIN RUSSELL

IN the hurly-burly of the Liverpool winner's enclosure the tentative inquiry was met with the predictable answer. "Would you come and say a few words?" asked microphone-holding Aussie Jim McGrath, in charge of the post-race interviews for closed-circuit television. The response was negative.

Pointing to the assembled press corps, their pens poised like daggers around Caesar, the question was repeated. The answer was the same. "I know them, and the boys know me." He shrugged, adding, with a wry smile, "I know you too, you're Australian, you should go back to Australia!"

The sharp mind, the wicked sense of humour in evidence just seconds after one of the high points of his long and distinguished career. It came just a day after one of the low points, but as he knows oh so well, that is racing.

Even by his standards last week was an extraordinary one in the life of Arthur Stephenson, doyen of jump trainers, and one of the most respected men in the game. On Thursday, with the big match just hours away, he had the misfortune to lose one of his star players, Grand National hope The Thinker breaking a leg on the gallops at Crawleas. A day later, the chestnut Blazing Walker enthralled the Liverpool crowd with a breathtaking performance to win the Glenlivet Melling Chase, a performance of such class it seemed to move even the trainer.

On Saturday the big one eluded him yet again, Durham Edition running another gallant National, but finishing only sixth. On Sunday he celebrated his 71st birthday.

For most of those 71 years Arthur Stephenson has lived at Crawleas, a square, stone-built farmhouse, perched just outside the village of Leasingthorne, just a field or two away from the town of Bishop Auckland, whose back-to-back terraced houses serve as monuments to a bygone age.

It is an unlikely setting for a training centre, but it is one that has served as home for almost the entire Stephenson career. Like his neighbours across the fields, there are no luxuries at Crawleas, none of the electronic gadgetries of the modern-day trainer. Training is by instinct, by feel, by knowing how horses think, based on 40 years of experience.

Born and bred into the world of horses, Stephenson initially made his name as an amateur rider, riding his first point-to-point winner at the age of 14 and his first under Rules just two years later. That experience was to prove the foundation stone of his training career, a career that began just after the Second World War and has become one of the most successful, if not the most successful, in British Turf history. To date his tally stands at 2,475 winners over jumps and a further 300 on the Flat.

Not that Stephenson is one for statistics – he is not a man to dwell on past successes, he lives for the future. Even after 45 years in the business he shows no signs of wavering, has no thoughts of retirement, horses are his life. When asked what keeps him going, there was no hesitation, just the straightforward reply: "I love every moment of it."

Like most in his profession he is a fine judge of horseflesh, eyeing up a horse like most of us eye up women. Whether it be the legs, the face, the ears or the eyes, within moments he can ascertain its strengths and weaknesses. Being right more often than wrong is the key to his success; he is not a trainer who is sent horses by owners, he buys them off his own bat and passes them on.

Most are Irish, because experience has taught him they are that bit tougher, and most are chasing sorts. They are a type who need patience, and they receive it. His no-rush policy is one that has brought him into many a conflict with the authorities, and it is a subject that still riles him. "They do not seem to understand," he argues strongly. "Most of my horses are backward sorts, not ex-Flat racers who know their job. They have to be educated, to be brought along steadily and it is no good at all giving them hard races when they cannot win."

Although holding strong opinions on this and many other subjects, Stephenson rarely gives vent to them in public. He is a man who keeps his feelings to himself, and gets on with the job of turning out winners. That is why there are never any behind-the-scenes action shots on the run-up to a big race like the National. Outsiders, particularly those bearing cameras, are simply not welcome at Crawleas. It is a place of business not of entertainment.

But as much as outsiders with cameras are barred, those armed with chequebooks are positively welcomed, because Stephenson is not just a legendary trainer, he is also a master horse dealer. "Come along and see, I'll have something to suit you," are well-rehearsed words in his vocabulary. Once there, most are caught, ensnared like flies in a spider's web. Few escape with bank balances unscathed.

Tough and persuasive in business, Stephenson is charming and sporting on the racecourse, being the first to congratulate those who have beaten him, and rarely being too busy not to pause for a joke with friends old and new.

That spirit of geniality wavers only when he is called upon for a formal presentation. Owning or part-owning many of the horses he trains, his ser-vices are frequently in demand to receive a trophy or memento. It is not a task he relishes, in fact nine times out of 10 his wife Nancy, brother Ralph or nephew Peter Cheesbrough are delegated the task, while the intended recipient slips away to saddle another runner, or watches unconcerned as the pleasantries are exchanged.

Stephenson does not court publicity, he shuns it. He is happiest saddling his runners at the small northern tracks like Carlisle or Kelso, well away from the television lights and microphone-bearing Australians. In the final analysis, it is not words that matter, it is performance. That is why Arthur Stephenson is more than content to let his horses do the talking for him.

10 April 1991

Fighting prejudice with guts and talent

Women in racing have to contend with not only the challenge of the sport itself, but also bias against their sex. Alex Greaves has proved that the battle can be won

by WILL O'HANLON

HISTORY was made at Doncaster when Alex Greaves became the first woman to win one of the major handicaps, my newspaper informed me on Sunday morning. True, but trite.

The race was won – in so far as jockeys ever win races – by one of the best apprentices of the day, riding with all the style which regular Southwell-watchers have come to expect from a thoroughly competent horsewoman. But in just the same way that Jenny Pitman has been patronised throughout her career (the first woman to train a Gold Cup winner, a Grand National winner, and so forth) so Alex Greaves can be certain that her every moment of glory will, in its turn, be both inflated and diminished by the same fawning appraisal.

A generation after show-jumping gave us champions of the calibre of Anne Moore and Marion Mould and three-day eventing produced Lucinda Green and Princess Anne, racing has yet to unburden itself of one of its most treasured prejudices – that women cannot compete with men.

Will Alex Greaves' success change that perception, or is this to be yet another false dawn, a case of thus far and no further, *vide* Lorna Vincent, Gee Armytage and Gay Kelleway? Each in her way helped to lead women out of the ghetto of 'ladies' races' in which the sport seemed happiest to contain them, but none could then build on that initial surge. But then none of them was in the position of being stable jockey to a successful 40-horse trainer such as David Barron, whose gamble on Alex has paid spectacular dividends. Her mother Val, herself

Life and hard times for a Turf heroine

Being an attractive woman and a jockey can produce some bizarre situations but, if you are Gee Armytage, you can plan to get your own back in a book

by MARTIN TREW

GEE ARMYTAGE sat alone in the women's changing room at Towcester last Saturday, hunched over a pad of A4. Having two hours to kill before her only

ride, she forced herself to work on her book.

She is writing it in collaboration with journalist John Dorman, whose idea it was. And despite the glamorous image she's very self-effacing. Discussing the book in the Crown & Horns, East Ilsley, she expressed the fear that people might find it dull. But there shouldn't be any shortage of material because it's been a remarkable year for Gee, who is now 23.

She turned professional at the start of the year and quickly found herself on the media treadmill. In the run-up to the Seagram Grand National, she was portrayed as Marilyn Monroe in breeches. The week prior to the National contained days of pure farce. When not serving tea to Fleet Street harpies she was being asked to undress for photographers (requests she flatly refused). Amid all these crazy goings-on, Gee the jockey was preparing herself for the ultimate challenge of a ride in the National. It says a lot for her that she gave Gee-A such a brilliant ride.

Without giving away too much of the book, here's something of the flavour.

Near the day of the race, Gee agreed to be photographed for a centre-page spread in The Sun for a fee of £800. They insisted she wear 10 different outfits, which they provided. The most generous consisted of a tiny jacket worn over the remains of a shirt. After a couple of shots, they asked her to take a pioneer on the women's trail – with the distinction of being the first lady rider to beat the men over hurdles – and head girl to Barron since his earliest days, had initially tried to deflect Alex away from racing. And with one second place from a handful of rides as an amateur, Alex's career might well have ended there had not trainer's wife Chris Barron stepped in.

It took just a little discreet lobbying by her to get Alex the chance.

Barron readily concedes that before Alex came along he, in common with most hard-bitten professionals, had little time for girl riders. "Most of them were too weak, but I never had any such doubts about Alex – she always was a strong rider," he remembers. "And whereas most apprentices are taught to be jockeys, Alex really could ride a horse. There's a world of difference."

But jockeyship, and in particular the ability to use the whip without horses veering away from it, did take time to learn. Barron himself had to administer the odd lash (of the verbal sort) in those early days, notably after a victory on Irish Passage at Southwell in January 1990, when his young rider was fortunate not to be stood down for careless riding.

Alex's identification with Southwell ('Queen of the Sand') was inevitable in the circumstances, and while she would now like to shake some of that sand from her feet, she is astute enough to recognise that Southwell has been an ideal nursery slope.

It was perhaps to be expected that she might struggle at the start of the 1990 turf season, as indeed she did. "I jocked her off a few at that time but I found I didn't improve one single horse as a result – and I used some good men too," Barron recalls. "So we sat down and had a good chat about it and decided two things needed changing."

The first was to accept that Alex's riding weight was to be 8st 1lb ("She'd been trying to do 7st 13lb but we agreed there was no point in riding light if it also meant riding weak"). The second was to excuse her from mucking-out and other routine stable duties ("We had been killing her with work") and to treat her as the prized asset she had become. Alex responded by going on to ride 17 winners on turf that summer.

Her all-action finish will never please the purists, but Barron would not have her change. "She's been attacked over the way she moves her legs about when she's driving a horse out, but that for me is where the power comes from.

"A lot of jockeys keep their legs still simply because they're not able to use them – Alex can and if she ever stops I'll fire her!"

27 March 1991

---

off the jacket. Gee declined. They were taking roughly 100 shots of her in each outfit. The least compromising pose involved her lying on her side with one leg stuck in the air.

"Eventually I just burst into laughter and the more I laughed the harder it was to stop. I was laughing and crying so much I felt sick. All the make-up they put on was ruined. I had to be sent out to get some fresh air."

When the pictures appeared, her make-up had been touched up "to make me look like a tart". Otherwise, they were surprisingly innocuous. However, Britain's biggest-selling daily had not finished with her. On the day she was to appear live on Wogan, The Sun ran a story by Steve Smith Eccles saying girls should be banned from the National.

Gee agreed to reply provided her quotes were read back to her before they went in the paper. She was riding at Ascot that day. The plan was to drive straight from the races to the BBC studios in West London. Unfortunately she left her clothes in the boot of her brother Marcus's car. He drove home, leaving his sister with nothing to wear on Wogan.

They made a rendezvous at junction 13 of the M4. As Gee hurtled towards London she remembered The Sun had not rung her back. She got through to the newsdesk on her car-phone and had the article read back. She had been so badly misquoted, she asked for the article to be scrapped. They said it had already gone to press.

The story had a happy ending. Having arrived late at the studios and been hustled through make-up as the show was beginning, Gee went on to give a performance of considerable poise.

In truth, Gee has a better story to tell than most. Her mail-bag alone would fill a book. Since she became nationally famous she has become a sort of Marge Proops, a shoulder to cry on for Britain's most indefatigable letter-writers. Perhaps the strangest incident of all to be recorded in her diary happened after she broke her collar-bone in February. She was being examined by physiotherapist John Skull. Her boyfriend, Carl Llewellyn, was waiting outside the surgery, in his best suit. As Skull manipulated Gee's shoulder, she let out a series of long, blood-curdling screams. Carl found it all too much and after walking around feeling faint for a few moments, he actually collapsed in an alley next to the surgery.

While we look forward to the book's publication, others wait with trepidation. The list includes the jockeys Martin Bosley, Mr M. Armytage, Luke Harvey and Jamie Osborne. I don't *think* she mentioned any other names.

2 December 1988

A tough guy on stage at Aintree

Bryan Marshall won the Grand National on Early Mist and Royal Tan, and recalled with sparkling Irish wit and a long memory the inimitable early 1950s

by PAUL HAIGH

BRYAN MARSHALL looks a bit like Victor McLaglen, the Hollywood actor who turned up in about a hundred black-and-whites as the battered tough guy with the heart of gold.

Age has had something to do with the way life has redesigned his features. But it wasn't age that knocked his nose off-centre or altered the set of his chin. The man still has a sort of steel-bitted bridle which a London dentist built to hold the pieces of his jaw together after they'd been jigsawed in a fall a few weeks before he won the National on Royal Tan. He only took it off when he rode at Hurst Park a week before the big race to prove he was fit for Liverpool.

Marshall has lived a lot of racing history and it shows. He was born in Kilkenny, the son of an American father and an Irish mother, and was 11 when he first came to England in 1927 at the invitation of Atty Persse, then Master of the Limerick Hunt, "who admired the way I rode".

Marshall was 13 when he rode his first winner on the Flat. Sixteen when, because of weight, he switched to jumping. Thirty-one when he was champion jockey. Thirty-seven when he climbed aboard Early Mist, the first of the two National winners he rode for Vincent O'Brien and owner Joseph ('Mincemeat Joe') Griffin.

One of the surviving greats of the Grand National, he went round Aintree 10 times. ("Not 10 in a row though; I watched with a broken arm one year.")

He has an exceptional memory, a forceful personality and is a superbly direct raconteur. Sips of scotch and a bad cough punctuate his stories. When he comes to a punchline he sits forward in his chair, fixes you with an unswerving gaze and dares you to be unimpressed. Here are two of Marshall's racing memories, each about one of his National winners:

"When the other jockeys heard I was going to ride Early Mist they were all saying he was dodgy. They all thought I'd get crucified. He was a nervous horse all right. He'd shy at a cigarette pack if he saw it on the ground. He'd see things that weren't there and shy at them. But really he was a brilliant jumper and he went round with no trouble.

"I hadn't ridden him in a race before, and I don't think I'd ridden him at school either, so the first time I was on his back was at Liverpool. He was an extraordinary-shaped horse – very high withers, very narrow shoulders, then he suddenly came out like a bottle. I had to ride him with almost a full length so that my legs were sticking out at an angle.

"The quickest line down to Becher's is near the outside. People don't realise that, but if you look there's a slight elbow. You miss a lot of the barging that goes on in the middle of the field if you go that way, too. I'd been told he probably wouldn't be quick enough early to go along the inside.

"He landed in front at Becher's second time. I thought for a while the others were being cunning and leaving me there. Then I thought 'All right, let's go. It's catch as catch can now'. We went clear. Then when we crossed the Melling Road he thought the race was over and I had to sit on my arse and give him a belt and say 'Come on, you bugger'. I had to ride him like a donkey, but it was just because he was pulling himself up. He still won by 20 lengths and he was only a split second outside Golden Miller's record. He was a terrific horse. Gold Cup standard really, but just idle.

"People ask me which was the better of the two but there was no comparison. Royal Tan was a completely different kettle of fish. Royal Tan was a handicapper pure and simple. He'd had so many hidings they'd had an effect on him, and I didn't discover how to ride him until a week before the race. I'd ridden Royal Tan five times already that season. Every time something went wrong. Once he nearly fell, once he did fall. Nobody could tell me exactly how to cope with him.

"Now Vincent is very, very thorough and he leaves no stone unturned. I was retained by him that year and he had me flying back and forward between England and Ireland every week for one thing or another. Royal Tan had run second in his last race before Liverpool, when I couldn't ride him because of

□ *Continued overleaf*

When Bryan Marshall, a man with a sparkling wit and long memory, was up against the odds, Victor McLaglen could not have done it better.

□ *Continued from previous page*

he jaw. I was walking around in a rugby cap for a while with this harness round my chin.

"Vincent wanted me to go over and ride the horse in a school at Gowran Park. I didn't see the point in it. I thought it was silly to go schooling an old horse but he insisted. He wanted to show me how well the horse was. He wanted to enthuse me, I think. So over I went again and stayed with Mincemeat Joe, who owned the horse."

Mincemeat Joe, the man with the Damon Runyon nickname, deserves an introduction and Marshall's description has to be condensed. He wasn't quite as sinister as his nickname implied – but not far off.

He was a qualified accountant who made his first fortune during the war, bagging sand from the seashore, adding powder to it to change its colour – and selling it to farmers as 'fertiliser'. For this service to Irish agriculture, he was rewarded by his government with a year's free accommodation.

When he came out of jail, the war was over, but his keen business brain drove him to inquire what other commodities had been in short supply. "Mincemeat," said someone. "We haven't seen mince pies for years." Griffin 'bought', on tick from the Greek government, a £100,000 shipload of dried fruit, a cancelled order from a British grocery chain; "got out the same cement mixer he'd used for the fertiliser"; turned the fruit into mincemeat or a facsimile thereof; and sold the resulting substance, in jars, to the same British grocers for £200,000.

Griffin won £100,000 in two bets – one with Jack Swift, one with Wilf Sherman – when Early Mist won the National. But by the end of the following summer he'd lost the lot – and Swift could think of

nothing to do with a rubber cheque for £56,000 except frame it and keep it in his office.

Marshall had been given a present of £5,000 for Early Mist and he'd been luckier – it had come, eventually and in dribs and drabs. "Anyway," continues Marshall after this digression, "Mincemeat Joe takes me aside that night and says, 'I'll be giving you a present if you win but I'm afraid I won't be able to make it quite as big as last year's.' I didn't show any delight. This man already owed me £600. I just wanted to win the National and I didn't really expect to do so on Royal Tan.

Joe Griffin was grateful after he had won but not so grateful he wanted to give his jockey any cash. He still owed the £600, and had used various subterfuges to avoid payment. Once he'd even parted with a cheque, then cancelled it before it could be presented. Marshall found him at dinner at the Adelphi and suggested that now would be as good a time as any to settle. Apart from anything else he knew Griffin had bought a share in the winning ticket on the Irish Sweeps.

One of Mincemeat Joe's friends remonstrated. "Shut your mouth," said Marshall, who swears he was never a fighting man but who was angry and "had had a glass or two of champagne" by this time, "or I'll punch your nose so hard you'll be looking for it in your trousers."

The man shut his mouth. Marshall got his £600. Victor McLaglen couldn't have done it better.

6 April 1988

Bryan Marshall, winning his first Grand National, in 1953, on Early Mist. He won again the following year on Royal Tan.

Penalties of the fasting business

Racing requires that its jockeys are lightweight. Ensuring they match up to its demands can drive heroes of the riding art to the most punishing extremes

by JOHN OAKSEY

HUNGER is all too common in the second half of the 20th century but starving millionaires are not. No doubt a few boxers qualify but jockeys are the only highly-paid sportsmen I can think of in whose life and work hunger and the weighing machine play a vital part both before, during and after the event from which they make their living.

The crucial difference between boxing and racing is that fighters are weighed out some considerable time – often hours – before a bout and never after it. Having sweated off the pounds they need to make the weight, they pass the scales – and still have plenty of time to replace any liquid lost and avoid the enfeebling salt deficiency that comes with dehydration.

For a jockey spending hours in a sauna, by contrast, that cup of tea he snatched after weighing out may *taste* delicious. But, poured into a sufficiently desiccated body, it is all too apt to add embarrassing pounds. For he, of course, has to weigh in after the contest as well.

Admiral Rous usually takes the blame, but long before he produced his still seldom challenged scale of weight-for-age, some other anonymous genius must have worked out the effect of weight on horses. The thoroughbred itself weighs up to half a ton, but there is no getting away from the fact that a single pound on his back (and, allegedly, even less on his feet) will cause him to take marginally – but measurably – longer to cover a given distance.

Of course, if the way it works was always precisely measurable, handicappers would be richer than bookmakers which, as we know, is not the case.

Nevertheless the Admiral's principles still rule. In their modern form (the level of weights was last raised eight years ago) they are still making an undernourished misery of grown men's lives – just as they were before poor Fred Archer shot himself.

At one dangerous stage in the 1960s, for instance, the word went round that a certain Doctor X in Harley Street had a 'magic' method for losing weight. His waiting room should have put me off to begin with – full of pale, anorexic girls waiting like a pack of anxious borzois. But I urgently needed to get rid of at least seven pounds, so in I went – to be relieved of £20 before the learned doctor started talking. What this bought was a massive, rather painful diuretic injection and a large pill box that the doctor filled with handfuls of pink pills.

Well, the injection duly pumped out five easily replaceable liquid pounds and the pills, which turned out to be pure amphetamine or 'speed', certainly did cut your appetite while they lasted. In fact, taken, as ordered, when you got up, they made you feel like a slightly drunk but quite clear-headed 'king' – turning the chilliest 'first lot' into a carefree joy-ride. But then, about 12 o'clock, just as you got to the races, the effects began to wear off – and suddenly the novice chase did not seem such a good idea after all. It was on account of days like those that I would have liked to have strangled Dr X, but luckily the BMA and CID got to him before me.

Quite apart from using a bit of common sense about dangerous drugs, there isn't much doubt that jockeys simply take better care of themselves these days. But the fact that jockeys are sensibly doing themselves less damage is not, by itself, an argument against the five- or even seven-pound rise, across the board. Much as trainers and handicappers would like to make the lives of men like Steve Cauthen easier, there is a real, almost universal reluctance to ask horses to carry more than the present maxima – 9st 7lb for two- and three-year-olds, rising to 10st in the July of a three-year-old's second season. There would, understandably, be even stronger resistance to making jumpers carry more than 12st 7lb. Even Lester Piggott, whose life-long battle with the scales was won with the help of no drug stronger than his iron will, is not now in favour of a change. So, sadly, that is, at least, reassuring news for horses.

But, just possibly, reading this, you are sitting in a sauna with an empty stomach and a parched mouth, trying to sweat off those last few ounces. You have my sympathy and should take Jack Leach's advice. "I used to take off an extra pound so that I could have a glass of champagne before racing," Jack wrote. "It made me feel like a new man so I had another glass for the new man too."

13 January 1989

Born to be the heir of a jumps tradition

The riding record of Peter Scudamore has left past exploits far behind. But the roots of his modesty and his skill can be found among some illustrious predecessors

by JOHN OAKSEY

THERE are 16 men alive at this moment who know what it takes to be a champion jump jockey of Great Britain – and 15 of them can scarcely believe their eyes and ears. Like the rest of us, they have been watching, with a mixture of admiration and incredulous amazement, as Peter Scudamore rewrites the racing history and record books. They know, from personal experience, that this is one of the hardest titles to win in any sport – and it took almost all of them the best part of a year to win it.

So here we are, in the second week of February. There are nearly four months of the season still to go – but the title is won and Jonjo's record is yesterday's news. How on earth can you rate a man who has gone that far beyond the bounds of probability?

The last thing Peter Scudamore would want is any comparison calculated to belittle his contemporaries, still less his predecessors. But such comparisons need not be odious and, like any other sportsman ambitious to improve his game, you can bet that Peter has been making them privately for years himself – seldom, if ever, to his own advantage.

Son of Michael Scudamore, godson of Pat Taaffe, retained by Fred Winter, co-champion with John Francome . . . all 30 years of Peter's life have been spent among top-class jockeys and those are just four of the 'examples' from which, consciously or unconsciously, he has had to choose. It seems to me that they and others like them are as good a background as any against which to measure his unique achievement.

Having spent much too long for her own peace of mind waiting for ambulances outside racecourse first aid rooms, Peter's mother always hoped he might become a land agent or take up some other nice secure profession. But the odds were heavily stacked against her. The year before his son was born, Michael Scudamore finished second to Fred Winter in the jockeys' table. He was always more a horseman than a jockey – but the sort of tough, sympathetic horseman on whom trainers could and did rely.

In that season, for instance, Fulke Walwyn chose Michael to ride Mandarin in seven of his first nine steeplechases. Hard-mouthed, headstrong and too brave for his own good over hurdles, Mme Hennessy's now-immortal little horse was widely expected to prove a jockey's nightmare over fences. But he never fell with Michael – winning three races and finishing second in the other four. The foundations of Mandarin's heroic career were securely laid and it is no surprise now to hear tributes from Martin Pipe and others to Peter's skill and attention to detail on the schooling ground.

Of many other lessons Michael gently taught his son, the most obvious was that, however much some things change, racing is still an old-fashioned, conservative world. With few outstanding exceptions, short hair, tidy clothes and a clean-shaven face make it easier for a young jockey to be accepted and get on. I have never heard what happened the first day John Francome arrived at Fred Winter's with his now-familiar version of an Afro haircut – but probably by that time his genius and lightning ever-ready tongue had made such little eccentricities easier to accept than criticise.

An exception to so many rules, John has, among other things, revolutionised the stuffy 'presentation' ceremonies to which racing is so addicted. The all-male champion jockeys' dinner, in which a single but funny near-printable story from Lord Willoughby de Broke used to be the sole comic relief, will never, post-Francome, be the same. The party had become mixed by the time John arrived and I shall never forget the shocked horror on the faces of some fairly straitlaced Jockey Club ladies as he told them a story which depended on the alleged similarity between the top of Richard Pitman's balding head and another rather less mentionable part of his anatomy.

Long before John had finished, his timing and total unconcern had changed horror to hysterical laughter but, in that respect as in so many others, he is an impossible man to follow. Peter Scudamore, doing things his way, has wisely never tried. He would, however, have enjoyed a party given by a Hereford Farmers Club in honour of his father's Grand National on Oxo – and of Michael's great friend Tim Brookshaw, who, after breaking a stirrup at Becher's, called across, "Look, no feet!" – and rode Wyndburgh, virtually bareback, into an heroic second place.

Peter will, please God, never have to match Tim Brookshaw's stubborn courage when he became a paraplegic and he has certainly never copied 'The Treatment' – the unique Brookshaw finishing method which would nowadays have stewards calling for smelling salts! And, although he did take a lot of good advice from an even greater friend of his father's, Terry Biddlecombe, their routes to the title could scarcely have less in common.

There have been a few exceptions since, but Terry's last championship was 1969 and his retirement in 1974 marked the start of the modern, more business-like dedicated and 'professional' approach to jump jockeyship – the age of the breathalyser, Mrs Thatcher, car telephones, more married jockeys and more expensive mortgages.

Brilliant, unorthodox and supremely effective on the course, Terry was, in a sense, his own worst enemy off it. Unlike Peter, he could never, latterly, do 10 stone but the present champion's usual dinner – Dover sole, spinach and a glass of white wine – would have reminded Biddlecombe of Belsen. Rocketing gaily from nightclub to Turkish bath and back again, Terry doubtless did lasting damage to his health – but was also an unfailing source of pleasure to his countless friends.

All this makes Peter Scudamore sound a bit dull – and, just at the moment, driving tirelessly up and down England with the car phone buzzing, constantly plagued by press and public and, just as constantly, churning out the winners – he could, I suppose, be said to lead a rather monotonous life. I know a good few men and some women who would give an awful lot to be 'bored' that way for just one week. But, in the whole racing world, I defy you to find a single trace of envy.

Modest, unassuming and courteous, Peter knows better than most that nothing in a jump jockey's life is ever certain. He also knows that an open winter has combined with Martin Pipe's miraculous run of success to put him in a uniquely fortunate position. It still could not be happening to a nicer man.

I remember a November day at Newbury in Fred Winter's last season when he rode four winners. When Fred came back into the changing room every man there stood up, as one, and cheered and in our cheers, delight, respect, yes even love were mingled.

Peter Scudamore is, we all hope, nowhere near the end of his career but, at this moment, given the same circumstances, I believe he could expect a comparable reception.

10 February 1989

Peter Scudamore learned early on that racing is still a conservative sport where short hair, tidy clothes and a clean-shaven face make it easier to get on.

Hawk-eyed Sharratt hangs up his bins

Even the doyen of racereaders had to finally retire. He was a man whose sharp eyes had homed in, conservatively, on something like 50,000 races

by PAUL HAIGH

THE most frequently read journalist in racing retires today and in the Press Room at Newbury there will be a certain amount of sentimentality because he will leave a bit of a hole behind him. You may not be familiar with his name, but every time anyone has read the form in the past 42 years – you know the sort of thing: "Held up, Improved two out, Wandered under pressure, Weakened" – there's a pretty

good chance it was written by John Sharratt, Raceform's senior racereader.

Sharratt is a stocky, conservatively-dressed fellow with a well-clipped moustache and a strongly developed sense of what he thinks is right and wrong. He is also the doyen of racereaders, a man who has carried his natural fastidiousness into his examination of something over 50,000 horse races since he began the job shortly after leaving the RAF in which he played his own, probably not inconsiderable, part in thwarting the ambitions of Goering's Luftwaffe.

Sharratt bristles. He has been, for as long as anybody now involved can remember, the man who's maintained the old standards and tried to impose them on what he regards as his relatively frivolous 'new' colleagues. He's also been the man who's always been willing to help anyone who's trying to write and who isn't quite sure about what he's seen. Sharratt was born into racing. He grew up in Bishop's Cleeve, close by Cheltenham, which was a jump racing village in the same way some are mining villages. In the village school at various times attended by the Hameys, Alf Newgate, Billy Speck and Billy Stott nobody wondered what they were going to do when they grew up. They knew they were going into racing. Sharratt went into the Avebury stables of C. Birch, where he 'did his two' with Tim Molony.

He was still only 16½ when he joined the RAF in 1941. When he joined Raceform after the war he found himself under the tutelage of Jack Topham and since then Sharratt's had more practice than

Psychic messages about Shergar

The kidnapping of Shergar, the 1981 Derby winner, has never ceased to fascinate. Since his disappearance in 1983 the search for him has grown ever more bizarre

by PAUL HAIGH

YOU probably thought the search for Shergar was more or less over and that inquiries, like the great horse himself, had probably come to a dead end. This is very far from being the case, as an article in this week's Psychic News (what d'you mean "never heard of it"?) reveals only too clearly.

The article, by a man called Tony Ortzen, who apparently wears dark glasses even when being photographed for his byline, tells of the help which has been given by psychics and seers in the continuing hunt for the great champion.

You will all remember Superintendent Jim Murphy, the senior officer of the Garda, who incurred such unjustified derision from the British press for the way in which initial inquiries were conducted. He was, and is, a likeable man, but one who is easily guyed. For example: he used to wear a special and rather funny type of hat to his innumerable press conferences.

One day the members of the press, who until then had busied themselves by making up dreadful stories found out where he got it. They went round to the shop in Dublin and bought the entire stock.

anyone else and has himself reached the sort of status Topham then held in the game.

When someone of such vast experience retires there are certain questions you have to ask him about the horses and riders he's seen. Sharratt has no doubts about his heroes. He isn't a man who ums and ahs.

"Nijinsky on the Flat," he says without hesitation when asked to name his favourite. "The last Triple Crown winner. He and Lester. What a combination! Amongst the fillies I suppose Meld should come first but she was never a filly with the speed of Petite Etoile. Petite Etoile didn't really get a mile and a half, which was why Aggressor managed to beat her that time in the mud at Ascot, but Lester used to kid her to get it."

Lester Piggott stands alone in his pantheon of Flat jockeys ("That man was magic. There's no other word for it") although Charlie Smirke ("One of the great characters") is another rider he had a lot of time for – particularly when he was riding Tulyar.

Sharratt is essentially "jumping orientated" though, and it's about his National Hunt favourites that he waxes most lyrical. Among the jockeys he's most admired have been Martin Molony ("A tragedy his career was cut short"); Bryan Marshall ("A wonderful horseman"); Fred Winter, and Scu "who's as great an ambassador as you could wish for the sport. But if I had to pick just one jump jockey," says Sharratt, "it would have to be Francome. Francome was the complete pro, arrogant, sometimes annoying but he was like Lester."

As far as horses are concerned he names among the hurdlers National Spirit, Hatton's Grace, Persian War, and Monksfield ("As brave as a lion"). But at the top of his list he puts Sir Ken: "A machine: he was never beaten over hurdles."

He's seen all the modern greats of steeplechasing and is not unwilling to give Desert Orchid a place among them. He went as a boy to see Golden Miller, "although of course I was too young to appreciate him". Then there was Prince Regent, "past his best when I saw him but still good enough to win the Gold Cup," Cottage Rake ("A very underrated horse, I've always thought") and Arkle, at whose memory he becomes both excited and reverential at the same time.

"There's no doubt about it," he says, "when you're talking about Arkle you're talking about the king."

Sharratt's enthusiasm for the sport he's served for so long is still that of the young boy he was when he started. It's absolutely untarnished by familiarity or by cynicism. He isn't weary of his job. He's begun to feel he's losing the photographic memory he's relied on for so long, though nobody else has noticed. "I don't want to go on after I've gone over the top," he says. "I've got no time for the amateur approach in anything. I'd never want anyone to think I was trying to live on a reputation."

He's a very gentle, good-natured chap really, and when he comes back to racing, as he's promised he will after a decent break, he'll be very welcome.

31 March 1989

When Murphy appeared on the steps of Newbridge police station next day for his morning briefing he was confronted by the sight of about 100 heads, all wearing his hat. Many of the heads were also busily mimicking in various villainous brogues Superintendent Murphy's rather distinctive method of telling us that he really didn't have a clue.

Well anyway, Superintendent Murphy has now gone on to even greater things in his career. It was he who, resplendent in a bemedalled uniform, masterminded the great evacuation and search of The Curragh grandstand just before the 1986 Budweiser Irish Derby, and the people who said then that he hadn't found a bomb but he had found some of Shergar's droppings should be ashamed.

But Psychic News reminds us that it was while Murphy was on the case that paranormal help was first sought. "We are concentrating our search in the Galway area because we have had many psychic messages that the horse is there," said the Super at one point.

A year later, according to Ortzen, another Irish psychic called Zak Martin "was called in at the request of Shergar's owners". Martin "saw" the horse standing ankle deep in water, which he thought might have been treatment for some sort of swelling. An American 'seer' called Jeane Dixon claimed shortly afterwards that "Shergar is alive and well and has been on English soil." He was being kept on an isolated farm and being used for breeding purposes, she alleged.

Now it seems that "Scottish parapsychologist Tom Robertson has been invited to Ireland" (no, we don't know who by) to try where others have failed.

This may not be a matter to be too frivolous about, not least because the disappearance is widely assumed to be the work of the IRA or one of its offshoots. But before Robertson gets down to whatever it is that parapsychologists get down to, we feel we should alert him to the fact that certain Irish part-time sages, many of them taxi drivers and several of them sober, claim to have "seen" the poor horse, or at any rate his carcass, at or near the Dublin premises of a fast-food chain, whose name it would quite certainly be libellous to disclose.

3 February 1989

A 40-year love affair with jump racing

On the occasion of the celebration of the Queen Mother's 90th birthday in 1990, this revealing appreciation of racing's favourite owner of jumpers was written

by JOHN OAKSEY

THE day after Lord Mildmay's memorial service in May 1950, a Times leading article written by Peter Fleming ended with these words: "He would not, perhaps, have disdained the reward he has won – which is a kind of immortality among the English."

The writer little knew how true he wrote because, less than a year before his death, by speaking a few words at a Windsor Castle dinner party, Anthony Mildmay had done the best and most-lasting of all his many services to the sport he loved. For those words were to launch Queen Elizabeth the Queen Mother on the happy reciprocal 40-year love affair which she and National Hunt racing have been enjoying ever since.

Mildmay, of course, had several other claims to sporting immortality but, in a way, that night at Windsor was still his finest hour.Royal Ascot was in full swing and, drawn between Queen Elizabeth and her daughter, the present Queen, at dinner, it was natural enough for Lord Mildmay to compare his own very different kind of racing with the glossy social fashion parade they had been watching that afternoon.

Who cares now how the conversation went? What matters is that the great amateur communicated enough of his own enthusiasm to persuade his listeners to try their luck as owners.

Their first choice, suggested by trainer Peter Cazalet's stable jockey Tony Grantham, was Monaveen, and to him, too, owned in partnership between the Queen and Princess Elizabeth, we owe a deep and, sadly, an apologetic debt of gratitude.

Poor Monaveen. He won a supremely appropriate victory in the first Queen Elizabeth Chase at Hurst Park and then ran really well to be fifth in Freebooter's Grand National. Lord Mildmay was brought down on Cromwell in that race, but both for him and for Monaveen the sands were running out.

They had not, in those days, had the sense to modify the water jump and, taking off too soon at Hurst Park in the race he had won the year before, Monaveen was caught by its treacherous lip and broke a leg.

Earlier, only two months after the National, Lord Mildmay had gone down, as was his habit, for an early-morning swim off Mothecombe beach. He was never seen again.

So, with her first racing mentor lost, Queen Elizabeth's career as a jumping owner was, from the first, a roller-coaster of triumph and disaster, delight and disappointment. Of her first four horses, Monaveen was killed and, after winning a King George VI

Steeplechase, Manicou, whom she 'inherited' from Lord Mildmay, broke down and had to be retired. The third, Killarney, was a failure and the fourth was Devon Loch!

Queen Elizabeth does not much like being reminded of that dismal Aintree day in 1956 and, frankly, hates the famous, too often repeated picture of Devon Loch's still inexplicable sprawl.

But neither Dick Francis nor Dave Dick (left in front on E.S.B.) nor John Hole, who led Devon Loch up that day, will ever forget the calm, sympathetic sportsmanship with which Queen Elizabeth bore her disappointment.

"Oh you poor old thing," John remembers hearing her whisper to Devon Loch when she came to see him in his box. Then, and ever since, in her order of priorities, the horse has always come a long way first.

But jockeys matter too and so, very much, do stable lads. David Mould, who before riding 106 winners in the famous colours (twice as many as anyone else), 'did his two' at Fairlawne and remembers with what delight the Queen Mother's regular visits were expected.

"She knew all of us and all the horses. There she would be, whatever the weather, in her wellies, watching you muck out or down in the Park when we were schooling. Talking to her wasn't ever frightening. It was *fun.*"

Nearly 40 jockeys, including half a dozen amateurs, have had the privilege and delight of riding a winner for the Queen Mother, and even writing that turns me an envious shade of green. For on two occasions I did come tantalisingly close. The first and most shaming was on a horse called Sunbridge who, although rather slow, seemed to his trainer Jack O'Donoghue and me, made to order for the four-mile National Hunt Chase at Cheltenham.

This is – or used to be – a race in which, with the leaders apt to be out of control or over-excited or both, economy of effort in the early stages pays rich dividends. Nerves make you talkative and I blush to admit that I almost certainly gave the Queen Mother a pompous pre-race preview on my cunning tactical 'plan'!

Coming back onto the racecourse (you went half way to Evesham in those days) it seemed to be working like a dream. But then, without consulting me, Sunbridge suddenly threw two huge leaps at consecutive fences. He passed five opponents in the air at one, six at the next, and there we were in front. About half an hour too soon.

Chaseform: "Led 17th, one pace flat" tells the painful story all too clearly and Sunbridge was third, beaten four lengths.

"Didn't he jump beautifully?" was all the Queen Mother said but although, as always, her smile cheered you up, we all knew he ought to have won.

But, oh, how I would have loved to ride just one winner in those colours.

I would also love to have written the lines with which, 21 years ago, Sir David Llewellyn greeted Queen Elizabeth's 200th winner. There have been another 180 since and will, please God, be many more. But . . .

Ma'am, if you'd never won a race
The Turf would still be blessed in you
Who, with the worst of luck to face,
Still come serenely smiling through.
And that is why in happier hours
When you stand in the winner's place
We count your wins, like you, as ours.

4 August 1990

In February 1976 at Ascot, Sunyboy gave the Queen Mother her 300th victory over jumps, a rare milestone.

This John leapt out of his cot to stardom

Jockey, author, trainer, commentator, owner, builder, tennis player, tipster, John Francome was blessed with much more than his share of talent and energy

by PAUL HAIGH

ONE of the easiest ways of making yourself miserable is to waste time envying the apparent happiness of others. People like John Francome make it difficult to stay out of this trap.

It isn't Francome's fault that he seems to have been at the head of a quite ridiculous number of queues when the advantages were being dished out. There's no point in talking any more about his career as a jump jockey, other than to recall that Fred Winter, many people's idea of his closest rival for the 'best of all time' title, has said more than once that he thinks Francome was better than anyone else there's been.

There is some point, however, in examining Francome the man. If you accept that a good jump jockey has to be very quick-witted, very athletic and very brave, then it follows that the best of them has probably been issued with each of these qualities in a heavy-duty soup ladle. Fortunately for most people's peace of mind those who are gifted in these respects are not often gifted in others. Francome is.

A lot of jump jockeys, who have possessed those qualities in equal or perhaps only slightly smaller measure, have also had a sort of personal recklessness, a seed of self-destructiveness like a lot of boxers, which makes them go on just too long, take one fall too many; flop when they've finished because they can't really think what to do next. Not Francome.

He's a fox; a survivor; someone who probably hasn't been short of an idea since he first climbed out of his cot.

He is also very hard-working. He is very funny. He is not entirely unattractive to women. And he is sensible enough to be able to use all this for his own benefit without giving any impression of being vain or manipulative or any more selfish than the rest of us.

His first book, realistically entitled Born Lucky, came out three years ago and surprised even those who knew him by its fluency, wit and readability. His fifth is called Twice Lucky and comes out this week.

Francome is now, if anything, an even busier man than he was when he was champion jockey. He plays hard as well as working hard, and time is probably the only thing he finds in short supply. "I'm a commentator, racehorse owner, author, and I run a tipping service," he says in his Swindon drawl when asked to describe his present occupation.

Until recently he was also a racehorse trainer: "But the training stopped almost exactly a year ago for one simple reason. I'd bought a farm to expand and sold my other place before I'd got planning permission for the expansion.

"When that was denied I didn't have anywhere to train."

So he does get some things wrong. Some might have said anyway that the training was the least successful period of his life but he's not having that, although he doesn't get even slightly defensive about the suggestion.

"No, funnily enough," he says, "the other way round really. I felt I was just getting the hang of it. You can't see things when you're on top of them but when you have time to stand back and look it's a bit like calling in a team of management consultants, I should think. You learn from your own mistakes, don't you."

He goes on to give an unregretful example of how he's lost money in the past: I designed a stopper to go into a can of Coke. You know how when you're driving you drink half of it and then it drives you mad because you have to stick it between your knees to stop it spilling. I thought it would be very useful but I couldn't sell it. Still use it myself though."

The books were his idea too. The voice that comes off the pages of his books is very obviously Francome's own, but you can't help asking the question about, well, 'assistance'. "Absolutely not," he says, again unperturbed by the notion that any of his work is ghost-written. "It all comes out exactly as I put it in. I don't think anyone changes any of the wording."

The commentating is something he seems to take a lot more seriously. "I really enjoy it," he says. "You know Andrew Franklin [producer] and Bobby Gardam [director]. All of them and the other commentators, they're a really nice bunch of lads." The idea that he might be doing the commentating (and maybe the writing) because he needs to be in the public eye, because he misses his days in the saddle and the celebrity of being the greatest jump jockey on earth, doesn't bother him too much either: "I did a lot of riding for 15 years and when I packed up I did it because I wanted to – not because of injury or because I wasn't getting the rides any more. I don't miss it at all.

"As for the celebrity, that's never been one of my problems. Never. There's not as much of it as you might think anyway if you're a jockey. People might recognise you if you went into a betting shop or something, but that's about all, and if you ever get too pleased with yourself there's always some guy comes along and gives you a bollocking so you keep your feet on the ground."

Sometimes the bollocking came from persons in authority. Hardly any champion jockey has gone through his career without someone, sometime, making at least the suggestion, however unjustified, that he hasn't tried, on some of his mounts.

Francome writes about skulduggery in his novels and you have to ask him how clean he thinks racing is. "A lot cleaner in real life than it is in books," is his answer. "But you can't write a novel about everything being rosy, can you? You write about the things that could go on, and do go on to a certain extent, but much less than anyone would think.

"Racing is as straight in this country as ever you'll get it, and definitely as straight as anywhere in the world."

Once again he's very relaxed and unconcerned –

as relaxed as he is about his own future. He isn't sure which of the hats he's wearing, or has worn, is going to fit him best in five years' time.

"I enjoy getting things going and then tend to lose interest a bit," he says, venturing some self-analysis. "My long-term ambition is about the same as my short-term ambition really: just to keep myself happy and get on with what I'm doing. I'm quite an easy-going character. It's only when bureaucracy gets to me sometimes that I come to the end of my tether."

Maybe you need big troubles before you can have complexes, because Francome doesn't seem to be a very complicated man. That isn't intended as an insult. He clearly has a very high intelligence, but he's done his studying in the university of life and doesn't seem to believe in encumbering his brain with too much theory.

He's a practical man. He loves building. He built his own stables at his old place, brick by brick and loving every minute of it. On Monday a 30-ton heap of tarmac was due to arrive at his new one and he was really looking forward to laying it down on the drive: "Lovely, I'll really be in my element doing that."

It's a bit of a relief to be able to say that the new book is just a book, not something that's going to win a Nobel Prize or change anybody's life. You'd have to say, really, that it reads like a verbatim report of what you might get if John decided to hold forth in a pub on the subject of racing to a bunch of people – including possibly a pretty girl or two – who didn't know much about racing at all.

It's no less amusing for that. It just doesn't tell you anything new about John Francome, but then he doesn't pretend it will: "It's just a light-hearted read for Christmas, that's all. People are always stuck for something for Christmas, aren't they? And being a genial sort of chap I just thought I'd give them this out of the goodness of my heart."

Outside the sun is shining and the Porsche is waiting. "That all right?" he asks, letting you know in a friendly way that he feels he's already been interviewed a few times too many in his 35-year-old life. "You can always make it up if you want any more, can't you? That's what most of them do anyway, isn't it?"

It's only after he's gone that you think you ought to have asked about his (brief) modelling career, a bit more about the fish shop he has a half-share in with Bill Shoemark, about the telephone tipping service and the John Francome Racing Club and whatever his next brilliant scheme might be.

But by then it's time to get down to the serious business of persuading yourself that your own life isn't that bad either, and that there's no need at all to envy the apparent happiness of another.

26 October 1988

The man with a song in his heart

Michael Stoute is an elite trainer nurturing immense talent among his horses. A writer captured the lyrics when he became part of his team for one morning

by TOM O'RYAN

YOU can hear him coming long before you see him. Like a leading baritone practising for one of Mozart's operatic masterpieces, Michael Stoute puts his vocal cords through a whole range of exercises as he pounds his daily beat amid the wide-open expanse of Newmarket Heath.

Sitting astride his faithful hack, Basil, Stoute's singing, humming and whistling is incessant as he busily canters back and forth from one end of his giant string to the other, interrupting his aria only to issue instructions, like a general supervising his troops. "Trot on, jockeys!" booms the trainer somewhere from the rear before easing Basil to the wide outside and cantering past, bursting into song as he goes. Out of sight within seconds, the only remaining evidence of his presence is a faint humming noise in the distance.

It's a privileged feeling to be part of the team. There are 68 of us riding out first lot – "It takes half a mile to turn the string round," reveals one girl riding alongside me – and the mood among the staff is one of relaxed high spirits. And no wonder. The seeds of Classic success were carefully sown last autumn. Now is the time to anticipate germination.

My mount, Lady Midas, a neatly-made three-year-old filly bought for 100,000gns as a yearling, does not have Classic pretensions. What she does have is potential. Stoute briefly reins-in alongside and rattles off her vital statistics with the ease of a teacher going through his two-times table.

It's a little after 7.30am as we make our way across the Bury Hill towards Waterhall at a pace clearly designed to keep the horses happy and relaxed. They're all there, Derby hope Warrshan ("He looks grand; really filled his frame," says Stoute); the exciting Mythyaar ("We've got the Nell Gwyn in mind for her"), and Russian Royal ("A very promising filly"). Sally Eddery, wife of jockey Paul, ambles along on the attractive Musical Bliss ("She'll probably go for the Fred Darling"), while Kerrera, who showed headstrong tendencies last season after her dazzling display in the Cherry Hinton ("The best two-year-old-filly performance of the year") walks away to my left.

All five starlets look well forward and are totally at peace with themselves. "Relaxation is all-important," stresses Stoute, providing further proof, if any were needed, that a trainer of finely-tuned thoroughbreds needs to be as expert in equine psychology as he is in physical fitness.

Andy Andrews, head lad at Beech Hurst, Stoute's other yard, trots back on a hack to liaise with his boss. Bespectacled assistant James Fanshawe, riding the retired No Bombs, comes up from the rear to join in the conversation.

The string is divided into groups of threes and fours. "Come up behind Tracey," Stoute tells me, "two lengths apart the first time. And Christine," he says to a blonde-haired girl riding a bay filly, "you drop her in last."

Christine looks rather shell-shocked. "How does he remember everyone's name?" she asks incredulously. "I only started riding out here this week."

It was another illustration of Stoute's phenomenal memory, which is a source of constant amazement – and some amusement – not least his peculiar

habit of scribbling an imaginary message on the palm of his hand with his finger before completing the charade by casually rubbing one hand across the other, as though to wipe the slate clean. Imaginary or otherwise, it seems to work. Very seldom, if ever, does the meticulous Stoute forget anything and not only is he able to identify any one of his 186 horses at the drop of a hat, but he can, more often than not, reel off two or three generations of their pedigree.

The flat ground at Waterhall rides well. Lady Midas moves freely under me as we do a brisk 4 ½-furlong canter before easing down. Then it's across the busy Thetford Road for a quick assembly before an equally bold stretch up the railed all-weather Equitrack. My filly again does it nicely over seven furlongs, most of it on-the-collar, and she is hardly blowing as we pull up. Conditioning work, it's called. "We don't do any more of it now than we used to, but I'd like to think we do it better," says Stoute.

Eighty minutes after leaving Freemason Lodge, we arrive back in the yard. Legs are carefully hosed down before the horses are returned to their boxes, rugged-up and fed. Chief work-rider Frank Conlon is putting the finishing touches to 2,000 Guineas hope Shaadi, who, according to Stoute, "is pencilled in for the Craven, with Pure Genius going down for the Greenham, providing the ground is decent".

The experienced Conlon, 48, is in no doubt that Shaadi is destined for top honours and he reveals, among some leg-pulling from his colleagues, that the unbeaten colt, along with Dancing Tribute, are to be "bankers" in his six-to-follow; a competition open to everyone in the yard willing to back their judgment with a fiver.

"It's usually one of the secretaries, gardeners or mucker-outers who wins it!" laughs Frank. "The nearest I got was three years ago. I was convinced that Shahrastani was a Derby horse – I was riding him most of the time – but on the day I had to have my entry in, a horse called Danishgar did a brilliant bit of work, so I put him in instead.

"Danishgar won only one race, Shahrastani won four, including the Derby, and I got beaten by two!"

Over breakfast, stable jockey Walter Swinburn, just back from a winter stint in Hong Kong, explains how he keeps a detailed record of all the horses he rides at exercise – "It takes quite a while to get round them" – and how he awards them a star-quality rating. "When one turns out to be good, it's nice to look back and see that you gave it four stars," says Swinburn.

"Is four stars top?" I inquire. "Oh no, five is top," he grins.

Second lot clatters out into the yard. Swinburn teams up with a handsome two-year-old colt by Bairn, called Ruling Passion (how many stars would he get, I wondered), while my mount is the year-older Haebeh, a sparely-made daughter of Alydar, who finished unplaced in her only race so far, at Lingfield last autumn.

"All right, jockeys, let's go!" shouts Stoute as we move out once more.

Frank Conlon moves alongside on his pride and joy, Dancing Tribute, an intelligent, all-quality individual. "She's maybe a 'speed' filly," says Stoute. "Her work over the next few weeks will tell us an awful lot."

As we make our way across the Bury Road to join up with the rest of the string, stabled at Beech Hurst, Conlon reveals: "There's a lot of friendly rivalry between the two yards, especially this year. We've got Shaadi, Musical Bliss and Dancing Tribute at Freemason, they've got Pure Genius, Mythyaar and Kerrera. But at the end of the day, it hardly matters. They're all trained by M. Stoute."

Conlon is in no doubt what makes his boss, trainer of 14 Classic winners in England, Ireland and France, especially good at his job. "He never misses a single thing. He trains 'em all as individuals. He's an individual trainer. Brilliant at it, he is."

Michael Stoute does not hear the glowing tribute. He is already hacking off into the distance . . . singing happily as he goes.

23 March 1989

Pounding his beat, Michael Stoute, accompanied by Basil and musical aria, supervises his huge team on Newmarket Heath.

THE DREAM

Everybody dreams in racing, of the great horse who will win for them. Breeders match prize stallions with prize mares in pursuit of offspring who will give life to the ambition. Fortunes are spent and stud animals live artificial lives in cosseted comfort. Charts going back centuries are studied, detailed plans are hatched, but the transfer of winning genes will always remain in the lap of the gods. So even stars are consulted and seers referred to. In the end, champion horses like champion humans can come from nowhere. And it is that fact that gives the dream its essential allure

When Possessive Dancer, with Steve Cauthen, won the Irish Oaks, Alex Scott, her trainer, could not contain himself. At that moment, the victory marked the biggest success of his training career.

A sheikh awaiting his Derby destiny

The Derby is the race Sheikh Mohammed has wanted most to win. In an interview in Paris, he talked about the great race, his horses and his involvement in the sport

by JOHN OAKSEY

WHEN Sheikh Mohammed sweeps into the Epsom paddock at the head of his entourage this afternoon, he does so as the most powerful man on the racing earth. But he also walks in a loser.

For despite his many studs, 200 or so broodmares and 600 horses in training worldwide; despite the Classic successes that have stretched from Epsom to the Breeders' Cup in America; despite £6 million in global prize-money last year; despite 50 winners and almost £500,000 already this season, Sheikh Mohammed has never got remotely close to winning the greatest race of all.

Since Jalmood first carried the maroon-and-white silks in the Derby parade as joint second favourite in 1982, there have been just six more Mohammed runners and the nearest was Sharrood, a distant eighth in Shahrastani's year. For the biggest investor the racing world has ever seen you could almost call it a catalogue of disaster.

"We thought it would be easy when we started," Sheikh Mohammed said with that strong, disarming laugh last Friday evening. "We bought three horses in 1976 so as to win the Derby, the Oaks and the St Leger. Luckily the filly Hatta was quite good (she won at Goodwood) but no-one remembers the other two."

Sheikh Mohammed was talking in one of those beautiful, incredibly high-ceilinged Empire rooms from which fortunate customers of the Ritz Hotel in Paris can look out. But his jeans and sweater were much more the action man than the sophisticates downstairs, who even included a particularly toffee-nosed hall porter.

When asked for "Sheikh Mohammed" this factotum demanded much more information. "You see," he drawled with that special Gallic sneer reserved for poorly-dressed English peers, "we 'ave so many sheikhs."

But attempting to pin Sheikh Mohammed down takes more than a hall porter. He can be as elusive in conversation as he is in his jetsetting life. It is not that he is all charm and courtesy, nor even that sometimes the language becomes a barrier if not a bond. It is the difficulty for any of us quite to comprehend what makes him tick. How is it that this third son of a tiny but now oil-rich desert sheikhdom should be so stirred by the attractions of our strange old racing game to combine with his brothers to launch the largest single equine investment that any country has ever seen?

It is, of course, the most extraordinary stroke of luck. Countless trainers, stable lads, stud hands, builders and bankers too must kneel down in thanks every morning. But the empire's sheer size has to bring with it worries over what might happen if it suddenly went away, or if the Sheikh and his advisers played things a shade less benevolently.

What happens as he and his brothers gradually rationalise their operations? How will we feel if many more of his horses are switched to chase dollars and francs? Indeed, how will he feel if the Derby continues to elude him? Why not take up some other hobby? These are most unusual problems for any activity to face up to, but this is no ordinary man and today's big race no small ambition.

The first Derby at Epsom that Sheikh Mohammed ever saw was Nijinsky's in 1970. He watched it on telly while attending a language school at Cambridge. It is still the one English race he would most like to win.

"The Derby and the Arc de Triomphe," he said last week. "Those are top of our list – but eighth is the closest we've come so far at Epsom."

Sheikh Mohammed was flanked by racing and stud advisers Anthony Stroud and Robert Acton. Though jeans and sweater would have earned a rapid elbow at Ascot, for a man who had just flown in he looked remarkably fresh, and your first impression of Sheikh Mohammed close up is one of crackling energy.

When something interests or amuses him his eyes really do light up. You feel almost in danger of an electric shock and when, as repeatedly happens, a wide grin splits the brown-black bearded face, you suspect that only a very faint-hearted maiden would object all that strongly to a desert ride across the Maktoum saddlebow.

A trained jet pilot, Sheikh Mohammed, 41 years old, is equally at home on horse or camel and did

☐ *Continued overleaf*

An owner? I'm dying for the day it happens

When you are a racing pundit, people somehow expect you to own a horse. They don't take account of the vagaries of life, or the mortgage or the bills

by TONY MORRIS

IF I had a tenner for every time I've been asked, "Do you have any horses in training yourself?", I would be in the owners' list now.

It never ceases to amaze me, the way that question recurs. It's tens on its coming out in the course of the first conversation I have with anybody in this business, anywhere in the world. People have only got to hear what I do and how long I've been doing it, and they automatically assume I can't just be an observer or commentator.

I've now got beyond the stage of being bored by hearing the question; I get bored by the sound of my stock replies. There are two of them: "Horses in training? I've got five kids in education." And: "The bank manager wouldn't hear of it." Depending on what degree of jocularity seems appropriate to the occasion, I choose between "Ha ha" and "Ha ha ha" to round the answer off.

I went through that familiar routine for the hundredth, or thousandth, time last week with a chap on the phone, and in the normal course of events I would have put it out of my mind the moment I replaced the receiver. But this time was different, because the call had interrupted serious business. When I turned back to what I was doing, I allowed myself an extra "Ha", and could scarce forbear a "Eureka". I had found the missing link, the route to becoming a racehorse owner.

The task on which I was engaged was writing my will. I had taken a bit of legal advice, I had immersed myself in a couple of DIY books on the subject, and I hadn't made an awful lot of progress beyond a few philosophical thoughts on the absurdity of life.

Well, I ask you. Here I am in a constant battle to meet my financial obligations, going through agon-

---

☐ Continued from previous page

ride some private races back home as a young man. But it was not until 1976, when Dick Warden and John Dunlop bought him three yearlings, notably Molecomb winner Hatta, that he became seriously hooked on British racing.

"Oh, we thought we would win all your Classics straight away then," he said. He laughed. "Especially the Derby!" In fact the Derby has been his least successful English Classic. While such fillies as Oh So Sharp, Unite, Diminuendo and Pebbles have brought the Sheikh his greatest triumphs, Sharrood's eighth, as we've seen, has so far been his closest in a Derby.

A brand of friendly, bantering argument seems pretty typical of his close but easy-going relationship with his trainers and advisers. "We talk on the telephone all the time," he said when I asked how on earth a busy travelling man could keep in touch with the doings of 600 horses.

"The videos reach me pretty quick and, when I've seen them, we talk again. I can tell you, we do not always agree about what happened either! Often they just don't *know*. No-one does. Horses are flesh and soul. They fool you. It all depends on the horse." That last phrase was his answer to several of my questions.

It underlined again and again that this is a man who both thinks and cares deeply about animals. It was, for instance, his answer to the thorny problem of how early successful horses should be retired to stud, having said, not for the first time, that money is not the object of the exercise.

"We do not need to show a profit," he said. "It must depend on the horses. They will tell you. Take Indian Skimmer, for instance. She just did not want to do it any more."

In this controversial field, as a matter of fact, Sheikh Mohammed's own record is pretty good – and he can hardly be expected to comment on his brothers' decisions.

Clearly the whole subject of training fascinates the Sheikh, whose happiest racing moments, by the sound of it, are spent riding out, sitting beside his trainers, watching the horses work. He will, I suspect, have read with very special interest Seb Coe's enthralling discussions with Henry Cecil published in The Times. Sheikh Mohammed is certainly far from convinced that traditional training methods are ideal. "For one thing, how can it possibly be right ies every month wondering whether I can meet the mortgage, terrified every three months over the VAT liability, and suicidal annually about the Inland Revenue's demands.

I'm frightened to pick up the mail every morning for fear that there's another bill. What's more, the freezer's damn near empty. And the solicitor has the cheek to tell me that I'm worth a fortune! Well, that I'm going to be liable for a substantial amount of inheritance tax, anyway.

What kind of a crazy world is this? If I'm so so-and-so wealthy, where is all my wealth? The answer, of course, is that, like most other people's, it's all in non-disposable assets. I shall come into my fortune when I die.

I'm bound to say that I'd reckoned on its happening rather earlier than that, but things never run quite as smoothly as you imagine they will, when you go out into the world, bouncing with ambition and optimism. You've only got to get divorced a couple of times and getting back to square one becomes an unattainable target.

But I did always say that I'd become a racehorse owner if it was the last thing I did, and that's precisely what I intend to do.

You'll have noticed that a set of Timeform annuals, from 1942 to 1989, was auctioned recently for £6,000. Cheap at the price, too, if you ask me – nearly half a century of racing, vividly described and expertly analysed. It's a collection of masterpieces,

bound to become more valuable as the years go by. Well, I've got an identical set, and it's inevitably one of my proudest possessions. In fact, apart from Chateau Morris, which I shall never be able to call my own, there's only one thing I have which is more valuable, a complete set of The Sporting Magazine.

So here's the plan. In my will I direct that the Timeform annuals be sold and the proceeds used to purchase a racehorse. And the set of The Sporting Magazine goes to finance training fees.

I'd been wondering how to recompense my executors (who are both jolly nice people and racing fans as well) for the diligent discharge of their duties over my estate, and here's the ideal answer. Neither has ever owned a racehorse, and each will be certain to get a lot of fun out of managing my horse's career in my unavoidable absence.

Of course, I shall have to make sure that I assess my liability for inheritance tax correctly. And there might be a technicality or two to iron out over the acquisition of property by my estate. But no doubt there are ways and means, and I'll trust to my trustees to find them and use them.

I'm really getting quite excited over this, the realisation of a lifetime's ambition. Just imagine reading it in Racing Post: "The winner carried the colours of the Executors of the late Tony Morris." Fantastic!

I'm dying for it to come true.

22 November 1990

---

to keep a horse standing in its box for 22½ hours every day?"

Saying that, of course, he fully appreciates the labour problems which any other more elaborate method might involve. But I was left with a feeling that he might just be the man with the will (and money) to have a go at solving them.

I wonder, too, how delighted he will be to hear that Henry Cecil, who according to Coe "never times a horse or takes a pulse", "will have none of" the various scientific approaches of which Martin Pipe has made such brilliantly successful use. Training, as the great athlete wrote, is an admirable art. But that does not mean that it might not yet benefit from the application of some modern science.

It was reassuring, last week, to find that Sheikh Mohammed and his advisers are at least partly aware of the uneasiness, justifiable or otherwise, which is caused by the huge and still growing scale of their operations. "But we want to observe your customs," he said. "We like it here and want to stay. We hope we have improved things by bringing in good blood."

On competition some of the Sheikh's views sound a fraction naive. "We all want it," he said. "But they

should come and compete with us."

I fear that, to a smallish trainer catering for one- and two-horse owners, and confronted by one who owns 600, such an invitation may not be irresistibly attractive.

At least, arguably, the protection of the weak is a job for the Jockey Club and its race planners, not for individual owners, however powerful.

Both Sheikh Mohammed and his advisers firmly deny that there is any intentional 'sharing', or avoidance of competition, between him and his brothers, or even between horses in different yards. On actually limiting the size of the operation, however, there does not, at present, seem to be any agreed policy. Surely one ought to be arrived at.

Sheikh Mohammed himself is certainly not opposed to a bit of culling.

"When a hawk swoops he always takes the weakest bird," he said. "Racing and breeding should be like that, a series of tests to find the strongest and the best. The Derby is that sort of test. We shall keep trying."

Sheikh Mohammed said firmly: "We are not going away."

6 June 1990

End of an emperor among horses

When a great sire dies, it's tantamount to an empire collapsing. The headlines are stark and racing folk often speak of the loss with unashamed sentimentality

by RICHARD GRIFFITHS, DAN FARLEY and GEOFFREY FABER

NORTHERN DANCER, the greatest thoroughbred stallion of modern times, has been put down at the age of 29. The 1964 Kentucky Derby winner was humanely destroyed yesterday at 6.20am American time, at the Northview Stallion Station in Maryland, USA, where he had been enjoying his retirement.

"He got a severe attack of colic on Thursday and we could not see him suffer," said Windfields Farm president Charles Taylor, Northern Dancer's syndicate manager and son of the great horse's owner/breeder, E. P. Taylor.

Northern Dancer, who covered his last mares in 1987, was due to be buried yesterday afternoon at his birthplace, Windfields Farm in Oshawa. "His illness was not prolonged," Taylor added. "We did not let him suffer."

Taylor, who stayed up all night monitoring the horse's progress by phone, last saw Northern Dancer in August. "He was in great shape for a 29-year-old horse," he said. "He was a bit arthritic in the right knee, but he was full of spirit, as usual. He was number one, and he always knew it."

In a stallion career spanning a quarter of a century, Northern Dancer sired the winners of 99 European Pattern races from 605 foals and at one point in his career he commanded a stallion fee of $1 million. His sons and scions have dominated the Derby since 1970, when Nijinsky was the first of three sons of Northern Dancer to win the Blue Riband. Six Northern Dancer-line colts have won the Derby and his sons Secreto and El Gran Senor finished first and second in the 1984 Derby.

In only his second crop came the Triple Crown winner Nijinsky, providing instant proof that Northern Dancer was one of the few top-class racehorses capable of siring horses of his own immense ability.

Trained by Horatio Luro, Northern Dancer won 14 of his 18 starts, becoming the first Canadian-bred horse to win the Kentucky Derby. He also took the Preakness Stakes and Canada's top prize, the Queen's Plate. His jockey Bill Hartack last night paid tribute to the pony-sized dynamo:

"I'll always remember him as a completely honest horse who could stretch his ability because he was so aggressive. Once you asked him for his run, you could never get him to slow down again," said the great rider, who is now a racing official. "He was extremely game, like a little tank."

His loss was also mourned last night by Vincent O'Brien, who handled the careers of Nijinsky, The Minstrel, El Gran Senor, Storm Bird, and Northern Dancer's possible successor as the world's top sire, Sadler's Wells. O'Brien said last night: "I am very saddened by this news. I have had the utmost regard for the progeny of Northern Dancer, who have provided me with some of my greatest moments."

Newmarket trainer Michael Stoute, who trained Northern Dancer's sons, Shareef Dancer and Ajdal, said: "It is very sad to hear the legend has gone, but his legacy will always be remembered. His line has given me great success and I for one am greatly indebted to him."

His stable jockey, Walter Swinburn, added: "That is very sad news. Shareef Dancer and Ajdal were the best sons of his that I rode. They were both genuine horses with a lot of speed and ability. He has left an enormous influence on the breed and I have ridden a lot of good horses for Mr Stoute that are by his sons and I am sure I will ride many more."

Sheikh Mohammed's stud manager, Robert Acton, said: "Of the seven stallions we have here (at Dalham Hall), five are sons or grandsons of Northern Dancer, which I think is a fair reflection of the influence he has had on the breed."

And Northern Dancer's effect on the world breeding scene was summed up last night by top US breeder Warner L. Jones, owner of the Heritage Farm in Kentucky.

"He was my greatest investment in over 50 years in the horse business," Jones said. "He was the greatest."

17 November 1990

PS. Northern Dancer was leading sire in Great Britain and Ireland four times – 1970, 1977, 1983 and 1984 – without ever entering the country.

Attended by a farrier, Northern Dancer conveyed a sense of dignified majesty.

The magic art of the Wizard of Dormello

Federico Tesio, the only thoroughbred breeder who merited being called 'genius', gave the world Nearco and Ribot, and 35 years after his death came a reappraisal

by TONY MORRIS

PART I

FANCIFUL though it may seem, it is arguable that Ribot owed his existence to a reckless young man's failure to seduce a married woman. The connection is tenuous enough, but it is accepted fact that Federico Tesio was summarily ejected from a hotel bedroom window in Pisa, that – in order to escape further unwelcome consequences – he forthwith fled his country and travelled the world, and that the daredevil gambler who departed returned as a settled and sober character, intent on devoting his life to the single-minded pursuit of mastering a craft as it had never been mastered before.

That Pisa escapade has understandably not figured conspicuously among the vast literary outpourings on the life and career of Tesio the breeder, but it is worthy of recall if only for the fact that it illustrates a human side to a man who is more often portrayed as superhuman, even a god. Worldwide he is revered – and much misunderstood.

A lot of the misunderstanding may be put down to Tesio himself, who unquestionably derived some mischievous pleasure from the air of mystique which naturally surrounded one so uncannily successful and of which he was profoundly aware. He was anything but a gregarious person by nature, he was not fond of giving interviews to the press, he did not make friends easily, and on those rare occasions when he opened out to an admiring audience, as often as not, he lied; he rarely told the same story twice in the same way.

Tesio also wrote a couple of books, one of which,

Breeding the Racehorse, has now been avidly devoured by two generations of horsemen, vainly searching for the secrets of the maestro's success. Much of it, no doubt, he penned with his tongue firmly in his cheek, conscious that he would be widely misinterpreted.

The proof of those misinterpretations are to be found in countless articles and books. Many writers have simply been baffled by the mystery and blinded by his science, or, rather, pseudo-science. Others, more disreputably, have presumed to unravel the tangled web of constantly changing policies, fitting that lifetime's work to formulae of their own construction, imputing motives to his operation which never existed.

The fact is, there are no answers. There is no set pattern to be found in the way Tesio operated, and the smokescreen of pseudo-science he put up in Breeding the Racehorse actually leads us further away from an understanding of his methods.

What Tesio students, virtually to a man, have neglected to notice is that he was an artist, not a scientist. Mere pedigree pundits, working retrospectively, conditioned by countless hours' poring over charts and by the habitual practice of identifying names with racing aptitudes, can never hope to guess what was in the mind of a genius when he created a masterpiece. Nine times out of 10, the key factors are not to be found on the printed page; if they were, others would simply follow the same principles and produce comparable results.

Just as obviously, the genius himself could not explain how he created an individual masterpiece, less still a series of them. One might as well have asked Beethoven how he came to arrange the notes so as to manufacture the Ninth Symphony. Genius has its roots in basic techniques available to all, but it is manifested in a personal, idiosyncratic style in which experience is harnessed to the intangible qualities of flair and intuition.

Tesio acquired much valuable experience on that round-the-world trip as a young man. He undertook a lone ride from Buenos Aires to Patagonia, observing horses in the wild; he studied nature closely and spent a vast amount of time on horseback, though almost certainly not to the extent of having ridden the winner of the Peking Derby, a tale he sometimes told to rightly incredulous audiences.

That lengthy foreign excursion took place in 1894, the year after Tesio had established himself as Italy's leading gentleman rider with 12 wins from only 24 mounts. On his return he professed no further ambitions in the saddle; his mission now, and for the rest of his life, was to be the creation of thoroughbred masterpieces, fashioned and developed through his own breeding and training.

This was more than the brash self-confidence that any young man might have felt as he entered a milieu dominated by amateurs. It was the attitude of a man emboldened by experience, already convinced of his genius. What is more, he never ceased to behave like a genius, for his 60 remaining years.

He was totally self-willed, he had no time for other people's opinions, and though he was subject to the same commercial pressures aseveryone else, he really did believe that the world owed him a living – or, rather, the opportunity to give the world what he knew he had to give. Fortunately, throughout it all, from 1896, he had the unstinted support of a wife, Donna Lydia, who worshipped him and saw her own existence only in terms of its role in assisting her husband to fulfil his destiny.

Lydia was already a racehorse owner in her own right at the time of their marriage, and for a short while afterwards the pair raced in partnership. But after the foundation of the Razza Dormello in 1898, Tesio became more than the dominant partner. At both the stud and the stable (40 miles away in Milan), every decision was his, and credit for all that ensued was his.

Tesio started out in racing and breeding with a little money, and he came into a bit more as a result of his marriage. But the expenses of running the operations were always high, and for much of his life his actions were to some degree dictated by financial considerations. In fact, his basic *modus operandi* never altered; his aim was always to breed and develop horses to a standard where they might be sold, to be replaced by stock which might enable him to breed and develop better horses.

As the biggest fish in the tiny pond that was Italian breeding at the time, Tesio might have been regarded as hugely successful, with 11 winners of the Derby Italiano to his credit between 1911 and 1926. Yet in 1930, already in his sixties, he had to go, cap in hand, to the Marchese Mario Incisa della Rocchetta for the finance necessary to bring his master plan to fruition.

He asked, and got, a fabulous amount for a half-interest in the stud and the stable. He at last had the wherewithal to go international on the grand scale, the path that was to lead to Nearco and Ribot was laid, and within 10 years Tesio's standing was such that the Aga Khan came to him and asked him to buy out all his own thoroughbred holdings. Had that deal gone through, the history of the breed in the past half-century would have been vastly different. The package contained not only the three Derby-winning stallions Blenheim, Bahram and Mahmoud, but also Mumtaz Begum, in foal with Nasrullah.

27 April 1989

PART II

AS a breeder, Federico Tesio was to Italy what Marcel Boussac was to France and what Lord Derby and the Aga Khan combined were to Britain over the same period.

That statement says plenty about Tesio's reputation, but it does not say it all. Uniquely among that exalted group, Tesio came from a relatively impoverished background and was compelled always to operate commercially; furthermore, whereas the others all had eminent advisers, the Italian exercised total control over everything he bred, from devising the matings to training the produce throughout their racing careers. The annals of the Turf disclose no parallel case of such multi-faceted success.

As I previously outlined, Tesio established himself as the outstanding breeder in Italy in a relatively short time. But in a nation whose racing and stud populations were tiny, by comparison with Britain and France, that did not amount to much; Italian racing was held in low esteem elswhere, and the fulfilment of Tesio's destiny, as he saw it, depended on his gaining an international reputation.

Remarkably, it was his 11th Derby Italiano winner (in the space of 16 seasons!) which finally brought him some foreign recognition. That was Apelle, who won the Critérium de Maisons-Laffitte and ran second in the Grand Prix de Paris, a race Tesio always

□ *Continued overleaf*

□ *Continued from previous page*
regarded as the supreme test of a three-year-old. Apelle was promptly sold to England, where he won the Coronation Cup two years later.

Apelle proved that Tesio could produce horses of international quality, but he might have been both the first and the last such celebrity if the Marchese Mario Incisa had not later provided the backing for the expansion of the trainer-breeder's operation. When that happened, there was to be no stopping Tesio. He knew that the masterpieces which he had dreamed of creating were about to be realised.

Much of the Tesio legend has centred on his purchase, often for derisory sums, of fillies and mares who were to become the dams and grand-dams of international champions. He bought Catnip, grand-dam of Nearco, for 75gns, Tofanella, dam of Tenerani, for 140gns, and Duccia di Buoninsegna, grand-dam of Donatello, for 210gns. There were countless examples, all of them inexplicable beyond the fact that Tesio was an exceptional judge.

Other people's attempts at explanations have always cited reasons based on pedigree, which would never have been more than a part of the reason. He did not buy mares to suit a particular stallion, and he paid as much attention to conformation and temperament as to pedigree. Equally, there was no special physical type that he preferred, and it was remarkable that his racing stock were never typically 'Tesian'; they came in all shapes and sizes, and there were champions and nonentities in every category.

Tesio's flair as a judge of a horse and his intuition when planning matings were facets of his genius which could not be translated into some form of instruction manual for novice breeders; thousands have learned that, and not much more, for the cost of a copy of his book, Breeding the Racehorse. And as Mario Incisa related many years afterwards, on the one occasion when Tesio offered to impart his knowledge verbally, the words "Here is how to do the matings" were followed by a mixture of platitudes, *non sequiturs* and gobbledegook. Nothing of value came across.

Yet Tesio undoubtedly did follow a set of guiding precepts in his rise to pre-eminence, some which he committed to print, others which may be readily deduced. A number may yet be applied to advantage.

The pair most commonly quoted are lessons he learned from history, namely that the Derby at Epsom has made the thoroughbred what it is, and that there has never been an instance of four consecutive generations in the direct line proving successful in either the Derby or the Oaks.

The Derby was always something special to him. He sent mares to 27 different Derby winners on a total of 121 occasions, and he was not concerned about the fact that many of them were far from fashionable as stallions at the time. What is more, he got his share of good runners from them, not least, at the end of his life, Botticelli by the long-discredited Blue Peter.

Tesio was certainly not the first to observe that inheritance of quality in the direct line generally has distinct limitations, but he was probably the first big-time breeder to act positively on the knowledge. He would never expect families to keep producing the goods, generation after generation, and he was constantly on the look-out for likely mares from different backgrounds to replace them. He was never sentimental about any of his horses, who were always but a means to an end, and he would cull ruthlessly when he believed that a family's potency was on the wane.

He would always use the best stallions he could afford, which might not always be the most fashionable but would, for preference, be proven sires. He liked to use horses who had established their merit as sires, rather than just as racehorses; when the only options seem to be unproven stallions, he invariably chose the winner of a great race rather than an apparently equally worthy runner-up in a great race, believing that winning was the name of the game and had to count for something.

He would never trust his best mares to reproduce themselves with second-class stallions, invariably (except perhaps in his first season) sending them to the best sires. Better to gamble on breeding one champion than a group of second division performers, he reckoned.

Though circumstances sometimes dictated otherwise, he did not like standing his own stallions, and he would not buy shares in syndicated horses. Both policies, he held, were apt to affect any breeder's judgment of how his mares should be mated; it was important that the widest range of options be preserved.

He had no special preference for either inbred or outcross matings, and recommended that both should be tried. He was happy to ring the changes, providing mares with chances to succeed with a variety of different mates, but he was equally adamant that a particularly appealing union was worth repetition even after a couple of failures.

He had an abhorrence of sprinting stallions, and would never use one – and he would never buy a mare with a purely 'speed' pedigree. If any of his horses proved precocious enough to win over sprint distances at two, fair enough, but that was not the purpose of his policy, and those who did not train on and stay a mile and a half in top company as three-year-olds were held to be failures.

Those were the precepts which governed the Tesio operation over a period when he produced no fewer than 22 winners of the Derby Italiano and a host of other celebrities in domestic and international competition. But they were not inviolable. At times circumstances dictated relaxations of the rules, and it is ironic that both his supreme masterpieces figure among the exceptions.

In 1934 he sought a nomination to Fairway for Nogara, and had his old friend Walter Alston still been in control of Lord Derby's stud, one would no doubt have been made available. But Alston had died in the previous year, and his successor was not disposed to grant the favour. Tesio reluctantly settled for second best, Fairway's brother Pharos, who had been runner-up in the Derby and who patently did not get a mile and a half.

The outcome was Nearco, who raced unbeaten in 14 starts, gave his breeder a long-coveted victory in the Grand Prix de Paris and produced, within hours of that triumph, a cheque for £60,000 from Martin Benson. Tesio would never concede the greatness of that 'accidental' creation.

"He was not a true stayer," he claimed, persisting in the opinion that his lightly raced and unsound domestic champion of 1929, Cavaliere d'Arpino, was still his number one.

Possibly to illustrate his contempt for Nearco, Tesio sent him in his first stud season only one mare, a 16-year-old who had produced a single winner and was an uncertain breeder to boot. To nobody's surprise, she proved barren, and Tesio never went back to Nearco, not even when the horse was established as the best sire in Europe.

Tesio would forget his rule about not patronising his own stallions in his beloved Cavaliere d'Arpino's case, and the war compelled him to shelve the rule completely. He used that horse's son Bellini extensively, and from a 1943 covering obtained Tenerani, who came to England at four to beat Black Tarquin in the Queen Elizabeth Stakes and the supposedly invincible Arbar in the Goodwood Cup.

Tenerani was a wonderful stayer, though with no remarkable turn of foot, and Tesio disliked him on that account. He gave him a stud home, until such time as someone would take him off his hands, and when the English National Stud, having first leased him, offered £20,000, his breeder could hardly take the cheque fast enough. Tenerani had never been worthy of his best mares, fit only for the likes of Romanella, a precocious wretch who had failed to train on, turned jady and developed ringbone as well.

The offspring of Tenerani and Romanella in 1952 was a small bay colt, and Tesio's vast experience told him that he would not be worth entering in the Italian Classics. There is a legend, commonly printed as fact, that Tesio was inclined to believe he may have been wrong about Ribot after he had watched

his progress in training. The truth, alas, is that Tesio's failing eyesight would have precluded him from passing an opinion even if he had been present on such occasions.

Tesio was already too frail and infirm to attend morning exercise by the spring of 1954. On 1 May he died, two months before the debut of the creature he always knew it was his destiny to produce – "the racehorse who, over any distance, could carry the heaviest weight in the shortest time".

2 May 1989

Ribot and Nearco were Federico Tesio's most famous creations. Here Ribot is being greeted after his six-length victory in the 1956 Prix de l'Arc de Triomphe.

The proof positive of forward progress

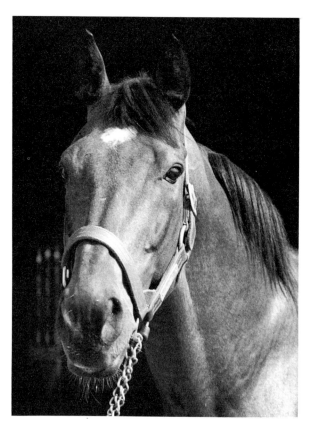

Making judgments about breeding and the relative merits of the great sires is a cerebral process not to be taken lightly, particularly when discussing Nijinsky

by TONY MORRIS

IF all great racehorses became great sires, life would be so much simpler for all concerned. But we have long since discovered that like tends not to beget like in quite the way we would prefer.

With very few exceptions, we do grant our great runners the benefit of the doubt from the start, supplying them with what we imagine to be the best opportunities to fulfil their supposed mission. Most of them disappoint us, and seemingly for reasons which we can barely begin to understand.

However, in the simplest terms it may be that the great horse – by which I mean a truly exceptional individual, rather than a typical champion – represents a natural climax, a state of perfection which cannot be improved. The only possible shift from that position is downward, however slight, in a process known as retrogression to the mean.

The superstar does not get horses superior to himself; the best that we can reasonably hope from him is that he will keep that retrogression to a minimum by getting a high proportion of stock whose level of ability approaches his own.

Meanwhile, it is the very good horse, rather than the great horse, who is apt to effect the more obvious progress, getting progeny who match him or excel him in merit. Sadler's Wells exemplifies the phenomenon in the modern era, an excellent runner, but one who nevertheless had the scope to generate further improvement. His sire Northern Dancer belonged in the same category.

As for the truly greats, the early 1970s provided four glorious examples, each representing a level of achievement which could not be exceeded by the next generation. In the cases of Brigadier Gerard and Secretariat, retrogression proved to be both swift and alarmingly complete; spasmodic successes could not disguise the fact that they were not even ordinarily good sires.

It made no difference that the one seemed to represent a startling advance over the achievements of his forebears, whereas the other was apparently the end-product of a gradually developing process of building quality on quality. At stud their records proved equally disappointing, and between them they got only a handful of progeny who might have been rated within 14lb of their own racing class.

Mill Reef was much better. Though powerless to extend the process of improvement through to the next generation, he was able to get a high proportion of runners whose abilities more closely approximated to his own. Sure, there was a wide disparity between him and the vast majority of his stock, but he nevertheless got plenty whose performances unquestionably placed them way above the average for the breed, with a select group of celebrities among them. He had 37 Pattern-winning offspring, who won 92 Pattern races, 32 of them at Group 1 level. He also sired the winner of one Graded Stake in North America.

Understandably, while we cherish the memory of Mill Reef most for his racecourse triumphs, particularly for his stunning Eclipse, King George, Arc and Ganay efforts, our respect for his stud contribution is also profound. The likes of Acamas, Shirley Heights, Glint of Gold, Diamond Shoal, Lashkari (that lone American Graded winner), Reference Point and

Doyoun did him tremendous credit. Twice champion sire, and with those 92 European Pattern wins placing him third behind Habitat and Northern Dancer on the all-time list, Mill Reef has to be regarded as the number one English-based stallion of the past two decades.

With that in mind, it is interesting to compare his record with that of the year-older Nijinsky, who was foaled in Canada 25 years ago next month. Based throughout his stud career at Claiborne, in Kentucky, he has one British/Irish sires' championship to his name, and 46 individual winners of 80 European Pattern races, including 25 at Group 1 level.

The pair are level at two Derby winners apiece (Shirley Heights and Reference Point; Golden Fleece and Shahrastani), but overall a comparative analysis of their achievements in Europe gives Mill Reef a slight edge. However, that does not entitle him to be regarded as the better sire.

While Nijinsky has been able to muster *only* 80 European Pattern wins against Mill Reef's 92, we cannot just ignore events in North America. Mill Reef, of course, was rarely represented there, and his score of one Graded victory, albeit in the immensely prestigious Breeders' Cup Turf, can say little about his merit in relation to that of countless sires whose stock habitually competed in that country.

Even so, no comparison between the achievements of sires is valid unless the total picture is presented in each case. Against Mill Reef's one Graded win, Nijinsky can show 104, the latest two of them from his six-year-old son Classic Fame in the first three weeks of 1992.

Needless to say, it is not completely fair to judge the pair comparatively on their tallies of Pattern and Graded wins. Nijinsky has lived longer, covered larger books and out-represented Mill Reef in one area to an enormous degree; he cannot simply be said to have been twice the sire that the National Stud's brightest ornament was. And yet, history surely will record that Nijinsky was, by a pretty wide margin, the more successful progenitor. If he has been fortunate in having two outlets for his stock instead of one, it is nevertheless much to his credit that his sons and daughters were able to flourish in one or other (or both) of those intensely competitive environments.

He has generated more success, over a wider area, than any of the other truly great racehorses in the history of the Turf. He has helped to raise the level of merit in the population on two continents by delivering a high proportion of superior runners, none of them as good as himself, but plenty with abilities not so far removed from his own. In brief, he has made a better job of fulfilling his 'quality control' function in the breed than any of his predecessors. He has stemmed the natural process of retrogression, while providing the base for renewed progress, exemplified by the phenomenon of sons capable of breeding stock better than themselves, e.g. Niniski (Petoski), Caerleon (Generous) and Green Dancer (Suave Dancer).

It is often erroneously stated that the justification of racing is the 'improvement of the breed'. That is a patent nonsense, but improvement of the breed nevertheless goes on, albeit imperceptibly, and it is the rare individual like Nijinsky who makes a major contribution.

Perhaps I should know better than to disagree with the eminent late Admiral Rous, who reckoned, around 1850: "The form of Flying Childers might not now win a £30 plate, winner to be sold for £40; and Highflyer and Eclipse might pull through in a £50 plate, winner to be sold for £200."

It was Rous's strong contention that the thoroughbred was constantly improving, which was fair enough, and he was around long enough to have noticed a rise in the general level of performance. But whether he was right to denigrate the form of early heroes is debatable; progress could, did, and still does take place without any need to view former champions in a derogatory light.

The improvements – no doubt much more gradual now than in the early history of the breed – are marked not in the form and quality of champions, but in the capabilities of lesser horses. Old-timers may crab the modern thoroughbred for a want of soundness, probably with good reason, but it is surely a fact that the average horse of the 1890s would not be a match for the average horse of the 1990s. It is at that level that progress has been made.

I remain as convinced as I was 30 years ago that Ormonde was the finest racehorse who ever lived, and I can easily reconcile that belief with my contention that improvements in the breed as a whole have occurred since his time. And if I get to that contest in Elysian Fields Park, when Ormonde takes on Ribot, Sea-Bird, Nijinsky, Mill Reef, Brigadier Gerard and Secretariat, level weights at a mile and a half, I shall put my money where my mouth is.

But judge that group by a different standard – which contributed most to the quality of racing through his genetic endowment to the breed - and Nijinsky, though still far from finished, is out on his own. He is the greatest sire of racehorses in our time, and let's hope that breeders are wise enough to ensure that his influence persists.

28 January 1992

On 15 April 1992, after being taken ill the day before, Nijinsky was put down. The progenitor of success, he has influenced the thoroughbred population of two continents to an unprecedented degree.

The star of the Arabian firmament

The influence of the Arab horse and now Arab owners on racing should be no surprise. The horse has been honoured in Arab culture for thousands of years

by RAMZI ILIYA

THE image of an Arab horseman riding over the sand dunes is a romantic cliché. But it does accurately reflect the extraordinary relationship that has developed between man and horse in the Middle East. It started when the horse-riding Hittites invaded Egypt in 3,000 B.C. and has continued to the present day, a relationship that has been one of war and poetry, bravery, killing and healing.

About A.D. 630 the Prophet Mohammed carved a place of honour for the horse in the consciousness of the Arab people. "When God the Almighty wanted to create the horse," said the Prophet, "he addressed the southern winds and said: 'From you I create a breed that will be the pride of my devoted ones, the humiliation of my enemies and the beauty in the eyes of my followers'."

Thus the horse gained religious sanction and a place of honour in the Jihad (Holy War) which swept Arab warriors like a storm across North Africa and into Spain, where Islamic culture flourished from 757 until 1400.

Mohammed, who kept 19 horses himself, had rightly judged that without horses the roving bedouin tribesmen would have felt emasculated, such was the horse's importance in the complex, clannish society.

In the earliest days, horses migrated south-eastwards from the Mediterranean coast of Africa to the Arabian peninsula. There, a horse's performance was intricately bound with the sense of honour which is so central to the bedouin code of ethics, including deep-rooted principles of generosity, hospitality and purity. In fact, the horse reached such eminence in early Arab culture that bedouin women reared them alongside their children with equal care and devotion.

The life of such bedouin people was routinely enlived by seasonal raiding, and the tribes shared long-standing feuds stretching sometimes over centuries. The horse was integral to the context of them and poet-warriors immortalised the noble deeds of the horsemen since the harsh nomadic life, full of long hot days and starlit, serene nights, prompted the bedouin to express his emotion through articulate and romantic verse, ranging over thousands of
□ Continued overleaf

Mystery of the modern racer

The evolution of the thoroughbred is shrouded somewhat in history but nobody doubts the influence of Arab, Barb and Turkish stallions

by TONY MORRIS

IN Britain mandatory registration of human births was introduced rather more than 40 years after the publication of the first volume of the General Stud Book.

From that simple fact it follows that the thoroughbred horse is the best documented of all animal species, the pedigree of each and every one traceable over a longer period of time than all but a tiny minority of our own race. But does that mean that we know everything we would like to know about the origins of the thoroughbred? There were centuries of unrecorded and poorly-recorded history which were inevitably instrumental in the evolution of the animal we came to celebrate as "man's noblest creation".

As in so many other facets of our nation's history, the Royal Family were trend-setters in the development of racing, and throughout the Tudor and early Stuart periods its studs were the biggest and best in the country.

And as leaders of the social set, the Royals inevitably played a leading role in establishing both the fashion for, and the value of, the imported horse. Many came from Spain and Italy, supposedly the products of crosses with Arabian and Barb stock.

By the time of the accession of James I (1603) it was already widely acknowledged, according to the noted historian C. M. Prior, that "the cross with the Barb was the most direct route to the winning post". But Gervase Markham, the great horsemaster of the first half of the 17th century, favoured the Arabian as a prospective stallion, with the Barb (which originated in North Africa) and the Turk as the next best.

There can be no doubt that examples of all three strains were extensively, if anonymously, involved in the development of what was conveniently referred to as "the native English breed" when, much later, the background to the thoroughbred came to be a
□ Continued overleaf

☐ *Continued from previous page*
lines that he committed to memory. These were his pride and it was poetry's central role in Arab and Islamic society that helped to immortalise the Arab horse.

If poetry and conflict were essential components of early Arab and Islamic society, the fame achieved by the warrior-poets and other raiders was commensurate with their riding skills. Raiding was carried out on horseback, and demanded great equestrian skills, which were traditionally developed through games, races and mock battles. These took place in the intervals between fighting.

The sporting events were very popular, and a source of great pride for the clans and individuals involved. There was also a great deal of betting on the races, in which the horses were often named according to their position at the end of the race. The prize was staked on the tip of a spear at the finish line.

The spread of Islam from the 8th century onwards resulted in the diversification of the Arab horse, due to selective breeding with the finest specimens from the Arabian peninsula, North Africa and Spain. From this, a number of breeds became popular in the Middle East, the most common of which were the Najdi (the most elevated), the Yemeni (the most patient), the Damascene (the most beautiful), the Peninsular (the best), the Lybian (the roughest), the Iraqi-Kuwaiti (the purest), the Moroccan (the fastest) and the European (the worst).

Over 600 years, the horse spread into the cities of the Middle East – Baghdad, Damascus, Cairo – where equestrian schools were founded. A number of veterinary and zoological studies were published. This golden age reached its peak between the 13th and 16th centuries under the Mamelukes, whose rule spread from Egypt as far as Syria.

Their rule was violent and chaotic, and in 1516 the people of Damascus welcomed the Ottoman Sultan Selim I as their liberator. As a token of their gratitude, they presented him with 300 of the finest Arabian horses, thus initiating the spread of the breed through the Ottoman Empire and later into Poland and Russia.

5 October 1988

☐ *Continued from previous page*
matter of interest to historians. Prior referred to "a continuous stream" of imported stallions over a period of a century and a half before the Restoration in 1660. And it was a process which continued for many years afterwards, with immensely consequential effects.

By 1760 the word "thoroughbred" was in common parlance, denoting a distinct breed. By 1810 a creature had evolved which was apparently incapable of improvement, for racing purposes, by further crosses with horses of Eastern origin. And by 1860, when the tabulated pedigrees came into vogue, every schoolboy seemed to be aware that the Byerley Turk, the Darley Arabian and the Godolphin Arabian were the founders of the breed.

For the sake of convenience, and with a substantial measure of ignorance, the latter simplistic view of the origins of the thoroughbred has been handed down as though the pages of the General Stud Book were tablets of stone. It is certainly true, and has been true for over 100 years, that every thoroughbred in existence can be traced in the male line to either the Byerley Turk, the Darley Arabian or the Godolphin Arabian. And nobody could deny the immensely significant part played by each of the three in his day. Yet none of them seemed any more remarkable than countless other contemporaneous imports, and their emergence as the tail-male 'founding fathers' of the breed was inevitably to some degree fortuitous.

Breeders' collective belief in the 'magic' of the sire-line chain had contributed vastly to the success story of the great triumvirate for more than a century before the science of genetics led some to think differently about the way heredity works.

In 1938, when Lady Wentworth advanced the notion that the unknown sire of a once-celebrated mare called Old Bald Peg was actually a more consequential figure in pedigrees than the Byerley Turk, the Darley Arabian or the Godolphin Arabian, many were inclined to dismiss her as an eccentric or a heretic. And only 10 years ago, the results of researches carried out in the Department of Genetics at Trinity College, Dublin, conflicted so starkly with traditional thinking that they have still to be widely accepted.

Everyone *knew* that the Darley Arabian was by far the most significant of the great imported stallions, so there scarcely seemed to be much point in going to expensive lengths to confirm the point. Unfortunately for the traditionalists, the researchers did not confirm what had always seemed to be obvious. On the contrary, they discovered, by means of a 'deep sample' pedigree analysis, that the Godolphin Arabian had made almost double the contribution of the Darley Arabian in present-day pedigrees. And just for good measure, they found that the Byerley Turk ranked only fourth in importance, with the unsung Curwen Bay Barb taking precedence over him.

Between them, those four horses are held to have contributed 32.5 per cent of the genetic make-up of the current thoroughbred population.

5 October 1988

An equine love story that bears repeating

Life at stud may not be absolute heaven for a stallion but it's better than ever today. Even so, in the past romance rather than planning could still produce a champion

by SUE MONTGOMERY

TURNING a racehorse into a stallion is not merely a matter of chucking a copy of the Kama Sutra into his box and saying: "Go get 'em, boy."

A significant change in the management of stallions these days, compared with even about 20 years ago, is the amount of freedom given to them. National Stud manager Miles Littlewort says: "The important thing is our stallions are out in their paddocks most of the day. Even in the season they go out after they have served a mare in the morning and come back in again when they are needed. Every year they seem to get more laid-back."

In the old days it was standard practice to keep a stallion cooped up, often in an isolated box, bringing him out only for a couple of hours' walking exercise or to serve a mare. Expected to show sexual arousal every time he was let out of his prison, it was perhaps no surprise if he became neurotic.

The act of covering a mare should be a natural one for a stallion, but not all take to it as quickly as others. The story is told of Brunelleschi, a reluctant Italian Romeo, who refused to cover a single one of his first book of mares. Blonde, glossy-coated virgins and voluptuous "been there, done that" matrons were paraded before him, aphrodisiacs and stimulants were administered, but to no avail.

Eventually his connections, increasingly losing patience, realised that he had had his wrist slapped so often in training for even thinking about sex that he regarded the mares as forbidden fruit. The problem was solved by presenting him with a filthy, unkempt mare, plastered in mud, that bore no resemblance to a shiny-coated filly in training. Brunelleschi cov-

ered her happily, and never looked back.

A new stallion in today's climate is expected to cover many more mares in his first season than were his predecessors. Littlewort says: "For a commercial stallion it is important to get as many runners as possible in his first crop. But on the other hand we don't have to use the stallions as much now, thanks to advances in veterinary science, like more accurate oestrus prediction."

A first-timer this season is Most Welcome, who has joined old-stager Balidar, at 24 one of Britain's senior active stallions, at the Meddler Stud just outside Newmarket. They are under the supervision of Dennis Atkins, who is about to start his 43rd season. Atkins said: "Most Welcome is a gentleman. He's covered his test mare successfully and we should have no problems with him.

"But they're not all so good. The act of covering is something that only practice can make perfect. Blue Cashmere used to forget to hold on with his front legs and lose his balance and fall off his mares. And Wolver Heights used to throw his front legs about and end up with them both on the same side, which was very awkward."

Most Welcome is led daily round the 1,000 acres of the Meddler estate. "They have to be fit, but it's a different sort of fitness than for racing. A horse will thicken and develop a crest as he gets older, but you can't have them too heavy. Covering is vigorous work and if you ask a fat man to do it regularly you're heading for a heart attack."

If this all sounds somewhat clinical, here to finish is a true equine love story. In Newmarket at the turn of the century there lived an eccentric Italian named Cavaliere Odoardo Ginistrelli. He bred, owned and trained his own horses, and the apple of his eye was the beautiful mare Signorina, a top-class racer.

In the spring of 1904, Ginistrelli had arranged for her to be mated with the mighty Isinglass, who stood, at the then huge fee of 300gns, at a stud at the other end of the town. Now, in those days it was common practice for the lesser, unemployed stallions to be paraded up and down the High Street, touting for business with their names embroidered on their rugs. The lovely Signorina was being led past them on her way to her tryst with Isinglass when Cupid's arrow struck.

One of the humble stallions, Chaleureux, espied Signorina and stopped dead. The mare, gazing admiringly at Chaleureux, did likewise. Neither would move a step, and a crowd began to gather. The romantic Ginistrelli summed up the situation. "They are in love," he declared. "They shall be married."

Isinglass got the money, but Chaleureux got the girl. And the result was Signorinetta, winner of the 1908 Derby and Oaks.

14 February 1990

Searching for the answer in the stars

William Hall Walker's story is indeed strange. He was ruled by astrology and it was he who persuaded the Aga Khan's grandfather to race horses in England

by TONY MORRIS

IT is arguable that if a certain Liverpool brewer's wife had produced her third son on, say, Boxing Day, instead of Christmas Day, Aliysa would not have finished first in the Oaks anyway.

That seemingly preposterous statement might be justified, on the 'for want of a nail' principle, by the following chain of reasoning. The Aga Khan would have had no horses in training if it had not been a family tradition, and his grandfather, who established that tradition, would never haved raced horses in England but for the persuasion of William Hall Walker, later the 1st Baron Wavertree.

Walker, one of the most successful owners and breeders of his era, was that Christmas Day baby, born in 1856 and from an early age imbued with the conviction that the time, date and place of birth were crucial to any (human or animal) individual's prospects in life. He was guided and influenced by astrology in everything he did. As he was a strong-willed, dogmatic and cantankerous fellow, few would have attempted to persuade him that the success he achieved in life resulted from anything other than the 'fact' that he was born under a lucky star.

A heretic might have suggested that Walker was not exactly harmed by the fact that his father had great wealth. The boy's rise to become Deputy Lieutenant for Lancashire and MP for Widnes was hardly impeded by his family connections and his Harrow education. When he registered his great achievements on the Turf, it seemed more than just coincidental that he enjoyed the services of William Chismon, the greatest authority on pedigrees around, and Harry Sharpe, the man whose un-

rivalled skills raised the status of the stud groom to unprecedented heights.

But no, it was all in the stars – the Classics he won with such as Cherry Lass, Witch Elm and Night Hawk, the production of his greatest champion, Prince Palatine, and the three epoch-making events for which he was responsible. He leased his home-bred Minoru to King Edward VII, who thereby became the only reigning monarch to win the Derby; he introduced the Aga Khan to English racing; and he sold what became the National Stud to the Government.

As a reward for disposing of his properties (at Tully and Russley) and all his bloodstock to the nation at less than their market value, Walker was given a barony in 1919. And only then, when he was nearly 63 years old, retired as an owner and retaining only a token interest in breeding, was he admitted to the Jockey Club. His late and – one imagines – reluctant acceptance by the hierarchy of the Turf surely derived from two factors. The first was his perceived want of class, for while his father had acquired a baronetcy, he was basically 'trade'. The second was that Walker was never one to court popularity; the generous reckoned him eccentric, but he was more commonly regarded as perverse.

Nobody found him more perverse than his trainers, of whom there were many, hired and fired at regular intervals, generally held to blame when his horses failed to fulfil the destinies supposedly pre-ordained by their horoscopes. Trainers of the modern era who complain about 'difficult' owners should count themselves lucky that they do not have to cope with the likes of William Hall Walker, who *knew* exactly what his horses were capable of achieving, courtesy of his female astrologer.

I obtained an insight into that phenomenon by the recent acquisition of Walker's book of horoscopes for 1911. It is the owner-breeder's own bound copy of a document which must have terrified his trainer – at that time a newly-installed fellow who rejoiced in the name of John Smith – and in the circumstances it is hardly surprising that he lasted only about 18 months in the job.

The book contains the astrological chart of all the breeder's foals born in 1911, together with an interpretation of it and all manner of deductions drawn from it on how they should be treated in training, how the stars foretold their temperaments and racing characters, and when they might expect to be fortunate.

John Smith might have reckoned he was fortunate with Callidora, for her expectations were not high, on account of "Saturn's affliction to Jupiter". But if he read on, he would have been concerned to see that "she will be able to win almost anything in 1913 in her class". Walker's expert (?) wanted her entered in "a big race in the first fortnight of April, which she ought to win", but the reprobate Smith did not get her onto a racecourse until July, and by the end of the season she had run unplaced in all five of her starts. Smith was 'obviously' to blame for this fiasco, because the stars also indicated that at stud Callidora would have "a tendency to slip her foals" and might also produce twins. Remarkably, they were right on both counts.

The trainer must have been puzzled by the equivocal remarks about Canidius. "His temper should be sweet, unless much upset, when he might be a bit savage" was the forecast, coupled with "he will have very marked success as a three-year-old". As it turned out, Smith never ran him and he was in other hands when his "very marked success" at three came in a maiden plate at Kempton.

It is tempting to think that the stars got Carrickfergus right, only for the astrologer to misinterpret the information. "When he is not expected to win, he will do it," was spot-on, because he was a 100-6 outsider when he beat odds-on Happy Warrior in the St James's Palace Stakes at Royal Ascot. Unfortunately, that was in 1914, which was supposed to be so bad for him that the advice to the trainer was: "You might just as well take his shoes off and let him run loose in his paddock all year."

One of the messages of the book is that if you make sufficient (apparently) wild predictions about any horse, the law of probabilities will dictate that some of them prove right. Dolabella was supposed to be smart as a two-year-old, to win when unexpected, and to be "not much good" in May 1914. In fact, it was in that month, aged three, that she scored her only win, and she started favourite. However, the astrologer also observed: "Sun in the 5th House trine Herschel makes that aspect exact in 1913; it falls from 5th to 1st House and promises her not only a successful racing career, but famous offspring." The first part may read like gibberish to you and me (and doubtless to John Smith), but there is no getting away from the fact that she did become the dam of the celebrated Myrobella, herself dam of the even more celebrated Big Game.

The prophetess expressed doubts as to Lady Killer's "qualities as a stud horse", which were realised to the extent that the colt had become a gelding before he ever set foot on a racecourse. The observation that "in 1916 he may have a bad accident, bad enough to kill him" may also have come true, as there is no record of his having raced after the preceding season.

Pursuing her fondness for prophecies of doom, Walker's astrologer predicted "a death quite out of the ordinary, possibly brought on through an explosion" for Lindisfarne. If she was right about that – and it is quite conceivable that the wretched beast was recruited for the cavalry – that forecast would have atoned for many that were wrong in his case. He did not have "a fine constitution, good staying power and speed". Nor did he become "a sought-after sire, with offspring very strong and sturdy". In fact, he was gelded and never ran.

The reasons for Walker's apparently sudden decision to abandon what had been his principal preoccupation for nearly 20 years has never been adequately explained. He intimated that it was because of his dissatisfaction with his trainer's handling of his 1915 Classic candidate Let Fly in both the Guineas and the Derby. But he could easily have changed those arrangements, as he had on plenty of previous occasions. It was also suggested that he foresaw the coming upheaval in Ireland and wanted to be rid of his Tully property before it occurred.

It would be refreshing to believe that he threw in his hand because he was at last finally convinced of the worthlessness of his astrology, but that assuredly was not the case. Within months of his own death, in February 1933, Walker checked out the King's horoscope and forecast – accurately – both a grave illness and a full recovery. He was a believer to the last.

20 December 1990

William Hall Walker, a man who was obsessed with astrology, persuaded the Aga Khan's grandfather to race horses in England.

PS. Fascination with Walker is widespread. See also 'The horse as an athlete', starting page 114.

THE WAGER

Betting and racing are blood brothers. The very origins of sport are rooted in the proposition that one man's horse is better than the other's. Bet you! The betting business, its folklore, its colour, its joys and its heartbreaks permeate every little niche of the sport. And however big and perhaps impersonal the bookmakers and the Tote grow, the wager remains to the individual a personal experience, the nearest most can get to walking one of life's most absorbing tightropes, a vicarious line to the challenge of the competition itself

Betting is not a business for the chicken-hearted. It requires nerve as well as study and contemplation, and here four punters, caught in mid-meeting, are totally absorbed in the events of the day.

How a tug (mug) was stitched right up

A tale of shameless skulduggery at Cheltenham is related here by the author, who is known to his intimates and Racing Post readers simply as At Large

by JOHN McCRIRICK

CHELTENHAM'S first day 18 years ago is recalled with no small feeling of ignominy – and only publicly now because the central participant has passed on.

In those days, At Large used to scratch a precarious living as an inept floorman, tea-boy, junior partner and arch schemer in minor rings. He had inveigled himself into a firm with a pitch in the centre enclosure, opposite the stands. Transport was a major headache but various pick-ups on the outskirts of London ensured a viable (i.e. trustworthy) car, loaded with guv'nors and workmen.

We set out that morning, like any other, buoyed up with hope. Syd 'The Snot' joined the three of us at White City with a mate of his. Now Syd, a flat-nosed ex-pugilist with permanent nasal congestion, belonged to the rough school of pre-war bookies and was one of those unpleasant characters you could do without.

Habitual loud abuse used to be heaped on his hapless clerk and floorman. And since he operated next to us, it was a quirk of fate not the least in our favour.

Syd, moreover, between incessant sniffs, could talk. His voice punctuated journeys to the races. Opinions, and occasionally hilarious one-liners, poured forth on every horse on the card, and about crooked plots. A persistent theme dwelt on how he was going to crack it "this time".

So we settled down, awaiting the monologue. For once it never came. Pensively settled in the back, Syd seemed morose. Since his pal kept stum, the rest of us were content to leave them undisturbed.

However, when The Snot pushed to the front of the queue in the transport caff and insisted on paying for all our breakfast fry-ups it became clear something odd was afoot. For the remainder of the journey the normally loquacious Syd let the banter pass and, by the time we had set up our joints, the atmosphere between us was more of curiosity than open hostility.

As always, readies were scarce, and if firms like ours reefed up more than a 'monkey' (£500) between us we were already flying.

Syd's policy never changed: come with little – go home loaded. Invariably, that was the plan, but the fact that he still scuffled around the barren outer regions like the rest of us showed how rarely it had been successfully executed.

In those days, the Aldsworth Hurdle commenced proceedings. Celtic Cone, unbeaten over hurdles, winner of the previous year's Ascot Stakes and favourite for that Cesarewitch, was the banker, napped all over the place, and regarded as a laydown. But he had been prone to jumping errors, so we set out to give him a right stripping which, for us, meant the full monkey touch.

A Celtic Cone victory would confine the rest of the day to ducking and diving.

The price we got him at was all-important. So we stood back amazed as Syd, not normally the most generous of our colleagues, chalked up 'wrist' (5-4) Celtic Cone when the tic-tacs from Tatts were sending first 'tips' (11-10) and then 'levels' (evens) 'with the thumb' (being taken).

Pounds, fivers and tenners flooded in as Syd took on all-comers and despite the ever-shortening price he continued trading over the odds.

Then I overheard him confirming he'd laid an even grand (£1,000) inside (to Tatts) twice! This was far beyond Syd's, and our, league and still he was smashing away, going 100-8 bar one (8-1 and 10s with us).

At such competitive prices we were virtual spectators as punters clamoured around Syd's joint, though having £500-£550 bet on Celtic Cone inside quite late suited us fine.

Near the off, he loudly confirmed £1,000-£1,100 and several £1,000-£80s and £1,000-£70s other contenders.

Heady stuff, and when Even Dawn, a 40-1 'skinner', beat the 8-11 shot by two lengths, we were ecstatic for ourselves – and not a little envious of The Snot's right tickle.

"How much then?" I asked his clerk as the euphoria subsided. "Took it, took the lot," he muttered shame-facedly, pointing to a single bet in the Even Dawn column of £5,000-£150 laid to the tic-tacs. Absolutely unbelievable. To stand Celtic Cone for more than four grand, take plenty out of the others, then get a blinding result, yet cop nothing when he could have had the bogey back at 40-1, having laid 'double carpet' (33-1) was stupefying.

So the momentous day went on. Second favourite Royal Relief was worse than odds-on Straight Fort for Syd, though not us, in the Champion Chase; the Tom Jones-trained double, Clever Scot (11-1) and Jomon (8-1), was "no good" for him, and the rucks after 20-1 Charley Winking took the National Hunt Chase were truly horrendous.

The air was alive with expletives (numerous) deleted: remarks such as "Should have backed it back" and "Why wasn't Syd told" something or other abounded, with "I told you so" and "Why won't you ever listen to me?"

Coming to the last contest, having gone 'bar one' (not laid) the Jones pair, we were enjoying the bonanza of our lives with Syd suffering his "worst day ever". He had to be the only losing layer on that Black Tuesday for punters, topped up when 16-1 Noble Life caught the future dual winner of the Champion Hurdle, Comedy Of Errors, in a desperate finish to the Gloucestershire Hurdle.

"We fell for it. They picked me out like a ripe lemon," snorted The Snot. His heart-rending misery only enhanced our perverse joy at the prospect of sharing out nearly six grand.

In the bar before leaving it was doubles all round for us. It was there that Syd's clerk revealed all. "Ignore his act," he whispered, "the steam tug (mug) can't believe what's hit him. He's confused with all those hundreds of bets we took and only knows he's done four long 'uns (£4,000) in readies.

"Syd decided a quick extraction was better than prolonging the agony over three days. There was no more to come from the steam tug. He was only playing up a fluked betting shop Yankee."

So that's who Syd's quiet pal was. A naive 'sticker in', doomed to last but one traumatic afternoon as a partner in the heady glamorous world of racecourse bookmaking. How the bloke ever left the track, with those results, not realising he'd been well and truly stitched up, none of us ever knew. The journey home was tactfully spent in reflective silence.

The next day there was an empty place in the car as The Snot obnoxiously bubbled. He was in top form, richer by nearly £10,000 after phoney 'bets' on long-priced winners had been rubbed out of the book. Why they came to be the last entries on those horses, the steam tug never got to find out. Syd simply regaled us with how he was going to "take on the ring" and stand odds-on Bula "for the bank" in the Champion Hurdle.

The plaintive, nasal whining and bitter recriminations on the return have scarred me for life. But in a strange way justice was, at least partly, done.

10 March 1990

Getting a buzz out of betting

Gambling intrigues everybody from the academic to the inveterate bettor alike, and in four articles an examination was undertaken of the pitfalls and the rewards

by NORMAN HARRIS

THE HAPPY PUNTER

IAN ROBERTSON covers rugby and racing for BBC radio. He was also, for a time, rugby correspondent of The Sunday Times. He is also famous as an inveterate bettor. It is a reputation established with a famous bet on the Varsity rugby match of 1975, though the actual details tend to suggest canniness rather than an impulsive betting streak.

Robertson felt that Cambridge, considered the outstanding team of that year and which he coached, was perhaps capable of winning by 20 points. Seeking odds against this improbable feat, he was disappointed to be offered only 10-1 and 8-1 by leading bookmakers, which he did not consider good value. Eventually, however, another offered 25-1 and he made the bet. When his team, having left it late, brought up the necessary points in the closing minutes, they turned in their coach's direction and collectively punched the air. Robertson's honeymoon started the next day, and his winnings would pay for it.

Greatly though his reputation soared, the fact is that he only bet when the price was right, and he only bet £10. Today, Robertson's stakes are equally modest. His regular Saturday bet is the Yankee. That's been his traditional bet since the day in 1968 when, as a Cambridge rugby blue, he was taken by the university club's vice-president to Newmarket. For a few shillings his Yankee bet won him several hundred pounds, a sum more than double his whole student grant. "This is easy," he thought. Inevitably, the Yankee has never come up for him like that again.

His other routine bet is made on the course, on each of the 40 or 50 racing days he covers for the BBC. He does the Tote Placepot, which costs him £6.40 and means that he has to have laid his money before racing starts. He knows the BBC worry terribly at the thought of his racing backwards and forwards to the betting shop. "But I work it all out on the train, get my bets on by one o'clock, and that's it."

What's important, too, is that the sums are small and, win or lose, they don't alter. "It's a question every gambler has to confront: what overall policy does he have? Mine is to keep my bets so small that they never detract from the enjoyment. That way my anxiety level is kept to a minimum. What the bets do is add that little buzz of excitement, a buzz which you wouldn't get just from watching half a ton of horseflesh thundering up the straight.

"But if your horse fades you're only momentarily disappointed. Then you can concentrate on the finish."

Robertson is, too, a small part-owner. It started with a 10 per cent share in a horse named Rugby Special, and now continues each year with various horses trained by Ian Balding and Gavin Pritchard-Gordon. It's for pleasure rather than money that he watches his horse run – "like watching my son score a try for his school" – and the bonus is that the trainers provide him with tips, as does his colleague Peter Bromley. But he doesn't bet at all on jump racing because, he says, he doesn't follow this side of the sport and doesn't have the contacts. And he hasn't, he says, bet in a casino in his adult life, so he's far from being a real gambler. "In fact I'm a typical mean Scotsman. I'm a windy gambler, a wimp!"

His bets amount to £50 a week during the summer and about £1,500 for the year. "A not inconsiderable sum," he says. But then, he usually ends up ahead, comfortably so on his Yankee bets. "The way I see it, I lay out what someone else spends on 20 cigarettes a day. It's less injurious to my health and a lot more fun. And I won't increase the stake when I win, because I don't need the extra burden. There's enough stress and strain in this life already. Even if I won a huge sum of money I would still bet in exactly the same way."

THE PRO GAMBLER

A FEW days before the Commonwealth Games opened Simon, who is a professional gambler, spotted generous odds against Peter Elliott winning the 1,500 metres. At 4-1, they were "clearly wrong"; they should have been, he reckoned, 2-1 or 5-2. So he immediately bet £200, and later the same morning the odds had already been cut.

It was a routine sum for a man who lays out around £½ million in a year. And he wasn't even sure that Elliott would win. "In a sense it didn't matter if he lost," he says. "The fact is, I knew I had the odds right. It was worth a bet. If I make enough bets like that it ought to swing in my favour in the long term, hopefully by eight or nine per cent."

Simon has been making a living out of betting for about 2½ years. To many, this will seem a glamourous existence, but he says: "It's hard work, like any other form of business, and often exhausting." He operates with a team of about 25, using others to get his bets on now that he's known to the bookmakers. He receives good advice, of course. But he doesn't talk much about horses, or athletes. He talks about data, about margins, about actuarial and insurance systems.

"The skill really is in getting the money on. That means assessing the early morning prices and looking for odds like 10-1 which will later come in to 5-1. Almost all my bets are laid in the first half-hour of the day. But equally, if the odds aren't right you don't bet, and there have been times when I haven't bet for weeks."

There are two myths in betting, says Simon. "One is that anybody's a winner. The other is that there are no winners." But it's clear he doesn't see ordinary punters among the potential winners. In fact he seems to side with those who take the view that "all

☐ *Continued overleaf*

☐ *Continued from previous page*

punters are utter mugs". They never remember their losses, he says. "How many people record their bets? And how many follow the rule that you don't bet if you're in doubt? Hardly any. On the other hand I'm surprised that people who do bet regularly don't invest more heavily. My impression is that a bet of £50 is pretty unusual in an average betting shop."

But such punters, as he points out, have a philosophy that is completely different from his own. "Let's imagine that you go into a betting shop and find a punter who's got a hundred pounds he's prepared to spend, and you say to him: 'You give me that £100, go off and have a nice afternoon, meet me at the end of racing and I'll give you £100 back plus £8 profit.' He'll tell you to sod off, because he thinks he's going to turn his £100 into £300. Well, to me he's already into a losing mentality."

THE ADDICT

EMIL GRYGAR was, or perhaps is, a compulsive gambler. When told of the betting method of people like Simon, the professional gambler, he marvels that someone can be "compulsive but controlled". He's somewhat puzzled by the argument that the professional *isn't* necessarily compulsive, any more than if he put his professional skills into the stock market or a High Street shop. It takes some time for that idea to sink in, for it contrasts so sharply with his own memory of betting.

"I'd feel above the rest of them in the betting shop but I would be humiliated by the end of the afternoon. The bookmaker would have seen me out again, as he knew he would. Having done my last loose change on the last race I'd try to slither out without him seeing me. That meant opening the door and the sunlight coming in, announcing that someone was going. That destroyed me, that moment. But even as I walked away I'd be formulating my big plan for the next day. I was going to be different, very calculating, go steady to start with, get a

little pot, and then *hit* them." Emil's gambling started, as a boy, with penny slot machines, then in looking for racing results for his father. He can't remember any point at which he got hooked:

"It just creeps up on you like an illness."

By the age of 25 he was, he now knows, a compulsive gambler. And he stayed on the treadmill for 15 years. He exploited the flexibility of being a self-employed builder as he kept a lot of balls in the air at once. He used the advances he received and then faced the prospect of working for nothing in order to finish the job. So he started doing a lot of jobs and dodged a lot of clients. More often than not he escaped to the betting shop. But he needed still more money to make good his losses. So he stole.

"My forte was stealing building materials, for which a friend paid cash." A lot of it was small-scale but occasionally it involved bigger items, like a couple of generators. And breaking into a yard at night could involve facing guard dogs. Inevitably, the police caught up with him, more than once, and he was lucky to escape with fines. He was also in court for mortgage arrears, non-payment of rates and, frequently, for driving without tax or insurance. At home, phone and electricity were cut off and furniture was re-possessed.

"If you have a big win you come home and you count it. You get up in the middle of the night and count it again, but you know that you're not going to give any of it to the family, or pay off the mortgage arrears. You're going to make the dream bet the next day. I have won £3,000, and lost it again the next day."

There is a somewhat pathetic element in all of this, which Emil recognises. He also acknowledges that he was never a racing expert. "I might have said I was, but I was as blind as the rest of them."

It seems as if the futility of it all got through to him one Saturday afternoon when two 50-1 winners came up. Emil, of course, had neither. On that same afternoon his £100 stake had gone down to £1, and then been lost again. "I thought, 'There's something wrong here'. It seemed to trigger off the thought that I had to do something about my gambling."

He rang the Samaritans, who referred him to Gamblers Anonymous. His admission, at his first GA meeting, that he was a compulsive gambler was the first step in starting a new life. Now, like a reformed alcoholic, he knows he must resist even one small bet, which would make "all hell break loose". He even has to be careful watching racing on TV. "When I turn the volume down," he says, "it's much easier." Says Philly, his second wife: "I don't think you should watch it at all. It's *not* good therapy." But Emil's feet seem to be pretty solidly on the ground. In the two years since stopping gambling he's become a stalwart of Gamblers Anonymous, one of 1,500 who, say GA, have faced up to their problem, along with another million or more who haven't.

"There are less stressful ways of earning money," says Emil. "It's called work. Gambling is a dream world. It's something for nothing. I accept it's not for me."

THE PSYCHIATRIST

Dr EMMANUEL MORAN asks a simple but important question about the nature of gambling. Since the gambling industry has to make a profit, which means that overall the punters have to lose, what is it that the industry is selling the punters and for which they are prepared to pay money?

"It has to be entertainment. So what's the nature of this entertainment? It's thrill and excitement. After all, we talk about having a 'flutter', which implies excitement. There's a progression of uncertainty,

build-up of tension and release of tension. It's what the Greeks recognised as catharsis, a very pleasurable and important part of relaxation."

Dr Moran, a consultant psychiatrist, is also chairman of the National Council on Gambling, a body set up by a number of people, including social workers, who were concerned at the effects on the community and the family of excessive gambling. Of course, he knows that many punters *don't* leave the betting shop feeling relaxed and thinking that they've had a great afternoon's betting. But he argues that this should be the philosophy which underlies legislation and attempts at education.

"The problem is that there's a tremendous amount of propaganda that gambling is all about winning money. Take, for example, terms like 'investment' and 're-investment'. The evidence is that most gamblers exaggerate the level of skill required, and the industry encourages them to think they *can* exercise skill." However, Dr Moran knows that the industry cannot be expected to discourage people who seem intent on losing their money (though

publicans will refuse to serve drunks, mainly because they have become a nuisance). Indeed, he's not anti-gambling, which he describes as an enjoyable activity for the majority who gamble sensibly. "It's a commercial enterprise and must be allowed to be entrepreneurial, within limits. What it mustn't do is entice gamblers."

Dr Moran has looked on in some unease as betting legislation first rejected a clause that there shouldn't be any 'loitering' in betting shops, then introduced race commentaries and has now embraced television and refreshments. He has mixed feelings: the facilities encourage people to enjoy their betting but they also encourage them to bet more, "and the fact is that if the shops are maximising their turnover they can't help but maximise compulsive gambling".

So what makes people gamblers? Are they compulsive by definition? "In the first place," says Dr Moran, "we're talking about an individual, inbuilt trait. These people tend to need a high degree of risk to get the same thrill as others. They have a need to purchase larger amounts of risk. So they lose more money. Often, too, they're exceptionally superstitious, so they have a tremendous faith in luck. But they also need the environment in which to gamble, and while it is convenient for the industry to see their problem as an illness, there's no evidence that they have an illness in the medical sense.

"It's a form of behaviour which is learnt and stimulated within a certain environment. Now, there's no doubt that people who have accidents tend to be accident-prone, but it would be totally foolish to say that accidents are solely the fault of people who fall under buses. Buses have some role in it too."

Dr Moran points out that gambling, like any other activity, can be represented by a spectrum. At one end are the people who are gambling "teetotallers". At the other are the compulsive gamblers. In the middle are those who, in varying degrees, gamble sensibly.

"And if you increase the betting facilities, everyone moves along a bit. At one point, a few people who don't gamble at all will have an occasional bet. At another, people who have been heavy gamblers become compulsive gamblers."

If Dr Moran's main theme is the need to control betting, another, possibly more promising approach is via education. Already, members of the National Council on Gambling talk to schoolchildren. "The message isn't: 'Don't gamble when you grow up'," explains Dr Moran. "The message is: 'Don't gamble in order to make money. It's for entertainment, it's for fun. Who ever told you that you could make money out of *fun?*'"

February 1990

Lament for a lost Fish

Residing in the mind of a writer are the cast of characters who inhabited the shop where he first cut his betting teeth. He recalls them with nostalgic affection

by PAUL HAIGH

THIS is a sort of requiem; an elegy for my first regular betting shop, in Aberystwyth, which closed its doors last month for the last time.

Corals in Bridge Street, always known by the name of its previous proprietor T. B. Fish (West Wales), was a place of something like pilgrimage for me. Whenever I went back to my home town I would visit it with much the same emotions another might feel upon visiting his alma mater.

It was there that I waded the first faltering steps into the great stream of racing. There that I found out what a Yankee was. There that I used to take my university grant, then my Giro money. There that I used to work briefly in the 1970s, sitting next to Iorrie the manager's son Creighton as we worked like a couple of Bob Cratchits at the weird T. B. Fish system of bet placing: a sort of double-entry ledger. The punters would approach and tell you their bets which you would then write down, often after a pitying glance. Then you'd give them the slip and leave the duplicate underneath.

It was in this shop that Dai Dog-ends used to sidle up and, with a look of enormous cunning, place his alliterative bets: multiple cross-doubles and an each-way 'acca' on all horses whose names began with a C, an R or an M. It didn't seem to matter which. All he'd say when we told him he was crazy was "It works", even though he must have known we knew it didn't.

It was in this shop that Peter, the brilliant settler, used to tear out what remained of his hair when people came up to collect before he'd had a

A day in Perth and you meet all sorts

Travel north to Scotland and a betting shop where the boss is Manager of the Year and everything turns out not to be quite as expected

by BROUGH SCOTT

SNOW on the Trossachs, a sign up for Bannockburn, Stirling Castle proud in the sunlight, Willie Carson on the carphone: but still the nagging thought "whose game is it anyway?" For sure it is Carson's.

Not content with heading the prize-money list over here for another season, he was planning this week's trip to Hollywood Park. But the auld racing nonsense belongs to a lot more folk than Willie Carson. Last Wednesday's journey on through Strathallan, over the River Earn and into the city of Perth was very much to the other end of the chain. To William Hills at 5–7 South Methven Street. It's the Betting Shop of the Year. Talking to punters like John Mitchell you could see why.

John is a pensioner now. He was 30 years in the army, he served all over, from Singapore to Stuttgart. But he and his children returned to Perth. They didn't need 1990's survey to tell them it had the Best Quality of Life in Britain. Nor where Dad should go for a club. Every day starts anew in a betting shop.

We had trekked up to present Peter Martin with his plaque as Manager of the Year. Tall, bespectacled, distinguished-looking but very much a son of Perth, he made a gracious little speech saying it was really a reward for his staff and for his customers, "especially for the winning ones".

They liked that, John and the others. Fifty hopeless little Robert Bruces of the betting game. Wasn't Bannockburn just 35 miles down the road? Who would stop them aiming, like Bruce's spider, "to try chance to do the sums. It was in this shop that a punter known only as 'The White West Indian' (a blond Jamaican who baffled us all by sounding exactly like other Jamaicans) once had a 50p eight-horse across-the-card accumulator on a Bank Holiday. Most of them were odds-on but he still walked out with £150.

It was in this shop that a strange student, who wore a black cloak and called himself Mr Shroud, once brought off one of the greatest coups, pound for pound, in the history of racing, when he convinced himself that New Chapter would win the Lincoln and backed it at every possible opportunity for weeks beforehand. I shall never forget his face during the 20-minute inquiry after New Chapter passed the post first, nor the way his hands shook as he contemplated his eventual good fortune.

We used to live in the same digs, and for some time afterwards Shroud would hire a fellow inmate, a Cream fan called Keith who thought Ginger Baker was God, to shave his face and trim his straggling goatee. The arrangement ended when Keith, anxious to get his chore over for the day, burst into the room early one morning and found the young master and his girlfriend 'on the nest'.

Shroud was a very odd fellow who had interesting habits. One of them was to borrow fivers from people "just for practice". He'd give them back all

right, but he had a theory that it was a good idea to establish the precedent. He had asthma, and a likeable sidekick called Tim, who preferred to be known as 'Slithe Golightly' and used to claim he'd lost the only girl he ever loved to Terry Biddlecombe.

Where have they gone now? *Où sont les punters d'antan?* The last I heard, Shroud was a guest of Her Majesty after a spot of embezzling. The White West Indian had gone back to the West Indies. Peter had had a stroke and retired, and Dai Dog-ends and the rest had vanished into the Celtic mists.

And now they've shut the shop and the wall beside it, on which we used to lounge like lizards soaking up the sun and the commentaries, is just a wall again for propping up a house. They've moved the shop up the road.

Corals have taken over the only university hall of residence in the middle of town and turned it into the most luxurious betting office west of Park Lane. A nice little comment on our society that, don't you think? Norton's Coin opened it in July and there's no doubt it's a great place with lots of TVs and chrome and loos and coffee and snacks on demand. What it doesn't have is atmosphere, or history. That's all lying there in the dark behind the bolted door in Bridge Street. T. B. Fish RIP.

28 August 1991

---

and try again" in the battle with Peter Martin's pay-out counter?

On the screens the first race at Kempton was already under way. Hexham's runners were circling at the start. The air full of the usual comradely mixture of shrugged-off suffering as the results run against you.

It was in Perth in 1559 that John Knox preached one of his great sermons. It wasn't the one about "the monstrous regiment of women". It was something about "idolatry" which led to much ugly business in the local monasteries. What he would have made of South Methven Street is an interesting thought. Isn't there something unwholesome in encouraging people to gamble away their money?

A former manager told of men pouring into one of the Glasgow shops on Friday afternoons and unsealing their pay packets to have a bet. The rolling-pin consequences when they later presented its depleted contents to the Gorbals equivalent of 'Er Indoors' are not for those of a nervous disposition.

Peter Martin is very clear. "It's their choice and their money," he says in that quiet Scottish voice which is a lot nearer Dr Finlay's waiting room than John Bank's pitch on the rails. "They may win off me, they may lose, but they know what they have to spend. There are not many fools around here."

But there has been a complaint. A couple of years back one of the regulars won the pools. Very soon the 50p doubles upped to a fiver, then fifty, then £500, then Peter Martin got a desperate request. "Ban me," said the punter. "I want you to stop me coming through the door."

Back on the screens the unpronounceable Achiltibuie was making people eat their words at Kelso, Ginger McCain's Sure Metal was boring holes in the fences at Haydock, while down at Hove the "one dog", Luna Pearl, was beaten back into fourth place by an 8-1 shot.

Outside, Perth stood unaffected in the icy November sunshine. Not unchanged; a frightfully swish new shopping arcade has been set up next to the town hall. Down by the river bank there is a weather-proofed copy of a postcard by the impressionist Seurat which raves about "Le Tay, Le Tay, Le Tay argentée". It takes all sorts.

It's 1,100 years since someone called King Kenneth the First brought the Stone of Destiny to Scone Palace up the road. Ten times a year Perth races livens up the royal grounds. John Mitchell doesn't make the trip. "I follow it, of course," he says. "But I am a bit chesty, and besides my sort of budget hardly equals the entrance fee."

28 November 1991

It was a day for discreet inquiries

How a 'cute little set-up' came good is the subject of a short story carried in Racing Post. The evocative tale is set in the autumnal chill of Brighton

by IAN CARNABY

LENNIE sounds guarded, of course. Not respectful, just guarded.

"Isn't this rather an unusual call?" he says. "I'm a jockey, not a trainer. It's Hopgood you want, surely?"

"Hopgood said she'd win last time," I replied coolly. "That was before she found more blind alleyways than anyone knew existed at Folkestone and came fifth." I try to keep the bitterness out of my voice.

He chuckles softly. It's a dry, Liverpool sound, timeless in its knowledge of human weakness. "Well, I didn't ride her that day," he says. "You'd have to ask good old Arnie. He's ridden for Hopgood since Methuselah shouted the odds. I shouldn't talk to him down the phone, though. These days you never know who's listening, do you?" The laugh takes on a harder edge.

He has me pretty well worked out and I haven't even come to the point. A deep breath. "Look, she's a syndicate horse," I begin. "Quite a few people in the group don't know that much about the game and it's a real let-down when she runs much worse than Hopgood says she will. All I'm asking is what you think about tomorrow."

I'm ashamed to feel my heart thumping insistently against my shirt. I wish I'd never rung him. That's the difference between three drinks and four.

He's too hard to let me get away with it. "Listen, Mr B, don't break my heart. Those people you've brought together are too flush to worry about the odd disappointment. They don't back horses for real, so it's you we're talking about, isn't it?"

It's pointless to argue, and he takes my hesitation to mean he's got it right. I wonder in passing how he views owners who normally command respect. I'm relieved that I let him go on, though.

"I rode that filly at Yarmouth, and if she can't win a poxy Brighton seller there's something wrong. I'll be trying, if that's what you're worried about, and neither Hopgood nor anyone else can change that. I can't afford to have my collar felt again, and I don't need phone calls like this."

He holds on just long enough for me to mutter thanks. He has no need to adhere to the usual jockey–owner relationship, and we both know I won't be contacting him again.

I GET through the morning. Part of it is spent making sure that the arrangements for placing money are well in hand. I don't bother much with the racing papers because the last thing you need at this stage is a couple of stars by her name, but in fact she's not widely tipped. I walk all the way along the front towards Hove, and as so often in the past I promise myself an identical journey 24 hours later, to compare moods.

Eleven o'clock isn't too early to arrive at The Grand. Vodka in heavy glasses and money everywhere. The members of the syndicate make their appearance soon afterwards. Nothing changes in the conversation. House prices are serious, the latest news from the City is all-important and school fees are scandalous, but horseracing is a game and this is a day out.

"But let's ask Mr B. He's the expert, after all, and he fancied her last time, isn't that right, Mr B?" In a perverse way they love you to be wrong. It probably strengthens their belief that they're not missing anything by staying at arm's length.

I smile winningly and make encouraging noises. I'm good with the blue rinses and check jackets. They know I know the game.

The atmosphere is much the same at the track. Hopgood comes on with that dreadful false bonhomie, flattering the women and joshing the men, but predictably things become more tense five minutes before she's due to canter down. Lennie arrives barely in time to offer a single pleasantry and says nothing to Hopgood, thus confirming the long-held belief that most meaningful trainer–jockey conversations take place a long way from the parade ring and conveniently bypass the owner.

It's not difficult to oversee the syndicate's investments yet still watch the race alone.

I go high up in the old-fashioned stand and try to let my mind go blank. My legs ache, there's a dull throbbing in my chest, and the first trickle from the armpits makes its descent. I look across the housing estate; thousands of people living mundane lives, and united principally by their complete indifference to the petty drama being played out above them.

NOT for the first time, this particular October meeting feels like the autumn of life.

How do I describe the ride he gives her? Indolent comes closest, I suppose. Indolent and slightly cruel. In a field of 12 he ambles along at the back for half of the mile journey. He pushes her through a gap where you have to on that final bend, but he doesn't send her on until they reach those caravans by the furlong pole. She's going to win anyway but he hits once, twice, to make absolutely sure. He's a tough little bastard.

And I'm shouting, of course I am, shouting and yelling until the sound of my own relief threatens to pierce the eardrums. Because when genuine excitement is dead, there's only relief and despair left. Today relief has it. Pathetic to you, maybe, but lifeblood to me.

Hopgood accepts his share of back-slapping and cheek-kissing and looks me in the eye for the first time.

"9-2 to 11-4, they tell me," he murmurs. "Well, well. Someone must think I know what I'm doing after all."

"Do we buy her in?"

He makes quite sure no-one else can hear. "I really don't care a tuppenny damn what you do," he replies. "You're the sportsman, you decide," and turns away without another word.

You want it to be perfect but it never is. We get her back cheaply and the champagne flows, but it's difficult to feel part of it now. Hopgood's words leave a nasty taste, and I need to be away from it all – a dark restaurant, a little self-indulgence and the usual calculations.

Even so I remain until the end and Lennie rides the last winner as well. It's a 25-1 shot, and maybe he stays for a little celebration himself, because the car park is almost deserted when I see him hurrying away from the Members. I have that instinctive feeling that he'd walk a brisk half-mile to avoid a conversation, but he passes so close that it's impossible. I startle him, but he recovers and nods curtly.

"Thanks for today," I say.

He shrugs, and that hard glitter comes into his eyes. "Quite a day, Mr B. You and Hopgood both have it away and neither of you knows what the other one's up to. The boys had a bit of a laugh about that." His mouth turns down in a mirthless grin.

"I don't think I can have horses with him any more. He knows I rang you, doesn't he?"

"So what? He's in no position to complain. He phoned immediately afterwards, as a matter of fact, just to let me know how much he fancied her. If it makes you feel any better, you were dead right about Folkestone. I asked around, and some of the lads were amazed Arnie wasn't pulled in. Still, win some, lose some."

I feel that tide of weariness which embraces all gamblers sooner or later.

"It doesn't make me feel any better," I say.

"Yeah, well, that's up to you. It's none of my business and I don't want it to be, but there's one big difference between you and Hopgood. He'll make today count for a good long time, but you'll need another cute little set-up in a couple of weeks. Just remember, I'm not on your list of contacts."

He's about half my age and he moves away quickly to where his BMW is parked near the exit. I watch him all the way, and catch the fragment of some current tune carried back on the breeze. He wears his loneliness well.

There's a definite chill in the air now and the lights are shimmering through a hint of sea-fret on the front.

I turn up my collar and set off down the hill.

10 November 1990

Tribute to the punter's friend

*When Phil Bull, the founder of Timeform,
died, the punter lost his most effective
advocate, a gruff socialist who knew how
to beat the system and win*

by JOHN McCRIRICK

NO man understood punting and the prominence of betting in racing more than owner-breeder Phil Bull, whose death last weekend at 79 robs us all of our most lucid, thought-provoking intellect.

His perceptive, all-embracing submission to the 1978 Royal Commission on Gambling would be a compulsive study for all future inquiries into horseracing. It stands as Bull's last will and testament on the game he loved and understood as few have ever done.

At times sharp, irascible, even boorish, diminutive ex-schoolmaster Bull was pedantic in the only tolerable way – when taking you on he was usually right and you ended up realising it. Like the late Lord Wigg, a formidable fellow socialist, he did his homework meticulously which no opponents were able to match. They were prophets and innovators, derided at the time but eventually recognised, albeit reluctantly.

Of course Bull couldn't square his luxurious self-earned lifestyle at the magnificent Hollins overlooking Halifax with his avowed left-wing beliefs, reckoning capitalism's hours, let alone days, were numbered and the barricades and banners of the proletariat would be up at any moment. Few exploited or benefited more from an economic and political system he despised. That the apocalypse never came, despite stuttering false dawns, proved to be one of the rare major losers he backed in life.

Staying at The Hollins was a privilege which stimulated both the palate and the mind into the early hours but proved costly on the snooker table. For his age Bull had to be as good as anyone on the

baize and it's said that his great friend Joe Davis was never at ease when playing on that unique table. Bull once did me like a kipper on the black, when giving 70 points. Though I've never managed a double-figure break in my life it was galling even so to be stalked to inevitable defeat by the perpetually cigar-smoking guru.

He was a prodigious punter in the days when, almost alone, he had access to reliable timing and form interpretation. Thanks largely to him, that information is now available to all, including bookies, through Timeform. But in those early years, he was afforded that rare compliment on racecourses of being tailed and earwigged.

"What's Phil backing?" was whispered repeatedly as he padded studiously up to the rails, Timeform in hand. Whether workmen or their guv'nors found out or not, all respected the sage.

Numerous hacks, and others, have made their mark through being Bull-trained. Never having possessed the brainpower, diligence or self-discipline needed even to apply, let alone graduate, through the strict old-style Timeform academy, this failure to be inducted correctly into the craft of reporting and analysing haunts me still.

Bull, like so many others it must be said, had no time for such as me bumbling along ineffectually with their half-baked opinions. Daily, if bothered, he could pick on something written or said and pull it apart. Thankfully he was usually merciful, though to be on the receiving end of a Bull lecture was a chastening, unnerving experience. How much worse it must have been for cowering employees at Timeform during his hands-on period after the war, and till the 1970s, is hard to imagine. But unscathed survivors owe their present careers to a mentor who, above all else, was a stickler for grammar along with accurate, impartial details.

Punters have lost their most feared and effective advocate – the Establishment their most resourceful and obdurate adversary.

His brief flirtation within the portals of Portman Square, as chairman of the talking shop Horseracing Advisory Council, couldn't last. Looking back to 1980, the only surprise is that action-man Bull took even a few months to rumble the powerlessness of the HAC. Anyway, although long-winded in his missions, he was no conciliator or formulator of meaningless compromises.

One way still to recall Bull's ever-critical gruff phraseology will be to wind up underestimated mimic, Timeform director Jim McGrath. He has his old boss off so expertly that you can almost smell the stale cigar smoke and see those alert glinting eyes peering atop the greying fuzz as he snaps back a typical Bull riposte.

All at Timeform House have been set innovative

standards unequalled in journalistic objectivity. Should these ever be allowed to slip, an irreplaceable hinge in British racing's integrity worldwide will have been severed. What finer memorial could any man leave to the activity he adored, however frivolous it may be in the great scheme of things, than the indispensable book of achievement and record?

As a final, fitting tribute, the Jockey Club, whose origins and trappings he loathed and whose members didn't all exactly meet with his approval either, should once and for all do away with the even more indefensible Rule 153 on disqualifications.

Bull's long campaign – one of the few yet to succeed – for the results of races to stand with, if necessary, draconian punishments to riders, gains credence almost daily and no amount of word-juggling will save hapless stewards from contradictory interpretations of *fact*.

Perhaps, when eventually we settle prizes and bets on a 'first past the post' system, Bull's stentorian voice will be heard round the table barking: "Should have done it 40 years ago!"

17 June 1989

Phil Bull, at times a sharp, irascible ex-schoolmaster, usually won the day in an argument.

The rare Bird who gathered the prize

In the normal course of events the luck of professional gamblers does not hold to the end. In the case of Alex Bird it did and he even died at an apposite moment

by CHRISTOPHER POOLE

TRIBUTES to Alex Bird have been both fulsome and heartfelt for he was that rare kind of man who possessed a total conviction in his own beliefs and, more often than not, proved them right.

Many admired such a single-minded attitude to the quirks of racing life; perhaps even more the fact that he once had the betting ring by the balls. His success left Bird light on humility, but he was the staunchest of friends and unique among big gamblers in my experience, for his ability to shrug at both triumph and failure. Alex Bird had style, manifest in his moated Cheshire country house, his immaculate Rolls Royce and his love of vintage champagne. He also had great staying power.

I have watched dozens of professional punters come and go over a period of more than three decades. Some of them plunged far deeper than Bird and consequently made far bigger amounts. Almost without exception, they dropped out, defeated by that old Turf truism that the bookies always win in the end. Alex Bird held on to enough of his considerable fortune to go on enjoying life. Although a casual acquaintance for many years, I only got to know him well during the 1986 Breeders' Cup at Santa Anita. We happened to be staying in the same hotel and developed the habit of discussing the meaning of racing life during a series of poolside breakfasts.

With his friend and colleague Peter Hurst, Bird had already taken a large slice of the action over

National dream with a silver lining

It is the earliest moments of a lifetime interest in racing that are usually remembered most fondly, and particularly when their fabric is pure Irish

by HENRY KELLY

MY fondest Grand National memories can be described as a Tale of Two Jimmys.

Jimmy Weldon, from a well-known Dublin jewellery family, sat beside me for maths class. Jimmy Gough, one of the best men and best teachers I ever met in my life, and who later became the first-ever lay headmaster of a Jesuit school in Ireland, did his best with our class.

On the morning of the Grand National in 1961 Jimmy Weldon and myself were in position in the front row as usual. Jimmy Gough said the prayer and started to write equations on the blackboard. He turned and told us to get on with them.

Then he winked at Kelly and Weldon and we went up to his desk, a big high-standing thing in the front of the room, the type of desk Dickens would have given a schoolteacher. From inside the desk Jimmy Gough extracted the folded-down racing page of The Irish Times and inquired if we had "anything for the 'Big One'?"

I fancied whatever Fred Winter was on. I always did. But then Jimmy Weldon stunned us into silence by relating his previous night's dream: a grey horse had won the Grand National. Begob!

Sure enough, there was a grey horse entered. Nicolaus Silver. What more could you want? Kelly and Weldon between them went half-a-crown each-way. Jimmy Gough's bet was a secret.

I listened to the race on the wireless at home and could hardly believe my ears. Nicolaus Silver won! It was rumoured that Kelly and Weldon had won "more than £10" and that Mr Gough had "made a

Dancing Brave for the Breeders' Cup Turf. He thought defeat for this hero of the Prix de l'Arc de Triomphe a highly unlikely contingency and had arrived on the West Coast simply to top up the bet and take pleasure in watching the spoils landed. Bird was convinced that another huge pot was about to be netted.

As luck would have it, we were on the same flight home, the day after Dancing Brave could finish only fourth behind Manila, Theatrical and Estrapade. I was still shell-shocked as were the rest of the British press party. Alex Bird, who had stood to win goodness knows how much and whose losses on this single race would have financed my gambling for years to come, was in tremendous form.

He had "got rid of a bit here and there" and backed another winner. It was, he told me, a damaging afternoon but might have been far worse. Win a few, lose a few but always come out on the right side by the end of the year. This was a prime example of the philosophical approach to gambling which Bird had developed over a lifetime and which provided him with an aura of calm assurance in the most trying of circumstances when a lesser man would have been reduced to abject panic.

He had more fully developed the theme in his best-selling autobiography which had been published the previous year and, in my view, remains required reading for anyone contemplating a serious tilt at betting for a living. "I have always said," Bird wrote, "that if worrying did any good I would be the world's greatest worrier." But having decided, early in life, that it was futile he dismissed the notion altogether. That was typical of his uncluttered mind, which always allowed a firm grasp of fundamentals and would, I suspect, have made him successful in whatever profession he had chosen.

Having flirted with bookmaking as a young man, he quite deliberately chose to stand the other side of the rails, a decision he never had cause to regret but which cost his one-time associates countless thousands of pounds. He became a noted form-book expert and, having developed uncanny accuracy in judging photo-finishes, was content to wager in huge figures for comparatively small percentage returns. It gave him no concern provided he had convinced himself he was right. Almost invariably, he was.

He is said to have collected on his last racecourse bet. It could hardly be otherwise. He even died on a day when the racing press was short of news and had ample space for his obituary. Alex Bird was a winner right to the end.

14 December 1991

---

killing". From then on maths never held any fears for me.

Our neighbourhood in Dublin was famous because Michael O'Hehir lived nearby and we went to Mass on Sunday in the same church. His now-famous sons went too and were like steps of stairs growing up. Racing men and footballers looked on the Great Broadcaster with awe. You should have seen them and heard them after Foinavon won the Grand National! All Ireland was proud that it had been Michael O'Hehir, and not some English fellow, who spotted the horse that survived the terrible fence, its fallers and refusals, and made history.

Our house was different on Grand National Day. My mother had a bet, and my aunt, but not my father. His father had been ruined by gambling in the early 1920s and, to his own death, he had a fear and dread of backing horses. He did, however, know a lot about them and was happy to impart knowledge each Saturday in March or April come the National.

The year I was born Lovely Cottage won the race and every woman in Ireland made a few bob, my mother included. A connection by marriage was not so lucky, however. He owned a bookies' shop near a large military barracks. It seems every soldier in the barracks backed Lovely Cottage.

The man himself was having lunch with a woman in town and had left orders not to be bothered. But for his clerk managing to back the horse with a bookie across the road my in-law's fate would have been worse. As it was, he just went out of business and became a carpet salesman.

In my home town of Athlone, Mrs Kit Hanley, who ran another bookie's shop, was ruined. Yet she bravely opened on the Monday morning, told everyone they would be paid and stuck to her words. There were rumours in the town that some winning punters had taken only half what they were owed because Mrs Hanley was a widow.

The year Highland Wedding won we decided it was an Irish victory. Our school got a free day off because Eddie Harty rode the winner and he'd been to our school. His brother John, who was a year or so ahead of me, was a great jockey also but never quite made the National. We jeered at other schools in Dublin for not having rounded men in their ranks: those who could do Greek irregular verbs and ride the winner of the greatest steeplechase in the world.

If Father O'Sullivan reads this today he'll know what I mean. If Jimmy Gough was near me now, he'd simply ask for a tip. Oh, and by the way, if Jimmy Weldon's phone rings early on Saturday morning, he'll know who it is. It'll be me phoning from London to hear about his dream.

6 April 1989

Norton's 'shock of the century'!

Sometimes a horse wins that nobody has given a chance. Such was the spectacular case when a 100-1 horse from Wales beat Desert Orchid in the Gold Cup

by TIM RICHARDS

THE impossible does happen. Norton's Coin, the horse who ran only because of an oversight by his owner-trainer Sirrell Griffiths, caused the biggest upset in the history of the Gold Cup when he landed steeplechasing's most important prize at odds of 100-1 at Cheltenham yesterday.

Desert Orchid, the nation's most popular horse and the 10-11 favourite, trailed in third. At Kempton on Boxing Day, Dessie had finished 39 lengths ahead of Norton's Coin when winning the King George VI Chase. The result, in record time, was close to fiction as Norton's Coin and Graham McCourt battled up the hill to lay the legend of the great grey champion. Norton's Coin won by three-quarters of a length from Toby Tobias, with Desert Orchid four lengths further back.

The sensational result stunned the 56,000 crowd into temporary silence. It was with total disbelief that they greeted the winner, only the seventh saddled by Griffiths in 11 years as a permit-holder. The golden victory was slightly marred when winning rider McCourt was later banned for three days for misuse of the whip on the winner.

Griffiths, 50, who weighs 15st 7lb, has a herd of 75 Friesians on his farm at Nantgaredig, five miles from Carmarthen, and rides Norton's Coin every morning after milking. Yesterday he was up at a quarter to four and had reckoned Norton's Coin could finish third behind Desert Orchid and Toby Tobias, granted a clear round. But he didn't have a penny on his 100-1 hero.

"A bookmaker friend of mine called round to see us on Wednesday night and asked me if I wanted to have £25,000 to £200 each-way," he said. "I must admit the temptation was rather great. But I've never backed Norton's Coin in any manner so I thought I'd better not start now. So I said no. And it doesn't bother me – we've won the Gold Cup.

"At the last fence I prayed, 'Please God, don't fall.' Once he'd got over I just hoped he'd keep going."

Desert Orchid's trainer David Elsworth said: "Disappointment was my first reaction. But results like this show just what a wonderful business this steeplechasing is. It's the stuff dreams are made of." Neither Elsworth nor owner Richard Burridge offered any serious excuses for Desert Orchid, and Griffiths said: "I know a lot of people will be disappointed that we've beaten Desert Orchid. It just hasn't sunk in with me yet."

After Norton's Coin had finished second to

Willsford at Cheltenham in January, McCourt suggested to Griffiths that he enter him for the Cathcart. Griffiths, who trains three horses under permit, said: "We found that he wasn't qualified for that so I thought we'd have a go at the Mildmay of Flete, but that had closed. So the only entry we had left was the Gold Cup."

Norton's Coin was not always the easiest horse to train and Griffiths believes the company of his farmyard chickens helped. "Up until 12 months ago the chickens used to perch on his back and their company helped to build up his confidence. Now the farm cats live with him in his box."

Norton's Coin has been wrong all season, and after his last race at Newbury last month he was scoped and was found to be suffering from a septic throat. Griffiths and his vet managed to work the oracle in the month between then and Gold Cup day.

Bald-headed Griffiths smiled. "This has got to be the greatest achievement of my life. Before this I suppose it had been marrying my wife Joyce." He said the result was like a dream and, though he had never anticipated such a fantastic triumph, he did dream that Norton's Coin would win before he produced the goods in a race at Cheltenham last April.

"The night before he won I dreamt he would do so. I wrote it down on a piece of paper and put it in a sealed envelope and left the note in a bureau. When we got back from Cheltenham I told my son to go upstairs, take the envelope from the desk and open it. He read out my dream to us."

16 March 1990

Norton's Coin, the rank outsider, gets up between Toby Tobias (right) and the favourite, Desert Orchid, to spring the biggest upset in Gold Cup history.

The man who was first past the post

In recent years the betting market has expanded enormously outside of racing and greyhounds. Ron Pollard was the pioneer of this modern expansion

by NORMAN HARRIS

AS all the world knows, bookmakers are not fond of the two-horse race. But sports other than racing *do* in the main offer the equivalent of the two-horse race. Ron Pollard refers to these sports as "head-to-head" contests: over the past quarter of a century they've given him some bad moments, but also made him Britain's most famous odds-maker.

It all started in 1963, when the unusual interest in the political scene prompted Pollard to open a book on the contest for the Tory leadership. He can still remember the odds; 5-4 Butler, 7-4 Hailsham, 6-1 Maudling, 10-1 the rest. A headline in the Evening News announced: "10-to-1 bar 3 for No 10".

For two weeks Pollard was a media star, as TV cameras were wheeled in and out of Ladbrokes. The firm took only £14,000, making a mere £1,400, but it had pulled off a major publicity coup. And at the following year's general election £600,000 was bet – including the world's biggest bet to that time, the £50,000 which won Maxwell Joseph £37,000 when Labour got home by three seats.

"As a result," says Pollard, "we realised that the public wanted to bet on lots of other things – aliens landing on earth, the Eurovision Song Contest, Miss World contests and sporting contests of all kinds."

One of the first sports authorities to accept on-site betting – and one of the least probable – was MCC. "Everyone said we wouldn't be able to," recalls Pollard. "But when I met them as a Ladbrokes man I was representing a pillar of the establishment, too." Initially, Lord's was anxious about the creation of noise in the betting tent, a worry which proved unfounded. What they did soon move to prevent, though, was betting on individual performances – i.e. on a certain player scoring 100, or 0.

To many, sport and betting may seem an unhealthy mix but Pollard remains sanguine. "What I've always said is that by and large the integrity of the sportsman, his determination to do his best, to be the Number One, is so ingrained that he wouldn't dream of doing anything else."

And the betting tents at Lord's, or the British Open, can be something of an illusion: most of the money laid at such venues is still on racing. Pollard estimates that horse and greyhound racing accounts for over 90 per cent of all sports betting, with football taking three to four per cent and all other sports sharing the tiny remainder. "What we get from these other sports is publicity."

At the same time he's developed a natural caution, not to say unease, about head-to-head sports. "It's easy to be too much influenced by one's experience of racing where, even though two out of every three races are won by the first or second favourites, you will have to decide which those two are, and you can put numbers on it. But in a lot of matches at Wimbledon, for example, the better player isn't 1-3, or even 1-33. You're just giving money away. In fact, I wouldn't bet on individual matches early on."

There's the same pitfall in certain team contests, like Worcestershire playing Glamorgan in the Sunday cricket league. "You're inclined to make the odds 2-5 Worcestershire and 7-4 Glamorgan, but they should really be 1-5 and 3-1."

In cricket, Ron Pollard's most costly mistake – if that is the word – was the 500-1 he offered when England were at their lowest point in the Headingley Test of 1981, only for Botham with the bat and then the England bowlers to perform like Boys' Own heroes. So, *was* 500-1 a mistake? "It should have been 5,000-1!"

That cost £21,000, a relatively minor sum compared with the £¼ million paid out when Southampton won the FA Cup, having been offered at a possibly generous 9-2.

Ron Pollard says he supposes that "if you do something that costs you a large sum of money you must have been mistaken". But it's clear he doesn't think of them as mistakes. After all, he wouldn't ever want to turn back the clock and withdraw the odds he once offered against Goldie the eagle, who had escaped his cage in Regent's Park Zoo, being recaptured by midnight on Xmas Eve. When the weather suddenly turned very cold Goldie voluntarily flew back into his cage on December 19, and Ladbrokes lost £14,000. But when their publicity director recently took semi-retirement they presented him with an eagle sculpted from solid silver.

17 January 1990

The joyous therapy of a betting battle

Backing your own judgment is the fundamental plank of the betting man's creed. Win some, lose some, he knows he is getting value for money

by PAUL HAIGH

BETTING shops get a bad press. The general view seems to be that they are places without a redeeming feature in which fat men with cigars and un- pleasant moustaches deprive the downtrodden.

They're supposed to be full of smoke and depression and masochistic relish of the certainty of long-term defeat. Every now and then, usually in one of the papers which believes it caters to persons of superior intellect, an article appears which confirms this view and gives the 'sensible' majority something to feel self-righteous about.

The problem with these articles is that they're never written by anyone who's even dreamt that you might be able to enjoy yourself in a betting shop. Of course they contain a certain amount of truth. There *is* tragedy to be seen and sometimes to be endured in there. But to say that's all there is to betting shops is as stupid as to say that cars exist to run people over, that holidays exist just so the foolish can squander the money they've spent the rest of the year accumulating, or that pubs exist just to make people so drunk they can be picked off by muggers on their way home to beat up the wife and kids.

There is a view of betting shops at the other extreme, but this view hardly ever gets into print. If you want to hear it, the man to listen to is Ron Pollard of Ladbrokes, whom I once asked how he could reconcile a life-long commitment to decent social- ism with his own participation in the process of stripping assets off the working class.

How the press tips itself into disrepute

The racing correspondent of The Independent was prepared to explode the myth of the newspaper tipster, for the Racing Post reader bothered to take note

by PAUL HAYWARD

EVER wondered about newspapers trying to tip the winner of every race? Or even more questionably, having six or eight shots at the target through a baf- fling array of so-called experts, each with their own catchy name and logo. Flicking through the national dailies makes you wonder how on earth we hacks can show our faces on the track.

I'm not saying that racing journalists are compara- ble, say, to the reptiles who instructed their photog- raphers to get "good coffin shots" after the Zeebrugge disaster, but should the sporting press be deceiving their readers in this way?

It would not be fair to include the two trade papers in this discussion because the quality of information imparted is so high, though again one wonders whether they should be encouraging people to bet in every race. Even Einstein wouldn't have deluded himself or his audience into thinking it was possible to go through the card, day in day out.

Nobody needs reminding that within 30 years of being legalised the big off-course bookmakers have grown into huge concerns. The reason bookmaking is so profitable is, of course, quite simple. It's be- cause people like you and me throw money at its practitioners indiscriminately.

It needn't be so, and the bookies know it. If news- papers really care about their readers they should be encouraging a culture of value betting, of selec- tive raids. They should have the courage to tip one or two horses on each card, always with value uppermost in their minds, not trudging through

To hear Ron talk you'd think betting shops were sort of way stations in the great marathon of life, laid on by Mother Teresa and a team of volunteer philanthropists.

"When a man goes into a pub," he will tell you, using his favourite comparison, "he has a couple of pints and he feels good for a very short time and then it all goes up against the wall and he feels about the same as he did before, or a little bit worse. If he goes into the betting shop and spends the same money on a set of cross doubles he buys interest. He buys excitement. He buys hope that'll last him all the way through the afternoon."

I don't know about all that, but I do know why I go into betting shops. I go in because I love the racing and I love to bet. I love to form an opinion and then see that opinion justified before my very eyes, with a financial reward thrown in if I've had the sense to support it with cash. And I'm prepared to go through quite a few races in which for some reason (moronic jockey?) my judgment is not vindicated in order to reach the one in which it is.

This can of course have serious financial consequences. But it's extraordinary how easy it is to sweep your losses under the carpet of your mind and dwell instead on the triumphs. Like every other betting shop *habitué* I have stumbled out at 5.30 numb with the horror of what's just happened. I have sworn to myself on many evenings that in future I'll bet only on Group races, or on non-handicaps, or on days when racing's on TV. Never, you will notice, that I will never bet again.

But in the morning when I pick up the paper and see the new day's card, my optimism returns. The horrors are forgotten. I am purified and renewed. All I can remember are days like last year's Ayr Gold Cup when Joveworth, the banker, came in at 50-1, and I am once again the Muhammad Ali of punting, The Man The Bookies Fear.

It may be self-delusion, but it's not a bad feeling. Some may say it hasn't done me much good, but I would reply that while I'm in there I'm free. No problem, no worry occupies my mind. The struggle itself is therapy. It may not do the world much good, but it doesn't do it much harm either.

As for the po-faced penny pinchers at home whose idea of a good time is a quick croon over their building society books, they may think they're richer, but they don't know that you haven't really lived until you've seen the last leg of a Yankee get up to win by a neck. And if you lose a few times in the process, so what? I still say it's better to have bet and lost than never to have bet at all.

2 October 1990

---

every race stitching their customers up. Who do we think we are? It's archaic.

The other issue is the use of multiple selections in each race. This is unlikely to make me popular in the press room, but the other day I conducted a survey after a visit to my local newsagent, a redoubtable chap who opens his shop at some ungodly hour. (On one occasion, making my way home after a particularly long night on the tiles, I was able to bid him good morning just as he was lifting the shutters for another day's trade.)

For what follows I will be accused of picking on certain papers, and had better hope The Independent never goes down the pan. But for firing buckshot at the target, Today must rank as the most flagrant hedger in the business. They carry tips under no less than 11 titles, if you include The T-Factor, a guide to long-distance travellers. Here they come, so prepare to wince: Henry Rix (in fairness, an excellent judge), Course Correspondent, Lambourn Tips, Northern Correspondent, Computerform, Pot Luck, Today Form, The Pro Bet, Newmarket Correspondent and Top Shot.

The Daily Mail emerges with scarcely less credit. On its pages you can choose from Robin Goodfellow, Gimcrack, Newmarket, Northerner, Placepot, Longshot, The Wizard and Captain Heath.

The Sun gushes advice under the guises of Top Rating, Templegate, Lambourn, Sunratings Double and something called Betting Spy. The same organ and the Daily Mirror also convey updated selections from their sister papers, the News of the Screws – sorry, World – and Sunday Mirror respectively.

Freedom of choice? Indeed you could argue that punters don't have to take the advice. But the final damning evidence comes when two or three good winners are tipped under one category or another. What happens? The boast gets blasted across the page and out come the lines about "bookie bashing" and "knocking the layers for six". Fine, as long as you can ignore the six losing selections in the same race.

Now comes the self-righteous defence of my own paper. Our tipping is done under the title of Hyperion, and we also have a form guide to provide an alternative view, as well as an essay on the race. That, plus a nap and next best from me, is about it, though we do preview televised racing in copy.

In mitigation I can tell you that the people on racing desks take tipping very seriously indeed (especially since the Coral/Racing Post National Press Challenge was instituted). But in the end we are all guilty of encouraging people to be mugs.

There is an answer, though. Wrap your chips in the racing page and make your own mind up.

10 February 1992

Gambling on a dizzy date at the Oaks

Going to the races with a lady who knows little about betting on horses, but still comes out ahead, can cool a swain's ardour quicker than a cold shower

by JOHN McCRIRICK

ONE fleeting vision of Noblesse, Ireland's first Oaks winner, is the last racing memory I intend having on my deathbed. Her sublime athletic grace has been captured and stored, a treasured memory in the mind, and nothing again will ever match it.

All of us can instantly recall great deeds of the Turf we've been privileged to witness, a Classic triumph, a photo-finish that financially meant so much, or tear-provoking bravery of a horse or rider. All the stirring acclamations, the releases of tension, remain locked in our memories. But for me, the pure, rhythmical elegance and seemingly effortless arrogance of that empress of fillies, Noblesse, on 31 May 1963, transcends all else.

A group of mates and colleagues had wangled time off work and study to spend at Epsom. Being poor – nothing's changed much, I'm afraid – it was the free Downs in the centre of the course for us. From there, I'd seen Greville Starkey secure my each-way Derby bet on Merchant Venturer some way behind runaway Relko; those grand handicappers Passenger (ridden by 5lb-claimer Bruce Raymond) and Be Hopeful battling out a tight finish; a Lord Rosebery favourite double with Gwen and Bivouac and France's Exbury routing Hethersett in the Coronation Cup. Come Friday, the final day of the meeting, just three of us remained solvent out of the original Derby Day dozen. It was time to rope in some girls.

Now fellas know what it's like taking a female to the races for the first time. They usually cling on, asking stupid questions all the time, or gush inane drivel. Unfortunately my choice, Sandra, a bit of a

raver on the dance floor and elsewhere, was a combination of both and not the ideal partner for a serious day at the sports.

Nevertheless, being English gentlemen, we did try to make an impression. No free entry on the hill, mingling with the riff-raff. Instead we went for the Hyperion enclosure, the furthest ring down from the Grandstand, right opposite Tattenham Corner.

The girls arranged the picnic grub and we brought along some plonk and somehow found enough cash for rail fares and entry. How much that was I can't remember but, to our minds, it bought them body and all for the day.

Sandra must have been thrilled and grateful to be escorted by such a good-looking, debonair, man-of-the-world turfiste. She couldn't stop staring adoringly into my eyes while chattering away. Well it seemed to me to be adoration!

Never can there have been a display of more profound ignorance of racing, betting and even horses. Rather than keeping quiet and trying to work out the basics like any sensible newcomer, she appeared to take a manic pleasure in flaunting her pathetic helplessness.

The four w's – 'why', 'what', 'where' and 'when' – took on a whole new meaning that sweltering afternoon. With machine-like rapidity questions assailed me from all sides. Anyone else would soon have wilted, but fancying my chances later, and being, as always, courteous and polite to ladies, the finer points were patiently explained again and again.

But when it came to betting we were sucked into a morass of misunderstanding. Trying to make Sandra comprehend that you win less than your stake when laying odds-on was a recurring nightmare. As for the difference between 6-4 and 13-8, it simply didn't add up to her.

However, as you've surely guessed by now, bubbly Sandra was destined to be the only one of us to leave the track in funds, though my best pal did manage to tap her for half the winnings!

Starting with 13-2 Miss Velvet she could do little wrong, except take under the odds: "Oh, I love velvet! How much shall I have on her each-way? Does that mean I win if we finish fifth?" An Australian link in her family was revealed on discovering the nationality of Scobie Breasley (two winners), Ron Hutchinson and Bill Williamson (one apiece). Win-

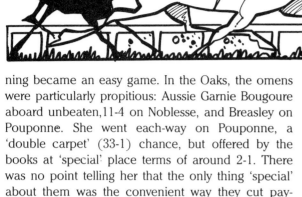

ning became an easy game. In the Oaks, the omens were particularly propitious: Aussie Garnie Bougoure aboard unbeaten,11-4 on Noblesse, and Breasley on Pouponne. She went each-way on Pouponne, a 'double carpet' (33-1) chance, but offered by the books at 'special' place terms of around 2-1. There was no point telling her that the only thing 'special' about them was the convenient way they cut pay-outs.

Going for the thieving each-way, my modest interest was in Jeremy Tree's Spree, beaten a length by Hula Dancer. The fact that she was returned at 100-7 – 11-10 'special' place odds – shows just how highly regarded Noblesse was.

Standing shirt-sleeved and not a little exasperated as the fillies swept round Tattenham Corner, I barely noticed Jimmy Lindley well up there on Spree along with the Queen's Amicable. Behind them on the outside nearest to us, Bougoure had hold of the white-faced Noblesse. The reins were tight, he wasn't moving.

In full flight, Noblesse, with her imperious, devouring stride, was an onrushing, unstoppable avenger, swooping down on her prey in what, for her, was little more than a canter. It was an unforgettable picture of power, harnessed to beauty. Up in the stands she will have been seen as one of the most impressive of all Classic winners.

Her 10-length rout of Spree and Pouponne equalled the race record, only to be eclipsed by 12-length Sun Princess six years ago. But Noblesse's performance swept her outside such mundane matters as statistics and money, though not for the nonplussed Sandra.

"Who won?" she asked.

"The favourite."

"Which one was that?"

"Noblesse."

"Did she have those pretty purple colours?"

"No, dear."

"What happened to my horse? What was it called?"

"Pouponne, dear, and it finished third."

"Would it win if it tried again?"

"No, dear."

"How do you know?"

"I do, dear, I do. Now, how about an ice lolly?"

10 June 1989

In 1963.. McCririck was young, "Noblesse" was the noblest of animals, and Sandra was not blessed with brains

Cracking the code at the Festival

The Irish look on the Cheltenham Festival as a home fixture, yet what are they actually saying when they talk to you? A Cheltenham veteran explains

by HENRY KELLY

THEY are safe when they approach you in groups. You are *even* safer. They will all talk at the same time. You will hear only in snatches and what you do hear will be in code. Even some of the words will be strange when you catch them. And you must understand the difference between an eejit and a *total* eejit. The first might occasionally do you a good turn, the second – never.

You must, however, particularly watch out for lone, wandering, silent types. The men who grasp you gently but firmly by the elbow and, glancing around, speak in calm tones thus: "Do you see that one there? [Pointing to a horse's name on the race-card.] That'll be there or thereabouts." He now disappears into the crowd. Next: "That ought to win, for it's strongly fancied at home. They reckon . . . [looks around] . . . they reckon it's there bar a fall." Note for English racegoers: make sure that you quickly absorb the fact that there are hurdles or fences in *all* the races this week.

Now you are ready to meet your first Irish trainer who, on being asked what chance his horse has in any given race, smiles and says: "We're not really happy with the ground but we're quietly confident."

Copping it in court at Bow Street

In 1986, in a celebrated court case punctuated by levity, the writer Jeffrey Bernard was punished for running a book in a Soho hostelry

by MARTIN TREW

A WHITE-HAIRED ex-boxer called Jeffrey Bernard – charged with running a book in Soho's Coach & Horses pub – headed an improbable cast at Bow Street magistrates' court yesterday. And a bizarre morning ended with Bernard being fined a total of £275 on two charges of betting without a licence and evading betting duty.

Last month police arrested Bernard, 54, who fought in circus booths before turning to journalism, moments after he took a bet on a Michael Stoute runner in a televised nursery at Newbury. Sadly for Bernard, whose column in the Spectator has been likened to a suicide note in weekly instalments, the punter was a Customs and Excise officer who had been watching him all summer.

Yesterday the many friends and colleagues who turned up to support him had to wait almost until lunchtime for his case to come up.

The award-winning columnist was preceded into the dock by a wonderful variety of alleged thugs and

There speaks a trainer. When his horse wins, it'll be: "There y'are now, we wouldn't put you off, would we."

Be particularly careful of trainers' assistants, lads, relations and cousins. They are deadly. Example: "Com'ere 'til I tell you something and for God's sake don't let it go further. Get out your racecard and look at the long hurdle race. There that one. Now: look, do you see that thing of O'Reilly's down at the bottom. Right. Well, there's a youngster over just for today, just today. A young fella who's goin' out with the trainer's daughter at home. Never has a bet. Never. Well: he's after havin' an hundred pounds each way this thing at 25-1. Need I say more? But for God's sake if it gets out I said anythin' I'm done for." Disappears in crowd.

There are, of course, resigned signs of hope: "If this doesn't win we'll be walking home." It never does and they never do. Or: "I'm down to me last tenner and it's goin' on this grey yoke in the hunter chase because there is a woman in our town is after takin' all her money outta the Post Office and gave it to a man she used to know who's over for the races with his married sister who lives in Bristol. They're not big gamblers but, Jays, they're cute hoors and I'd say they know a thing or two."

Beware of priests. Since they have stopped wearing polo-neck pullovers and sunglasses they are easier to spot but just as lethal. They are rarely wrong but they are rarely loquacious. They tend to be quietly sipping a Power in the corner after a race. Then you see them queueing to collect at the Tote. And even that's only a front, because if they have a winner they've backed it in Ireland *and* with Terry Rogers on the way over on the plane anyway.

On the other hand, information coming second-hand from or about priests can be very useful. "Do you know that big, tall man that's a parish priest somewhere in Mayo? Ah, Jays, you must know him. He's here every year and goes dog racin' in the ev'ing and he's always down at the little tea-bar near the end of the ring. That's the one, you have him. Well, Jays, he's a shrewd judge all right and do you see that thing of Paddy Mullins. Well, according to Father, the lad who rides that at home says it's the best horse he ever sat on. And guess what? Go on. Guess? What used he ride at work 25 years ago? Go on. Guess. Arkle that's who, the great Arkle himself. Jays, you'd need to be on that wouldn't you with that sort of a reference."

Isolated examples of excuses are easy to come by and must be treated not with scorn but shoulder-hugging understanding. They range from: "It's come back not quite right," through "Patsy thinks it didn't like the going," to the classic "Every other race it's carried a stone more. It didn't like havin' such a small weight . . . and the boy didn't really help."

As I enter the greatest racecourse in the world tomorrow, shortly after noon, a few friends from Ireland will greet me and I them. We meet but once a year. For the past 10 years, maybe a bit less, we've exchanged information. I've always been the gainer. I am quietly confident that tomorrow will be no different. And how will I know? Well, unfortunately it will be in code and just at the moment I haven't the room to explain it to you. But, do you see that thing of Dreaper's in the Foxhunters'? Well, now, looka . . . there's a fella here who has a butcher's shop in Killorglin . . .

13 March 1989

---

villains. Then Bernard, pale and penitent, stepped into the dock.

Prosecuting solicitor Robin Spencer told how Customs & Excise officials were alerted to Bernard's illegal bookmaking by a piece he wrote in a London magazine. During the next four months, Customs officials visited the Coach & Horses on a number of Saturday lunchtimes to bet with Bernard. They were embarrassingly successful.

Mr Spencer then quoted from Bernard's statement to the police. He had told officers he only accepted bets from friends. They then asked him why he had accommodated the Customs officials. "I must have been pissed at the time . . . which is quite likely," he said. Bernard, who pleaded guilty to both charges, left it to barrister Geoffrey Robinson to make a plea of mitigation.

Claiming the officials had acted as *agents provocateurs*, he said: "My client assumed that they were regulars . . . and indeed they were regulars by the

time he was arrested. The pity is that the police did not indicate to him that they were taking the matter seriously. The last horse which the Customs officials backed was Aid And Abet. That is in effect what they were doing. It could have been stopped earlier and it wasn't."

The barrister's speech over, Bernard and his friends waited, rather like punters hanging on the result of a photo, for the magistrate, Mr Tom Waring, to pass sentence.

"Now listen carefully," he told the defendant. "I appreciate this case has caused some levity but the law must be obeyed. You will be fined £100 on each of the charges and you will pay £75 costs."

Afterwards Bernard joked: "When I was arrested there were nine police officers, three Customs and Excise officials, a squad car and a van. Perhaps when Cheltenham Gold Cup day comes round, the SAS will burst into the pub with stun bombs."

21 October 1986

THE POWER

Racehorses are not Nature's ultimate expression of fast animal movement over the ground, a superlative that belongs to the cheetah. But they have become that of man, who has intervened to perfect an animal of power, stamina and primordial explosions of speed. Racehorses are, in essence, superbly developed athletes. The attention paid today to the study of them is immense. The methods by which their performances can be honed are the subject of constant experiment. The knowledge that is emerging is, in truth, amazing

A Ferrari can go from 0–60mph in 5sec, while a jockey aboard a thoroughbred – here Alan Munro on Firm Pledge – is riding an animal capable of 0–42mph in 2.5sec, achieved in a mere six strides.

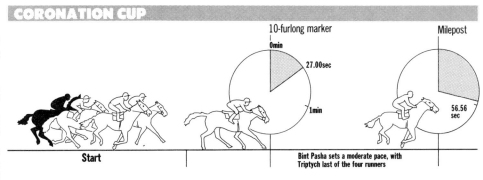

CORONATION CUP

10-furlong marker
0min
27.00sec
1min

Milepost
56.56 sec

Start

Bint Pasha sets a moderate pace, with Triptych last of the four runners

The criticial comparison

A fine recent example of the value of sectional times, in accurately describing the distribution of pace within a race, was to be found at the 1988 Epsom Derby meeting.

The Coronation Cup and Oaks were both run over the same 1½-mile course, on similar ground (good) within 48 hours of each other, and in virtually identical overall times (electrically a difference of 0.18sec; hand-timed a difference of 0.16sec). Yet, the similarity ended there.

Whereas the Classic fillies benefited from the pacemaking efforts of Atropa (on behalf of Bahamian), the Coronation Cup was a four-runner, cat-and-mouse affair, in which Moon Madness (strong on stamina) had to burn off the finishing kick of Triptych and Infamy without burning himself out in the process. The ebb and flow of two differently run races, and the crucial sections, which brought about victory for Diminuendo and Triptych, are highlighted here.

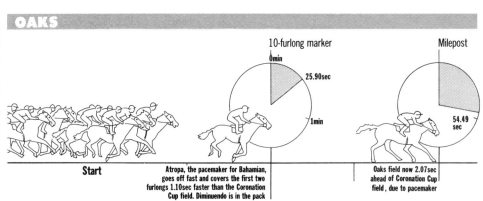

OAKS

10-furlong marker
0min
25.90sec
1min

Milepost
54.49 sec

Start

Atropa, the pacemaker for Bahamian, goes off fast and covers the first two furlongs 1.10sec faster than the Coronation Cup field. Diminuendo is in the pack

Oaks field now 2.07sec ahead of Coronation Cup field , due to pacemaker

A case for catching up on the stopwatch

The suggestion that sectional timing should be introduced in British racing provokes instant and heated debate. The author is a leading advocate of its value

by MICHAEL TANNER

FOR a country that more or less gave horseracing to the world, Britain has been rather slow to adopt a number of innovations that benefit the sport. The camera took its first photo-finish here 11 years after its debut in the USA and we were two years behind the French with starting stalls, some 30 years after their widespread introduction in America.

Now Britain lags behind in the field of sectional timing.

Critics stress the fact that the comparability of any form of race times in Britain is eroded by the enormous diversity of track topography – but they miss the point. The principal object of sectional times is to compare the distribution of speed within a race – not between tracks. In so doing, the accuracy of our race-reading is enhanced and we are provided with irrefutable evidence when attempting to assess a horse's merit. What singles out the true class horse is the ability to display exceptional speed at the competitive stage of a fast-run race.

Let's use as an example Dancing Brave, a horse universally acclaimed as outstanding and one whose exploits were sectionally clocked. Sectional times repeatedly emphasised his class, not least in the 1986 Arc, where his final pair of 200-metre splits, officially timed at 11.4sec apiece, capped a 2,000 metres 4.90sec faster, for example, than Rainbow Quest in 1985 (2min 5.55sec), Sassafras in 1970 (2min 5.20sec), and Levmoss in 1969 (2min 5.50sec) run on similar ground and which also resulted in above-average overall times.

Of course, when interpreting sectional times it is prudent to remember that each one is triggered by the leading horse at each mark. For instance, Dancing Brave's last 200-metre time in the Arc was considerably faster than the 11.4sec officially given since he must have been a good three lengths behind the leaders when they initiated that figure. At the Arc's pace that deficit was worth about 0.3sec, making Dancing Brave's individual split nearer 11sec. A clock put on him at Epsom recorded a 10.30sec penultimate furlong that almost snatched victory.

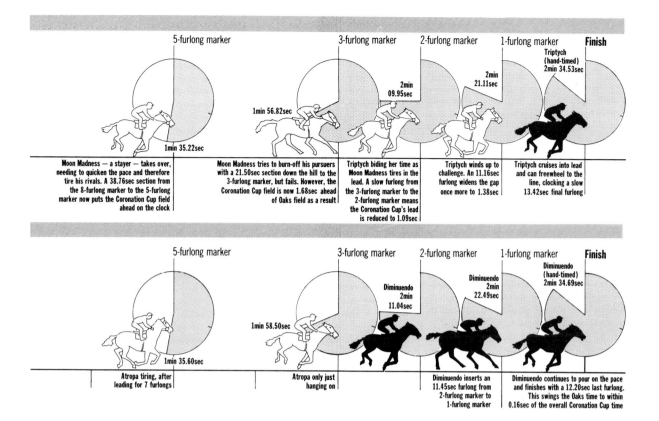

5-furlong marker   **3-furlong marker**   **2-furlong marker**   **1-furlong marker**   **Finish**

Triptych
(hand-timed)
2min 34.53sec

2min
21.11sec

2min
09.95sec

1min 56.82sec

1min 35.22sec

| Moon Madness — a stayer — takes over, needing to quicken the pace and therefore tire his rivals. A 38.76sec section from the 8-furlong marker to the 5-furlong marker now puts the Coronation Cup field ahead on the clock | Moon Madness tries to burn-off his pursuers with a 21.50sec section down the hill to the 3-furlong marker, but fails. However, the Coronation Cup field is now 1.68sec ahead of Oaks field as a result | Triptych biding her time as Moon Madness tires in the lead. A slow furlong from the 3-furlong marker to the 2-furlong marker means the Coronation Cup's lead is reduced to 1.09sec | Triptych winds up to challenge. An 11.16sec furlong widens the gap once more to 1.38sec | Triptych cruises into lead and can freewheel to the line, clocking a slow 13.42sec final furlong |

5-furlong marker   **3-furlong marker**   **2-furlong marker**   **1-furlong marker**   **Finish**

Diminuendo
(hand-timed)
2min 34.69sec

Diminuendo
2min
22.49sec

Diminuendo
2min
11.04sec

1min 58.50sec

1min 35.60sec

| Atropa tiring, after leading for 7 furlongs | Atropa only just hanging on | Diminuendo inserts an 11.45sec furlong from 2-furlong marker to 1-furlong marker | Diminuendo continues to pour on the pace and finishes with a 12.20sec last furlong. This swings the Oaks time to within 0.16sec of the overall Coronation Cup time |

This begs the question of how to interpret sectional times when you've got them. Did the winner quicken at the end of a true-run race or merely decelerate more slowly than his rivals, after a suicidal early gallop?

Take the flying finish of Trempolino in the 1987 Arc. The last quarter of 25.10sec was the slowest of the race bar the first. In the wake of Reference Point's 10 furlongs in 2min 1.20sec, Trempolino was appearing to accelerate only as most of his rivals tired.

One can safely assert that most horses are capable of running a 24sec quarter-mile somewhere in a race but, unless the initial mile is run at a dawdle, only the class horse can break this figure in either the penultimate or final quarter-miles of a one-and-a-half-mile race. This pattern is exacerbated by the cat-and-mouse tactics which, as in an Olympic track final, are frequently adopted when talented individuals clash, whereas a field of handicappers tend to show no such inhibitions. However if a pacemaker runs as is so often the case nowadays in races like the Arc and King George, courage is equally as important as speed during the last two quarters and split times will deteriorate accordingly, whoever the combatants.

In the King George VI and Queen Elizabeth Stakes, Dancing Brave's relatively slow final quarter-miles of 24.73sec and 27.03sec bore testimony to both the pacemaking and his own courage. For, although he personally did not cover the first mile as fast as they, he had to make his effort off their gallop, a task demanding exceptional determination.

One of the principal lessons hammered home by sectional times is the appreciation of a horse's need to change gear at some point in a race, for the rhythm of a race is seldom constant. The majority of races are settled by the injection of one comparatively brief, yet telling, burst of speed. Time and again Dancing Brave showed his ability to sprint when required in just this manner.

In a race over a middle distance, this telling acceleration usually comes in the penultimate quarter (occasionally the first furlong of the final quarter) and in races of a mile or less during the penultimate furlong. This tendency reflects the launch and delivery of potential or race-winning challenges.

In the 1986 Eclipse, a penultimate quarter of 22.78sec sandwiched between a 23.66sec and an uphill 26.35sec signalled the start of Dancing Brave's victory drive. In the King George a sequence of 26.14sec, 24.73sec and 27.03sec depicted the selfsame change of pace obligatory at the conclusion of a Group 1 middle-distance event. Dancing Brave's outstanding class, however, enabled him to reproduce this speed at any point during the final stages of a race. He clocked the fastest 1986 quarter over middle distances courtesy of his 22.10sec penultimate quarter-mile in the Derby and the fastest over a mile with his 21.50sec final quarter in the 2,000 Guineas.

Speed and the priceless ability to increase it at will constitute the criterion of the true class horse and only sectional times can spotlight this characteristic with authority.

12 August 1988

Success at the end of a needle

One of the leading advocates of acupuncture for horses is a distinguished vet now based at Roger Bolton's Whitcombe Manor complex in Dorset

---

by BRIAN EAGLES

ACUPUNCTURE literally means sharp puncture; the strange treatment techniques involving inserting through the skin needles of varying lengths into specific sites in the body to alleviate the symptoms of diseases or to reduce musculo-skeletal pain

This technique was practised by the Chinese 3,000 years ago, but was unknown to the Western world until about 300 years ago, when medical officers employed by the Dutch East Indies Trading Company saw it being used in Java. Over the centuries the Chinese have evolved the art and practice of acupuncture, and we have now grasped its value.

From its earliest beginnings, the practice of acupuncture has been closely associated with a philosophy of life and an appreciation of the holistic approach to medicine. It seeks to harmonise forces within the body, which should always be in rhythm and equilibrium, but become disturbed with injury or disease. Acupuncture in its simplest forms attempts to restore the balance by stimulating or depressing various specific body sites: the acupuncture points.

At this moment you may wonder why a veterinary surgeon with a highly specialised scientific training should consider this method of treatment for horses. In 20 years of equine practice I have come to realise that we have only a few of the answers, and that one of the fundamental problems with sports horses of all types is that the nature of the occupation leads to a high level of musculo-skeletal injury – all of which are associated with some degree of pain. Relief of this pain is possible with medication of varying types, but it is being recognised that pro-longed medication may result in some serious side effects.

When a horse injures himself inflammation occurs, characterised by pain, heat and swelling and, if the skin is visible, redness at the point. These symptoms are the body's defence mechanism against further insult. The pain stops the horse moving the injured part too much. Accurate diagnosis becomes essential. Is the pain caused by a muscular tear, a chipped bone, a bad fracture or just simple bruising? All the most sophisticated techniques can be used to diagnose the condition, but we are probably still left with a horse which is in pain and cannot move properly.

Horses are by no means stupid, and if they feel pain for a prolonged period of time they will adjust their gait to make their action more comfortable, and potentially this will produce differential muscle wastage. Acupuncture, by its powerful, pain-relieving properties, has an integral part to play in restoring normal functions, once an accurate diagnosis has been made.

Treatment usually takes the form of twice-weekly or weekly sessions, usually of 20-30 minutes' duration, and a course of treatment invariably takes a month to complete. In the majority of cases, improvement is noticeable within the first week. Sometimes this relates initially to the general well-being of the horse rather than an improvement in gait. As a general rule, however, if no improvement has occurred in three weeks I have either not devised the right prescription of acupuncture points to stimulate or acupuncture is not going to be successful as a treatment technique.

I now feel comfortable using acupuncture in my daily equine work and apply it on an increasing basis for the treatment of acute injury; bruising and soreness can be relieved very quickly and, when combined with controlled exercise, can produce a much quicker return to full performance, without the problems associated with medication.

Acupuncture effects are also produced by many forms of physiotherapy equipment, all capable of stimulating acupuncture points if applied over large areas. This can also be said of a number of chiropractic techniques that are performed, as these also produce a transient acupcunture point stimulation, albeit on a hit-and-miss basis. The deeper understanding of the acupuncture points, however, allows more precise treatment and provides a powerful therapeutic tool.

Acupuncture may have its roots in ancient history, but as Western medicine unravels its mysteries, its use in the treatment of athletic injuries of horses will continue to increase and its true benefits in the veterinary armoury be realised.

25 June 1991

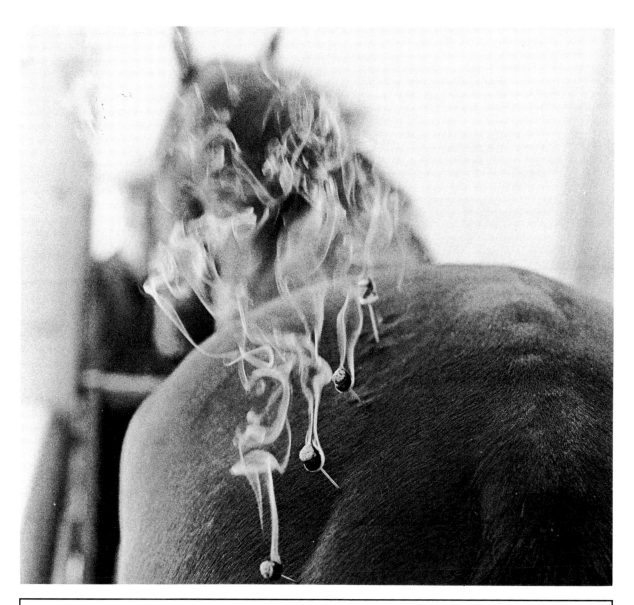

Putting some devil into a racing machine

In the picture above deep heat is being transmitted down the needles by using nuggets of moxa, made from the dried leaves of mugwort, which combust intensely. Complex Chinese charts show acupuncture points, with complex names, linked with lines designated as meridians. Western interpretation has simplified the nomenclature and simply given the points a meridian relationship and a positional number.

"What we're trying to achieve," says Brian Eagles, "is what the Chinese call chi." If the needles are in the right place, the sensation a human being gets for example is either deadness or tingling or warmth.

The results of chi can be sensational. A horse performing poorly on the gallops one day can, after acupuncture, be sensational the next, a fact noted by one jockey in the past. "What in the devil," Greville Starkey once asked Eagles, "have you done? He's a different horse today."

Eagles himself became interested in acupuncture a decade ago, while he was at Guy Harwood's where he was responsible for the treatment of several star horses, including Dancing Brave. While Eagles was at Harwood's another vet

came to treat five of the horses with acupuncture. It worked with three of the five and Eagles was hooked. He studied the subject at a centre of alternative medicine and has progressed from there.

"We're really talking about internal medicine for the horse," says Eagles, who demonstrated acupuncture for this feature on a quite undisturbed five-year-old colt called Follow The Sun (the horse in the picture).

Basically Eagles uses acupuncture to treat orthopaedic conditions, ranging from sore muscles to chronic backs.

A past president of the British Equine Veterinary Association, he has by now a long and impressive track record, working conventionally at first with horses trained by everybody from Ryan Price to John Dunlop, and in more recent times less conventionally but more frequently with acupuncture needles.

To transmit deep heat down the needles Eagles uses nuggets of Moxa, made from the dried leaves of mugwort, which combust intensely.

The silky way to go forward into 1990s

Jockeys' silks have been put under close scrutiny as the search to make the horse's power and speed more effective has become increasingly scientific

by PAUL HAIGH

NOTHING irritates like innovation – particularly in racing. It was not therefore surprising when, in the aftermath of the Breeders' Cup, news of aerodynamically styled outfits for jockeys should have been greeted in some sections of the British press with dyspeptic growls of contempt.

It was a bad time for British racing. Indian Skimmer had been beaten. Warning had failed to raise a gallop. And Triptych, our adopted heroine, had just run her last race.

If we wanted to hear anything about what was going on in America we wanted to hear about their 'medication' addictions and about how their artificial and automatically-drained turf tracks can produce unraceable going, not about how Wayne Lukas was sending out his jockeys in sissy old body stockings.

But the turn of a year is as good a time as any to look at new developments, and if those who sneered at them look again now, they may be forced to agree that there may be something in this aerodynamics business.

Other sports have known it for ages. Think about athletics and the cling-film costumes sported by Florence Griffith Joyner. Think about the way competitive cyclists are equipped nowadays with slick suits, taper helmets, and even blocked-in wheels to prevent the very spokes from pushing against the air in front of them. Think about skiers who considered the problem of wind resistance even before the cyclists and who, once upon a time, used to dress up like snowmen. Now no self-respecting downhill racer would dream of taking to the piste in anything but a

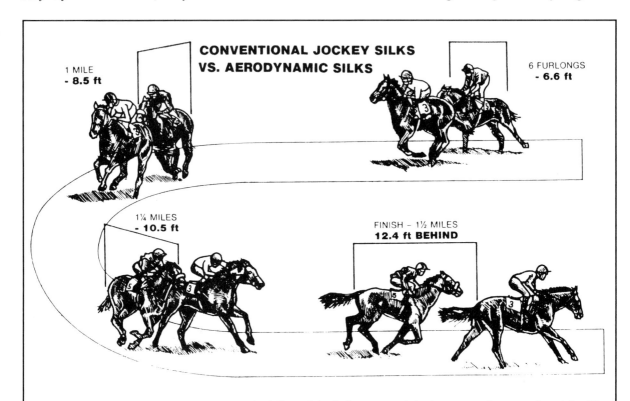

CONVENTIONAL JOCKEY SILKS VS. AERODYNAMIC SILKS

1 MILE
- 8.5 ft

6 FURLONGS
- 6.6 ft

1¼ MILES
- 10.5 ft

FINISH – 1½ MILES
12.4 ft BEHIND

A physicist's comparison, based on equal ability of both horses and jockeys, carrying equal weight. The resultant figures illustrate how much distance is lost by conventional jockey versus aerodynamic silks. Flapping of old-silks interferes with the horse's performance. The calculations assumed a zero wind velocity, since any wind could increase figures by up to 50 per cent, depending on strength and direction.

drag-eliminating, head-to-toe outfit. These, sceptics will point out, are sports in which the human frame and human strength are pitted alone against the elements. Racing is a bit different. The horse, not the jockey, is the means of propulsion. And the horse is so big and so strong that surely it can't make any appreciable difference to his speed if the wind slides round his jockey's clothing instead of going through it?

The fact is that it can. If you doubt it ask why the makers of cars, even more powerful than the horse, should spend so much time and money on wind tunnel research to determine optimum shapes for the improvement of performance.

Racing is not exempt from the general laws of science; and scientific research has proved that subsidiary items which may seem of the most extreme triviality make a quite ridiculous amount of difference if they are allowed to obtrude and create wind resistance. Jim Hendry, Chief Executive of the Cycling Association, provides some extraordinary statistics to show the effect of clothing on his sport. The statistics were compiled by Dr Chester Kyle, who is based at the US Olympic Center at Colorado Springs – although most of the pioneering work in the field has been done by the East Germans.

According to Kyle and his team, the saving to a cyclist wearing a skinsuit instead of a woollen jumper on a 25-mile run at a speed of 30-34 mph is no fewer than 29 seconds. The faster you go the bigger the difference, but since 30-34 mph is something like a relaxed racing speed for a horse it's probably a good bracket to choose in this context.

An aerodynamic helmet, which reduces turbulence behind the cyclist's head, besides cutting through the air more quickly, makes a difference of about 47 seconds in 25 miles. Taping over your shoelaces can save seven seconds. Shaving the hair off your legs could save "up to five seconds", depending presumably on how butch you were before you reached for the razor. And if you only wore lycra-backed gloves you'd probably go around two seconds faster over the test distance than you would if you wore leather ones.

For obvious reasons involving the difficulty of setting up the experiments, nobody has done quite such detailed research into the effects on the speed of a horse of all the various items of equipment – jockey included under this heading – which he has to carry during a race. But now some has been done on the effect of the silks and what happens if the wind gets into them.

It was instigated by Rhonda Allen, a sculptress and wife of Joe Allen, a leading American racehorse owner. Mrs Allen looked at some of her husband's horses in races, saw the jockeys' silks ballooning in the wind and reasoned that if a parachutist's fall can be slowed substantially by such a material then so can a horse's speed.

Dr Richard Brandt of New York University was approached and asked if there was some obvious flaw in her reasoning. He was sceptical at first, then came to the conclusion that she, and her precursors – apparently jockeys in Italy have been trying out slicker clothing for years – were absolutely right.

Mrs Allen then developed her own silks which were made out of a substance which is both form-fitting and waterproof – to reduce the amount of moisture and therefore weight which a horse has to carry in wet weather – and her husband has used them ever since.

By the time of the Breeders' Cup, D. Wayne Lukas, who is to American Flat racing more or less what Martin Pipe is to our jumping, and who is a man who never tires for one moment in his search for anything which will improve his competitive edge, was so completely sold on the new silks that he insisted on all his jockeys wearing them.

Nobody is suggesting that he wiped floors at Churchill Downs just because he was clever enough to save his horses a bit of extra wind resistance, but nobody in America is laughing any longer. As Angel Cordero, who finds the new racewear very comfortable and who also thinks it suits him, puts it: "When I first wore the new silks the other jockeys made fun of me. But I always think about the wind when I ride. You've got to take anything that gives you an edge or you're a bobo."

Perhaps the most significant race of the day on 5 November as far as the silks argument is concerned, as well as the most exciting, was the Breeders' Cup Distaff, in which the superb Personal Ensign retained her unbeaten record by getting up on the line to beat the Kentucky Derby winner, Winning Colors. It would have been even more significant if she had just failed.

Randy Romero on Personal Ensign carried traditional silks. Gary Stevens on Winning Colors carried the new ones. The University of New York thinks that the difference between the two sets can be as much as 8.5 feet in a mile race; 8.5 feet is something like three-quarters of a length.

The pressure to wear the new silks will eventually come from the owners, and once the resistance begins to go, which it will – particularly if a Derby or an Arc is one day settled in this way – horses will run that little bit faster, just as they began to do at the turn of the century when jockeys learnt to sit in line with the neck instead of bolt upright. Of course weight distribution had a lot to do with that, but so did aerodynamics.

Who'll be the last whom Cordero will be able to accuse of being a 'bobo'?

29 December 1988

Dessie's world jumping record

The ability of a horse to jump is one that has been encouraged and honed by man. Desert Orchid may well have jumped further than any horse or man

by SUE MONTGOMERY

IT is not beyond the bounds of possibility that Desert Orchid broke the world equine long-jump record with the leap that carried him over the second-last fence in the 1990 Racing Post Chase.

The official record, as ratified by the Fédération Equestre Internationale (the body that looks after showjumping and eventing), is 27ft 6¾in (8.40m). Desert Orchid's jump was not measured but it looked well over 30 feet from take-off to landing. The white plastic wings at Kempton are 20 feet long, and Dessie launched himself into the air level with the end of them. The wings overlap only the sloping apron of the fence, which is around five feet deep from guard-rail to back-rail, and the horse landed a good eight or 10 feet clear of the obstacle.

But whatever distance he cleared, it was certainly more than the FEI record, set by the showjumper Something in Johannesburg in 1975.

As far as statistics are concerned, men can jump further than horses. The human long-jump record is Bob Beamon's phenomenal 29ft 2½in (8.90m), set at altitude in the 1968 Mexico Olympics. Dessie, though, won't be the only horse to have unofficially leapt much more. The annals of the Turf and of hunting are filled with reports of prodigious leaps. Lottery, the first Grand National winner (1839), is credited with clearing 33 feet at the last, a stiff upright post-and-rails topped with gorse.

Horses can propel their bodies, weighing half a ton or so, remarkable heights and distances. And their ability is all the more remarkable because nature did not design them for jumping. They are heavy, their spines relatively inflexible and their limbs fragile under stress. In the wild, a horse will make every effort to go round an obstacle rather than jump it. But, nevertheless, horses *can* jump, and once they passed the stage of being solely beasts of burden and became beasts of pleasure, man started directing their energies in that direction.

Steeplechasing, of course, had its origins in the hunting field. The sport began in the 18th century in Ireland, with pounding matches. Two horses would set off together with the leader, decided by lot, setting as stiff a course as he dared over natural country. The winner was the one who first 'pounded' his rival to an often-fatal standstill. From this developed matches over an agreed distance, usually from village to village, using the steeple of the local church as a guide to direction.

The earliest recorded steeplechases in England were held in Leicestershire in 1792, and 19 years later the first run over a specially constructed course took place at Bedford. There were eight fences, each four-feet-six high topped with a strong bar, and the races were run in heats. Only two of 11 subscribers completed the course.

The first organised showjumping came later, at Leinster Lawn, Dublin, in 1864. Events included the High Jump and the Wide Leap, and were intended to test the abilities of hunters.

I have said horses were not strictly designed for jumping, but that is not to say they are not good at it, or that it is cruel to make them do it. Horses are taught to do many things nature probably did not intend, starting off with the basic premise of carrying a man. They adapt very well to jumping and many

appear to positively enjoy it, Desert Orchid being a prime example.

To see how horses jump, let us talk Desert Orchid through his mighty leap at Kempton. Probably most surprising is that the initial upward thrust comes not from the horse's hind quarters, but from a single foreleg. The horse is already airborne before the hind legs come into play.

Like all steeplechasers, he approached the fence in gallop. Speed is not necessary to jump high – showjumpers can jump large obstacles out of a slow canter or trot – but it is necessary to win races. One thing the best chasers, showjumpers and eventers have in common is balance, physical and mental.

On the approach to the fence, Dessie was leading with his near-foreleg. As he reached his take-off point, he switched his leading leg, instigating his jump by springing off his off-fore, while his hind legs were still on the way to the ground.

The forehand of the horse is pushed into the air by the straightening of the bones and muscles of the leading forelimb (the last to leave the ground at the end of a gallop stride), from shoulder to pastern, putting brief, but enormous, strain on the flexor tendons.

Simultaneously the horse uses his head and neck as a balancing pole, first bringing them up and back to shift his centre of gravity backwards, and then extending them forward while airborne. Back muscles contract, arching the back as much as possible and helping to raise the forehand.

A split second after the forefoot lifts, the high feet, one after the other, are slammed into the ground.

The hind limbs – hips, stifles, hocks and fetlocks – straighten and the horse is launched upwards and forwards. The final impetus, again, is given by the straightening of the fetlock.

Chasers normally take off some 10 feet in front of a fence, fold their front legs up, more or less tidily, as they describe a parabola over the obstacle, before extending them to land on. Desert Orchid, whose *joie de vivre* prompts him to take off sooner rather than later, had to get extra reach for his airborne extravaganza at Kempton by extending his forelegs early, bringing his toes up to his chin in mid-flight.

He was already on the way down as he crossed the fence, and brushed it with his belly. He landed first on his off-fore, with the near-fore placed in advance of its fellow almost instantly, providing a firm base to travel over. A horse jumping fast will spring off his forefeet before the hind legs touch the ground and start the first non-jumping stride, pushing away from the fence.

28 March 1990

PS. Bob Beamon's world record was beaten in 1991 by Mike Powell, who long-jumped 29ft 4½in (8.95m) at the world athletics championships in Tokyo.

Desert Orchid's jump (above) at the second-last fence in the Racing Post Chase made him, unofficially, one of the few horses to surpass Bob Beamon's fabled leap (opposite page) of 29ft 2½in at the 1968 Mexico Olympic Games.

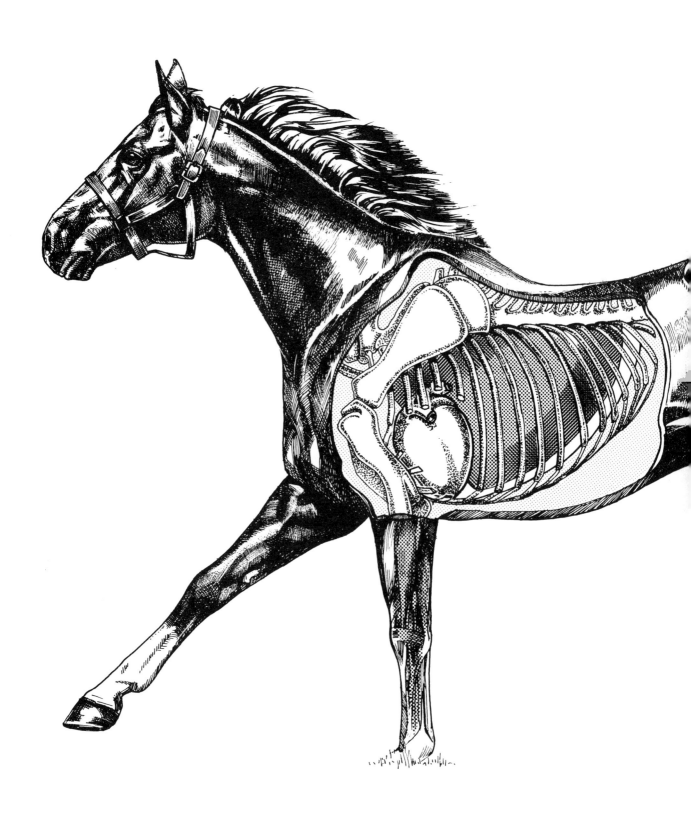

The horse as an athlete

by BROUGH SCOTT

MOST racing people know a tremendous amount about their speciality. The trouble is, hardly any of us know much about the most important speciality of all – what actually makes the racehorse run. Amidst all the talk it's easy to forget that the essence of racing is none of these things. It is no more and no less than Equine Athletics.

But compared with human athletics, knowledge and discussion of the four-legged version has been minimal, for two reasons. Firstly, because only one fan in thousands has been aboard a galloping runner. Second, because until recently it was much more art than science, described in terms of mystery rather than measurements.

This is all about to change because the latest work on equine physiology has the potential to spotlight the champion long before he reaches the track and to make a knowledge of heart size and oxygen efficiency as important as the form book.

But how far has science got? In the past 10 years there has been a tremendous amount of research worldwide into exercise physiology in racehorses.However all the research has suffered from two basic problems: lack of adequate funding and the unavailability of elite horses.

So we turned to a man who has daily care of a very large number of high-class horses in their developmental stage. The renowned veterinarian Michal Osborne who now runs Sheikh Mohammed's ultra-modern new enterprise at the Kildangan Stud in Co. Kildare. There has never been such an opportunity for study.

Coincidentally, a distinguished athletics writer, Norman Harris, has long searched for the point where talent and training divide. And so we invited him to ask Michael Osborne how much of the thoroughbred's mystery still remains.

4 May 1989

☐ Continued overleaf

Questions about the heart and mysticism

by NORMAN HARRIS

YOU don't have to be a racing man to have heard of famous racehorses who were found, after they had died, to have large hearts. Likewise there have been autopsies on human athletes – like a veteran American marathon runner, Clarence DeMar, whose 70-year-old heart was shown to be very large and liberally supplied with extraordinarily wide coronary arteries.

But is it cause or effect? Were the human and equine athletes endowed with hearts which gave them a flying start, or did their hearts simply grow larger and more efficient as a response to training?

That's just one of several key questions which Michael Osborne finds pleasure in contemplating as he monitors the high-bred foals and yearlings of Kildangan and speculates on which of them will prove to be stars. It's a fascinating game and also a tantalising one, for the growing bank of physiological data contains so many components that may hold the key to reliable forecasting. But, if the heart is only one of several possible indicators (*see panel page 119*), it is obviously the one on which the scientists first focused. The benchmark that has been established, the Heart Score, has attracted a certain amount of scepticism.

Perhaps that's because it was seen to be related to Timeform ratings: an early set of Heart Scores at Kildangan ranged from 144 to 90 but the following year a second set went from 171 to 80, which seemed to need some explaining. It doesn't, of course. The score is simply a measure of the electrical impulse which created the heart beat, the theory being that the time it takes to pass through the heart muscle must be related to the size and power of the heart.

Dr Osborne sees it as no more than a benchmark, one that will indicate which of his horses are in the top bracket, which are in the bottom bracket, and which are in the middle. Even being able to dispense with the bottom 15 per cent would mean significant savings. For the moment, he will say no more than that Heart Score probably has a 65 per cent relevance in determining athletic elitism, at least at the level of horses in his care. "A toss of a coin would be 50-50, so it's better than that." That's not saying a lot, for Osborne is cautious when quoting figures.

It's Osborne's hunch that the great horses have been endowed with larger hearts, though as yet he hasn't got the scientific proof. That will come when the data being collected – including videotapes from the ultrasonic imaging of the heart in action – can be related to performance. In part, his hunch comes from his experience as a vet in listening to horses' hearts. But as yet, says Osborne, it isn't known whether it's the size of the entire heart that's important, or the size of its main chamber, the left ventricle, or the thickness of that chamber's main wall, or the blood volume of each stroke of the heart.

It is also not known whether the main physical component in the elite racehorse will prove to be the heart, stride cadence, the ability to inhale air without impediment, or the ability of the muscles to extract oxygen.

"We're just starting," Osborne says. "We haven't followed enough horses for long enough. But we're cutting down on the variables, and in time the results will start to be meaningful." But that doesn't mean, he adds, that they will ever go out and buy horses on such a basis. "We're just interested to *know* what makes one horse superior to another."

He's well aware that the information now available contains uncertainties and contradictions, and they fascinate him. For example, the comparison between leg length and stride length. "A long-legged horse would have had an inside leg measurement of, say, 37 inches, compared with the 30 inches of a short-legged horse. But it doesn't necessarily follow that the long-legged horse is going to have the longer stride. A survey of American racehorses showed that Secretariat had the longest stride of all, 27 feet, but he wasn't particularly long-legged." Then there are the horses for whom no training will bring an improvement on a time of 40 seconds for two furlongs – barely faster than the human world record for 400 metres – while others can run 26 seconds immediately and, with training, 24 or 23.

"They're born to run," enthuses Osborne. Indeed, while this former head of the Irish National Stud is employing every tool that modern science can provide, nothing seems to delight him more than to tell of the mystical success of William Hall Walker. It was the legendary Hall Walker who founded Tully Stud (later to become the Irish National Stud) and who, influenced by Zen Buddhism, later created the

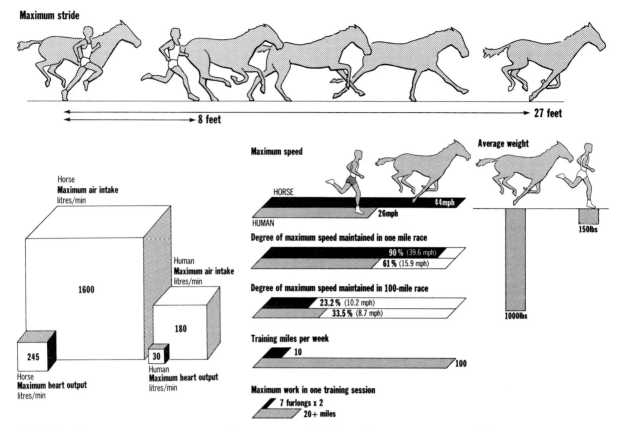

Maximum stride

← 8 feet →   ← 27 feet →

Horse
Maximum air intake
litres/min

1600

Human
Maximum air intake
litres/min

180

245

30

Horse
Maximum heart output
litres/min

Human
Maximum heart output
litres/min

Maximum speed

HORSE   44mph
                              26mph
HUMAN

Average weight

150lbs

1000lbs

Degree of maximum speed maintained in one mile race
90% (39.6 mph)
61% (15.9 mph)

Degree of maximum speed maintained in 100-mile race
23.2% (10.2 mph)
33.5% (8.7 mph)

Training miles per week
10
100

Maximum work in one training session
7 furlongs x 2
20+ miles

Athletes: a comparison of the horse and human

The horse has a remarkable capacity to create oxygen-carrying red cells in its large spleen, which responds to the demands of exercise like an instantaneous reserve tank. Their muscle cells also extract oxygen very efficiently when they're at peak effort. "Energy production is much higher in horses," says a leading horse physiologist. "Partly that's due to the horse, being a quadruped, using 90 per cent of its muscle mass when running, whereas humans have more areas of muscle that aren't employed when they're running. The horse can maintain a high speed very effectively, though over long distances dehydration and salt loss are more marked than in humans."

● All the figures are for elite athletes and racehorses, with the exception of the 100-mile 'endurance' event. Further, both the endurance horse and athlete would actually be performing at a slightly higher percentage of their *own* maximum speed, though the percentage figures given here are true of horses and humans as a breed.

Japanese Gardens at Tully. When Osborne came many years later to take charge of the same stud, men who had worked there from boyhood told him of the book in which Hall Walker recorded the date and hour of all foalings, and how the only windows in the stables were in the roof. Thus were the horses in direct contact with the firmament. Hall Walker recorded in his notebook the "horoscope" of each foal at the moment of birth.

There is another story which Michael Osborne can tell, this one from his own experience, which suggests that relying on the firmament may provide better predictive data than linear measurements. The measurements in question were those of Northern Dancer: 33 inches inside leg, 66 inches body length, 88 inches overall length. The team with whom Osborne was working at the time felt that 33-66-88 perhaps represented a kind of Golden Mean. They sought to match a son of the great horse, with exactly those measurements, with a mare of identical dimensions. They also identified three other physical formulae which seemed significant, and used a computer to bring all the formulae together in a consensus which would, they hoped, represent the perfect mating.

"The outstanding prognosis was one which scored 98 per cent," says Osborne. "But the horse that resulted won only one small race and was a rather poor performer." In the final analysis there may be

□ Continued overleaf

☐ Continued from previous page

attributes that defy all measurement. Osborne cites the hyper-sensitivity of all the great horses he has known." If you were to toss a little handful of barley seed in the air," he says, demonstrating, "and a seed landed there on the horse's back, he'd react. Whereas you could throw a pebble at another horse and he'd not feel it. Rarely do you get real slobs of horses that are champions."

At times it is hard to know where Michael Osborne's instinct is taking him, or where he wants it to take him. Is he the scientist who would like to predict elite equine performance, or is he the romantic who distrusts his own stethoscope?

"You can sum it up by saying that I don't believe you can predict athletic prowess by strictly scientific means. There are other dimensions that make it more difficult, more exciting and more fascinating. The components of anatomy, feeding, training and development are, I would guess, 85 per cent of the situation. That leaves the jockey, an element of luck, and other components – including extra-terrestrial.

"What we can't quantify is the charisma of champion horses, because there's no doubt that the great horses have that superstar look. They give the distinct impression that they know they're the best, and I would think that these horses are dominant from the time they are born . . ."

Nashwan, winner of the 1989 Derby, epitome of the thoroughbred ideal, now stands at stud.

A horse to win the Derby?

In June 1991 Racing Post, its appetite whetted, looked specifically at the qualities a thoroughbred horse needed to win England's greatest Flat race, the Derby. It went without saying that it had to be a superb equine athlete, like Nashwan in the photograph above, but conformation, breeding and temperament, it was said, all contributed to the chemistry. The resultant information proved to be a fascinating extension of the original study of the horse as an athlete.

Heart

At rest approximately 36-42 beats a minute, rising to 210-240 beats a minute when full-out, the amount of blood pumped at each beat is approximately one litre. The average cardiac output for a 455kg horse at rest is 35 litres a minute, but at maximal exercise this increases to 225 litres a minute.

Blood

A volume of approximately 42 litres. The blood carries red cells that contain haemoglobin pigment (approximately 33%), which transports oxygen. At rest approximately 12.4% of the blood flows through the muscle but when the horse is full-out this may increase to 80%.

Speed

37-38mph, which requires energy generated in muscle, the fuel burnt being not petrol but a carbohydrate glycogen – to achieve this, oxygen is required.

Stride

5.5m to 7.3m when galloping, the variation depending on height. The complete stride, from when the left fore leaves the ground to when it hits it again, takes place within the space of 0.4second.

Breathing

At rest a horse breathes 10-12 times a minute, but when galloping this can rise to as high as 150 breaths, equivalent to 2½ breaths a second (impossible for a man), each breath taking in approximately 10 litres of air.

Clues to the superhorse

● **BIRTHWEIGHT**. Around 112lb for fillies and 114lb for colts will produce, with uncanny certainty, an ideally-sized horse of 15.3 hands and around 1,000lb. That does not necessarily mean a champion. But a foal of under, say, 80lb will almost certainly be an inadequately small racehorse.

● **STRIDE CADENCE**. This will be established quite early in a horse's life and may be analysed by video. The hooves should make minimum contact with the ground and give the impression of spokes driving a smoothly turning wheel. The difference between 'stance time' and 'swing time' can be measured in milliseconds, as can the degree of overlap in stance time between two or more hooves. This may distinguish the outstanding horse.

● **HEART**. Heart size may be judged by ECG pulse, producing a Heart Score. Additionally, ultrasonic imaging can show the size of the heart's main chamber, and the blood volume of that chamber when full and empty – and therefore the stroke volume. It is thought that heart size in thoroughbreds may vary by as much as 30 per cent.

● **BREATHING**. The alarm bells are ringing, following the controversial discovery of a high percentage of laryngeal paralysis: the result, it is said, of a recessive gene in the thoroughbred breed. The 'switch gear' that admits air to the larynx (or food to the stomach) is already extremely narrow, given the other proportions of the horse and the amount of air it inhales. This now is compounded by a partial paralysis of the laryngeal nerve, meaning that the passageway does not pull open fully to accommodate increased air flow. Hence, the whistling or roaring of horses who are badly affected.

Lungs

Large lungs that suck in oxygen, absorbed into the blood, and pumped by the heart to muscle, releasing energy. Power is generated and speed is the result.

Weight

On average, a body mass of 446kg, plus or minus 36kg. Of this 42.9% is muscle and 9.7% blood.

Breeding

The man who decided there was no such thing as a badly-bred Derby winner simply pronounced all previous winners as well-bred (they must have been to have won the Derby!) and trusted all future winners to meet an acceptable standard. Generally, that arbitrary standard would encompass all the runners anyway. A more definite, but in essence equally silly, 'rule' had it that a prospective Derby winner must have a high-class performer over at least 10 furlongs in the supposed 'key' positions of sire and maternal grandsire in his pedigree, in order to stay 12 furlongs and quicken at some point. Usually that tended to take care of most of the entries, and Hard Ridden (1958) represented a rare embarrassment for the theory's proponents until America threw a spanner into the works, inundating us with horses whose antecedents had proved their merits in a different racing regime.

Temperament

The demanding preliminaries before the Derby constitute a unique 20 minutes in a thoroughbred's young life. So temperament is all about how this inbred, highly-strung, finely-tuned animal can cope with the razzamatazz. They are like Formula One cars revving up on the grid before a Grand Prix – waiting to explode into action.

Conformation

The thoroughbred's conformation has given him large lungs, a big heart and a long stride in relation to his body weight. Common sense dictates that to run 12 furlongs over Epsom Downs faster than any other contemporary three-year-old requires a superior cardio-vascular system; training and fitness bringing about increases in blood volume and haemoglobin concentration, improving yet further the respiration and oxygen intake. This is the vital key to superior performance, well recognised by the Koran, in which the horse is described as a "drinker of air".

The real key to an appetite for victory

Feeding winners is no simple matter. Racehorses, like human athletes, need carefully designed diets and they feed on everything from garlic honey to Guinness

by SIMON CRISFORD

CLIVE BRITTAIN'S feedman, Mick Leaman, gets his job satisfaction from seeing a licked-out manger and counting the prizes won by the stable for best-turned-out horses.

The lads responsible for leading horses up at the races take the credit for 'best turned out', but the feeding programme for horses in training is what makes them look well in their coats. As Leaman says: "If a horse is not well inside, then he will not look well outside."

So for Leaman, feeder for the past six years at Carlburg Stables, it has been satisfying that the yard's runners have consistently picked up best-turned-out awards. Lapierre has been among them.

Leaman's day begins at 4.45am, when he checks all of the horses in training to see how they have done overnight. He explained: "I check that they have eaten up, and I give them their first feed, which is one 3lb bowl of oats. Their next feed is at midday, when they get a basic feed consisting of bran and oats mixed into honey with chaff and lucerne.

"The art of feeding is to keep the horses interested in their feed, and that is why, when they have their main feed in the evening, I will sometimes put in a bit of sweetness such as glucose, and different vitamins which are mostly for energy and to keep the blood thinned. They also get garlic honey and wheat germ oil, which is good for their coats.

"Twice a week, on Wednesdays and Saturdays, they will get a mash feed which clears them out. The bran mash consists of barley cooked with linseed. Molasses, which is black treacle, is mixed into

the mash to give the extra iron, and this particular feed is a good laxative. Into this we put some sulphur, which thins out the blood and cools them down.

"The other five nights a week they get a normal feed, and I try to keep them interested. I do the feeding round at midday on my own, so I know all of the horses and their various requirements. A horse in full training weighing 460kg can be expected to eat 18lb of oats each day, though they do vary. In the evening the colts can get 9lb of oats mixed down with half a bowl of damp bran, garlic honey and salt. At this time of year they sweat a lot, so I like to put the salt back into them.

"Added to this are the various supplements, such as the green pellet Twydil, which is calcium for boning, and iron vitamins. There are eight vitamins attached to this main supplement. There is also the Twydil Hemopar, for iron again, and vegetable oil. So much of the goodness is taken out of the coat with all of the dressing-over, but the vegetable oil can put that back.

"They have three eggs and three carrots mixed in every night, and a handful of chaff and lucerne. The eggs and the Guinness that they get are used to keep their appetites up, especially with the fillies. Some of the smaller fillies wouldn't eat 14lb of oats, and so we have to help them along as much as we can.

"The horses are given a pick of comfrey leaves – which are good for the liver – mixed down with chaff, twice a week. The important thing is for the horses not to be purging. When I check round I like to see a nice sort of firmish dropping."

Brittain's assistant trainer, Jock Brown, 47, who has overall responsibility in the yard, said: "A lot of races are won in the manger. The horses get one wedge of hay in the morning, and one wedge of hay at night. The morning hay comes from Devon, which is good bulk feed, but the evening hay is Canadian and has much more goodness and protein. There is no wastage at all with the Canadian hay, and it is very palatable. The oats we use come from Australia, which are very dry, clean and not so dusty as other types.

"As the horses have their work built up, so their feeds get adjusted until they reach their ideal racing weight. Every horse is weighed before racing, and on the morning after, and if they are not racing at all, they are still weighed once a week. By weighing horses you can tell what sort of a race they have had, and how much it has taken out of them. It also gives you a very good indication of how fit the horse is but their best racing weights vary.

"Horses do not put that much weight on from two years to three, and quite often their best racing weight is the same as it was in the autumn of their

two-year-old careers. Weighing horses will tell you how much they are doing in their work, whether too much or too little. For example, Lapierre's best weight is 466kg. If the horse doesn't do a stroke of work in his race, he will show you that when he is weighed. And by weighing them you can see how well or badly the horse has travelled.

"On average they should lose between six and eight kilos after a race, and if they lose more than that then you need to look at them to find out why. Some horses can lose up to 16 kilos."

24 August 1988

LAPIERRE'S FEED

1. Hay (Devon); **2.** Sack of Australian oats; **3.** Tub of Guinness; **4.** Hay (Canada); **5.** Tub of chaff and lucerne; **6.** Comfrey leaves; **7.** Tub of mash (Wed and Sat only); **8.** Wheat germ oil; **9.** Twydil pellets; **10.** Twydil Hemopar; **11.** Eggs; **12.** Carrots; **13.** Molasses; **14.** Garlic honey; **15.** Super E glucose; **16.** Electrolytes; **17.** Salt; **18.** Sulphur

Pictured from left: Mick Leam (feeder), Lapierre, Lapierre's lad Phil Chambers.

Mystery of of equine movement unravelled

It was not until the latter half of the 19th century that a thorough understanding was achieved of the mechanics of a horse's movement

by SUE MONTGOMERY

ONE of the things that set Nashwan on a different plane from other horses was his extraordinarily elegant movement. He was a big horse, nearly 17 hands, yet there was nothing cumbersome about him. In all his paces he moved like silk rippling softly in a breeze and gave the impression that he could have cantered on eggs without breaking one.

There is little more majestic than a thoroughbred horse, in graceful control of his frame and limbs, running at speed. It is the racehorse's justification, and if he can do it properly, all else is forgiven. How often do we hear: "He's no oil painting, but he can't half move."

Classical looks are not a prerequisite for athletic ability, which is just as well, because very few horses do conform wholly to what is perceived as perfect. A handsome horse is as capable of moving like a square-wheeled bike as a plain one. But how does he move? What are the mechanics of it? You can hear a horse's feet going clip-clop on the tarmac, or durrum-durrum on the turf, but what are they doing with them?

It wasn't until the 1880s that we really knew. Up until then racehorses in paintings had been represented at the gallop with their legs stretched out like rocking horses. There were no cameras to freeze the movement in those days and horses galloped and cantered too fast for the eye to see accurately how their legs worked.

Then photographer Eadweard Muybridge solved it. He set up some cameras along a track, the shutters of which were released by a horse breaking a thread attached to each as it galloped past. The result was a series of photographs which showed the progression of the horse's limbs in a stride.

A horse has four basic paces, or gaits: walk, trot, canter and gallop, each with its own rhythm, which should have equal stress on each beat.

The walk is a four-time pace. You can hear that as the horses clip round the parade ring, one-two-three-four. The sequence of footfalls is near-fore, off-hind, off-fore, near-hind. In walk, there are always at

A horse at the gallop. This four-beat. . .

1 *Moment of suspension: All four legs off the ground. The horse is about to instigate an off (right) fore lead stride by bringing his near-hind to the ground.*

2 *Beat One of the stride. The near-hind comes to the ground, bearing the horse's full weight as he pivots forward over it.*

5 *Beat Three of the stride. The near-fore has hit the ground and the weight of the horse is briefly on both it and the off-hind.*

6 *The horse pivots over his near-fore, bearing his full weight on it as the off-fore reaches for the ground.*

least two feet on the ground at any one time.

The walk is, to many good judges, the most important pace by which to assess a horse. The theory is that a horse that swings along at a walk will be able to swing along at a gallop, which is also a four-time pace. One of the things that show a horse is 'a good walker' is if his hind feet overstep the front feet. If the hind foot lands well in advance of the print left by the front foot on the same side, then the horse is using his hind legs, which are the power-house, properly.

Ideally the hind feet should follow in the same line as the front feet, in any gait, so that only two tracks would be visible if the horse was running on, say, sand. Horses tend to carry their quarters sideways if they tense up, for instance when they are about to leave the paddock and canter to post, but a large number move like crabs anyway and would leave a three-furrow track like a Reliant Robin.

This is actually a required movement in some dressage tests, but a racehorse is more efficient on two tracks.

The trot is a two-time pace, with the limbs moving in pairs diagonally. Racehorses are rarely required to trot in public – they generally go straight from walk to canter going to post – but they will jig-jog, one-two, one-two, in the parade ring. There is a brief moment in a true two-time trot – the period of suspension – when all four legs are off the ground as the horse springs from one diagonal to the other.

There is a variation of the trot, rather confusingly called the pace; hence the differentiation between trotters and pacers in harness races. A pacer moves his legs in pairs laterally, the two on each side moving together. It is perfectly true to say of such a horse that he moves like a camel.

The canter is a three-time gait, with either foreleg leading. Each stride starts with a distinct moment of suspension, and it is the hind leg which comes to the ground first that dictates the foreleg lead, which will be the opposite. For a near-fore lead the sequence of footfalls is off-hind, near-hind and off-fore diagonal together, then near-fore. A horse is physically capable of a disunited canter of off-hind, near-hind and near-fore lateral together, off-fore; but it is unbalancing and feels horrible.

The gallop is the important gait for a racer. Like the canter, it contains a period of suspension, but after that there are four distinct footfalls as the hind legs lever the horse forward and the shoulders and forelimbs reach out to grab the ground. Like the canter, too, there is a leading foreleg.

For an off-fore lead, which is illustrated, the sequence is suspension, near-hind, off-hind, near-fore, off-fore, suspension, and so on.

Knowing how a horse should work does not guarantee the identification of a winner, because all sorts of crabs, camels and Reliant Robins can, and do, win races. But the upper echelons are generally the preserve of horses who move most efficiently. The blueprint of the perfect galloping machine is what everyone is after and the magnificent American Triple Crown champion Secretariat probably came closest to it. His stride length was measured at 27 feet.

21 March 1990

. . . stride is one of four basic gaits

3 *The horse continues to swing over his near-hind leg as the forelegs unfold and the off-hind moves forward and down.*

4 *Beat Two of the stride. The off-hind comes to the ground and begins to take up the weight of the horse as the near-hind flicks backwards. The near-fore is about to come to the ground.*

7 *Beat Four of the stride. The off-fore hits the ground and moments later the near-fore is lifted. The hind legs begin to fold up.*

8 *The horse has pivoted over his off-fore in the final phase of the stride. In a second all four legs will be off the ground again.*

Wet and wonderful, a racing Pegasus

There is an increasing awareness of the value of swimming for horses in training, and pools are not now viewed as an eccentricity but by some even as a necessity

by JOHN LOVESEY

SCENE: a morning dip in the cool, translucent blue of the equine pool at Whitcombe Manor Stables in Dorset, where Toby Balding is currently in residence as trainer. It is a picture conjuring up visions of Pegasus, the fabled winged horse of Greek mythology.

It is also proof positive that, despite a natural buoyancy and despite all those river-crossing scenes in old films about the Wild West, horses do not take to the water like ducks but in a manner more akin to humans. In fact, swimming is decidedly *not* a natural pursuit for racehorses, and they can rapidly become exhausted in water.

For example, Super Morning, pictured here, may swim with equine elegance, the legs pedalling in a rhythm that is much easier on the eye than the dog-paddle managed by most humans but, lordy, note how he keeps his nostrils closed tight! Indeed, when first cajoled into the water, most horses breathe deeply and clearly desire to make it through the ordeal without inhaling again.

Horses often have trouble, too, with their very style of swimming, having to spend much time in the pool before developing steady, even movements. Some try to 'climb', using their front legs only, and others roll from side to side. Yet others use both forelegs but only one hindleg, while some will not use their front legs. But as time passes most manage the matter of breathing well enough and become proficient in the business of swimming itself.

There is no doubt about the benefits. Water is weight-bearing so limbs are exercised and the muscle beneficially toned up without the hammering the ground can impose. Most important of all, the effect on the cardiovascular system is miraculous, working it at almost racing pitch. The heartbeats per minute shoot to as high as 200, compared to 210-240 beats a minute during a flat-out gallop on land.

At Whitcombe, swimming is considered so effective that many of the horses do regular stints in the pool, while most are likely to be introduced to the water at some stage. One Balding horse, with an arthritic fetlock joint, swims, out of necessity, five days a week while having outings on the gallops only twice a week. Super Morning is not swimming here because of injury but is in the water after running, as a welcome break from training.

In warmer countries than Britain, swimming has

been not simply a therapy, but an integral part of training for years. Clive Brittain, with his own equine pool at Newmarket, is a successful leading exponent, and other British-based trainers not already in the swim are planning to follow suit. Brittain was largely inspired to incorporate swimming into his training regimens primarily after seeing the benefits derived from it in the USA. He has had an equine pool for 17 years and, out of his current crop of horses, all of them swim apart from a pair of recalcitrants who have a pronounced aversion to the water.

"It is the best training you can get, outside the gallops," says Brittain. "After a hard run, swimming for a couple of days keeps horses fit and refreshes them mentally." At Whitcombe, horses start by doing two or three laps (approximately 30 metres a lap) of the circular pool. Once they take to it, then the work is increased.

The current Whitcombe record for laps is 21, equal to a non-stop swim of some 600 metres. Eat your heart out, Adrian Moorhouse? Not quite, but not bad for a noble creature of the animal kingdom, designed not for swimming but flight.

3 September 1991

Super Morning swimming in the pool at Whitcombe Manor. It is a form of exercise that can set a horse's heart beating at a rate of 200 times a minute.

World's greatest horse trainers

It says much for two of the greatest horse trainers in history that they are linked, over a period of 100 years, by a common code of kindness to the equine breed

by SUE MONTGOMERY

IT'S great news that master horseman Monty Roberts will be at the Brent Walker Festival at Ascot on Saturday to demonstrate his incomparable skills. But if you reckon the American is the first horse trainer with ideas out of the mainstream to cross the Atlantic and create a sensation, think again. A hundred years ago Professor Norton B. Smith came from Canada to astound British audiences with his displays.

The moustachioed young professor's speciality was the handling and taming of difficult animals, and his methods are spelt out in his Practical Treatise on the Breaking and Training of Wild and Vicious Horses. This slim volume was first published in 1892, and it would be easy today to poke fun at the illustrations – some of which are reproduced here – and some of the advice. But Professor Smith, if the letters of approbation included in the book are a guide, was, in his time, extremely successful.

He was also very much a showman and, judging by the posters advertising his act, modesty was not one of his greatest failings. But then, hype has always been part of the horse business. And Smith and his English agent Nat Behrens would have little to learn from today's promoters. At the horse-handling exhibitions it was possible to buy Professor Smith's books (1s), patent bits for riding or driving (6s), whips (2s), halters (1/6d) or special automatic rein holders (2/6d), which, attached to one's carriage, were guaranteed to end trampled rein misery.

Although to modern eyes some of Smith's methods look extreme (the instructions under the heading To Approach A Biting Horse begin "Always

do so with a revolver heavily loaded with blank cartridges" and there is also a section on Whirling A Horse By His Tail), there is one thing that he and Roberts, a century apart, have in common. It is the use of kindness when dealing with their subjects.

That quality is not so unusual today, and its advantages have been known by enlightened horsemen since Xenophon, but the Victorian era was still in many ways a brutal one, as anyone who has read Black Beauty will know. Riders commonly drew blood on their horses' flanks with spur and whip, docking of tails was legal and fashionable, and the RSPCA had yet to be founded.

Monty Roberts stresses that his method of starting (he calls it that, rather than breaking) young horses involves no pain and the minimum of mental stress. He uses no magic hocus-pocus; his understanding of the horse's natural instincts and way of thinking means he can turn them to his own advantage.

Back in 1892, Smith wrote: "In dealing with my plan, you are not wasting your time with a mysterious trick. The three fundamental principles of my theory are first, control; second, let kindness run through all your actions; and third, appeal properly to the horse's understanding.

"In all my time I have not injured one horse, or found it necessary to be cruel, and a horse may be taught to perfectly submit to anything, however odious it might have been to him at first."

Roberts' display takes place in a small pen or lunge-ring. He uses his own 'advance-and-retreat' method of gaining the unbroken horse's trust, chasing the animal from him if it will not come to him,

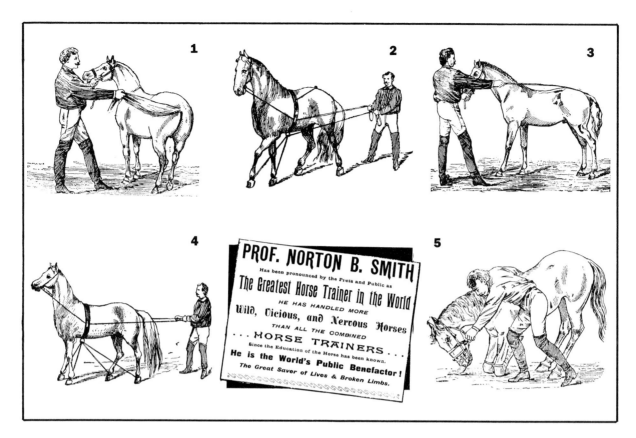

and rewarding it with gentle hands and soft words when it follows him freely.

Here are Smith's views: "The first lesson to give a young horse should be to turn him into a box stall or enclosure of about 20 feet square, taking in your right hand a whip, and approaching the colt. If he runs away from you, give him a crack of the whip round the hind limbs and follow this up until he will turn his head towards you.

"Then place the whip back under your left arm and hold out your right. If, as you approach the colt, he turns to run, give him the whip again. When he comes to you, offer him kindness. You will teach him that it is wrong to turn his heels towards you, but that the right way is to keep his head to you."

Most of Smith's work seems to have been with driving horses, and he was very keen on various rather extraordinary patent gadgets to teach recalcitrant pupils. But he advised their use only for education, not for permanent control by force. He was dead against one of the harness horrors of the time, the bearing rein (a device which held the head artificially, and supposedly smartly, high) and, interestingly, firing, which he described as "brutal".

His views on the whip would stand today. He wrote:

"The whip in its place is a good instrument, but is very often misused by parties. For instance, how many do you see driving through the streets of our cities, and in our public parks, and when a horse becomes frightened of a bicycle or a band and makes an attempt to shy, will get him by [the obstacle] the best way he can, while the moment he has passed brings out the whip with the words 'I'll teach you to shy' and then the horse receives a severe punishment?

"The horse, not having the reasoning power that you have, associates the punishment with the object that he was so much frightened of."

A book like Professor (if, indeed, he genuinely held such a title) Smith's Practical Treatise is nowadays something of a curiosity, but a fascinating one, not least for what it can teach us about contemporary social attitudes and customs. Its author, however, though on one level an entertainer for commercial gain, clearly had an understanding of horses, uncommon in his time, and, also unusually for then, a desire to share his knowledge for the benefit of horsekind.

Monty Roberts is another of the same, and those who are lucky enough to see him at Ascot on Saturday will gain much from the experience, just as those far-distant Victorian audiences must have done from Professor Norton B. Smith.

25 September 1991

Opposite: Monty Roberts, who practises no hocus-pocus, is the natural heir to the Norton B. Smith tradition.

Above:
1 *Whirling a horse by his tail.*
2 *Handling and driving a colt.*
3 *How to make a colt follow you.*
4 *Driving and breaking a bad kicker.*
5 *How to handle a vicious, biting stallion.*

Alan, the invisible jockey, cashes in

It seems logical to Alan Munro that to ride low in the saddle not only brings you more into tune with your horse but provides an important aerodynamic advantage

by TOM O'RYAN

THE pencil-slim jockey crouches low. So very low, that for one awful moment at Doncaster last Saturday it was feared he wasn't there at all.

From his lofty position in the grandstand, Raceform's senior race-reader, Alan Amies, binoculars focused on the Lincoln field had thought his eagle eyes were deceiving him as Evichstar blazed a trail down the stands side of the course. "Is there anybody on that one of Fitzy's?" he muttered, as the ant-sized figures thundered towards us amid a sandy spray. "Oh yes, there is," he chuckled. "It's 'Cash'!"

It wasn't the first time that the experienced Amies, who is renowned for being able to spot a non-trier more quickly than any man on the northern circuit, had mistaken a horse ridden by Alan Munro for a riderless one. And it won't be the last.

"It's easily done," he admits. "He gets so far down, you just can't see him."

It was inevitable that Munro should have earned the nickname of 'Cash' for his distinctive fold-away style and subtle technique that makes him look like a carbon-copy of the multi-skilled Asmussen. That said, he claims not to have modelled himself on the lanky Texan, or anybody else for that matter.

If imitation is the sincerest form of flattery then it is American jockeys in general, rather than Asmussen in particular, who should have been well pleased with Munro's faultless exhibition of mimicry on Evichstar, the Lincoln hero, not to mention the other two winners he rode at Doncaster's opening meeting and the five since.

Munro is a man with his head very much on his shoulders, and his feet very much on the ground.

He thinks carefully about what he says and is clearly conscious about not wishing to sound cocky or conceited . . . just ambitious.

"You wouldn't believe how ambitious," he says. "My career is all that matters to me."

It is that hunger for success that first led Munro across the Atlantic and consequently brought about such a drastic transformation in his riding style. The turning-point for Munro came one day at Beverley in 1986 when he rode a horse called Hot Ruler, for Mel Brittain, whom he had joined that season. It was a rude awakening for the York-born, Stevenage-raised youngster, who, having left school measuring 4ft 10in and weighing in at 5st 7lb, spent 2½ years with Barry Hills before heading north with only one winner to his credit.

"If you'd seen that race at Beverley, you wouldn't have thought I had a future," confesses Munro. "I was falling off the horse and the stewards, quite rightly, dragged me in to ask me exactly what I was doing. They showed me the film and it looked terrible. I was riding very, very short and, being weak as well, I was just so unbalanced."

The lessons learned from that day were not lost. "Looking back on it now, it was so stupid. I was very immature then about taking advice. I thought I knew best, but I wasted quite a few years finding out how to ride the correct way."

Munro says he discovered the key almost by accident. "Things weren't going brilliantly here and I was looking for back-doors more than anything else. It was through going over to America and riding American-style, which you had to do to earn any

money, that started it all. I found it came quite easily, but I'd never even thought about it until then. Before I went to America, I didn't know *how* to ride.

"Don't get me wrong. I admire and respect the English jockeys, but I prefer the American way. Over there it's all about balance, which is a big thing throughout a race. If you can balance a horse and get in rhythm with it, like the Americans do, you can become part of that horse and provide it with so much assistance."

Munro has let his leathers down quite a few notches in order to perfect the style he craves. "You can only go as low as your knees, so if you ride with your knees below the pommel of the saddle, you can get as low as the saddle. It's common sense, really," he says. "And with your knees dropped, you automatically get more of a feel with the horse, which in turn helps your balance. I also find that by putting just your toe in the iron it's better still, because you can use your ankle as a pivot."

As for the aerodynamics of the whole business, he is equally convinced that the streamlined style has the edge over the traditional British seat. "It's obviously an advantage. It's logical isn't it? Take Doncaster the other day for example. There was a strong wind coming straight at us. Well, if you're stood up or sat back in the saddle, it's going to catch you more than if you're sat down behind the horse's head. It's common sense really."

Munro has, of course, gone the whole hog, by carrying his American-style whip in the American-style way, held permanently in the forehand, in an upright position. It looks more like a car aerial, bob-

bing about above a horse's ears, but it is, he says, "readily available in an instant and much quicker to switch."

He has come a long way since all but disgracing himself on Hot Ruler at Beverley. And he possesses all the right credentials to go a lot further. "I'll always be grateful to Mel Brittain for standing by me. He kept pushing me and I don't think I would ever have found an opportunity anywhere else to equal it," he says.

Munro is his own severest critic and, although now on the threshold of the big time and widely tipped for future stardom, he needs no reminding that racing is the greatest of levellers. Far from resting on his laurels, he is still far from satisfied that he has got it right.

"I've always taken the view," he explains, "that as soon as you think you're at your best, that's when you start to back-pedal. I refuse to accept I'm at my best yet and feel that there's still room for a lot of improvement.

"I think, compared to the likes of Pat Eddery, I'm still a bit green, particularly in the mind, simply through inexperience. But it'll come."

In the meantime, Alan Munro will continue to ride the all-American way by striving to become even more a part of the horse. Alan Amies and fellow race-readers, please note . . .

31 March 1990

Riding on Evichstar in the Lincoln at Doncaster, Alan Munro used his streamlined style to winning effect in a wind that was blowing straight at the jockeys.

Ear! Ear! Both work hard for a horse

The hearing of a horse, though not as sensitive as a dog's or a bat's, is still quite extraordinary. Its ears, capable of turning through 180 degrees, are also rather special

by SUE MONTGOMERY

A HORSE'S sense of hearing is one of his greatest attributes, but it is one that his human masters do not always utilise properly. Those sensitive equine ears can be actively abused, through being subjected to loud or unnatural noises, or simply wasted as a means of communication.

There is no doubt that horses can hear better than humans. The internal ear of the horse is built along fairly standard mammalian lines, but the external ear is particularly well constructed to capture sound. Horses can not only hear more acutely than humans, but have a better range of hearing at both high and low frequencies.

Man, in his prime, has a top range of 20 kilohertz (20,000 cycles per second); tests on horses have established that they can hear up to around 25 kilohertz.

Equine hearing, however, is nothing like as good as canine (up to 100 kilohertz), and both pale into insignificance beside that of a bat. The members of the order cheiroptera have a range of between 1-200,000 kilohertz.

Being funnel-shaped, a horse's ears greatly augment the sounds they receive, like an ear-trumpet. The ears are also wonderfully mobile – each is independently controlled by 16 muscles and can rotate through 180 degrees. Thus a horse can pin-point a sound – and possible danger – coming from any direction.

Horses do not only utilise this ear mobility as individuals. When they move together, for instance as a herd or a troop of military horses, and particularly at night, the leading horses direct their ears forward, those in the rear point their ears back, and those in the centre turn them sideways.

A horse's ears, though relatively small in comparison to its size (think of an elephant or some breeds of dogs), are one of its most prominent and visible features, and so have evolved not only as listening devices, but also as indicators of its mood. Originally this was for the benefit of fellow-horses; but soon man learned that a horse with ears pricked forward was attentive or startled, but at least non-hostile, whereas ears laid flat back meant anger or fear. And to compound any trouble, a horse with his ears flat against his neck cannot hear any placatory noises.

There is a range of positions between the two forward and back extremes. Ears sideways, especially in a young horse, is a submissive signal; and the same position, or turned slightly backwards, is a sign that a ridden horse is listening to what his rider is saying.

Closely allied to the horse's ability to hear through his external ears is his ability to 'hear' through the transmission of vibrations in the earth, via the bones of feet and forelegs, vertebrae and skull, to the middle and inner ear.

This, as well as superior conventional hearing, may explain why horses can detect the approach of another animal, or even the onset of a natural disturbance, long before humans. People who live in earthquake zones have noted that horses

in the area often become agitated before anything happens.

Horses hate loud noises, although they can accept a temporary racket if, after the first alarm, they realise that the noise is not harming them. The noise of a cheering raceday crowd must be baffling to a young thoroughbred, although the ones that enter the winner's circle often enough may begin to associate their reception with the end of effort and pleasant pats.

'Show-off' horses, like Desert Orchid, seem to enjoy the sound of adulation.

Dick Francis is convinced that noise was the downfall of Devon Loch in the Grand National. The Queen Mother's horse, ridden by the jockey-turned-thriller-writer, led over the last, only to collapse mysteriously 50 yards from the post. Many theories as to the cause of the incident have been advanced, but that of Francis is entirely credible.

In his autobiography, The Sport of Queens, he writes:

"From the last fence onwards the cheers which greeted us were tremendous and growing louder with every yard we went, and although I knew the reason for them, they may have been puzzling and confusing to my mount, who could not know that his owner was a Queen.

"In order to hear better what was going on he would make a horse's instinctive movement to do so, and into those newly pricked and sensitive ears fell a wave of sound of shattering intensity. The noise that was uplifting and magnificent to me may have been exceedingly frightening to Devon Loch.

"I remember how startled I was when I first heard the cheers for M'as-Tu-Vu (another of the Queen Mother's horses) at Lingfield, and they were a whisper compared to the enveloping roar at Liverpool."

Horses respond quickly to sound, and this marvellous hearing is a great aid to teaching them. They can easily learn to associate sound with an action. A hunter will prick his ears up at the sound of a horn, or bay of a hound, even years after he has retired from the field.

It is not difficult to teach a horse – especially the finer-bred types, who have better hearing than their common cousins – to walk, trot, canter or stop by verbal command. This can be extremely useful, as the great trainer Fred Darling discovered. In 1922 his Derby winner Captain Cuttle got loose as he was being boxed up for Epsom and was just about to set off down the main road when he heard his trainer's voice calling 'woo-oah' just as he had when schooling the colt on the lunge. Captain Cuttle's brain, reacting to the sound, dropped into obedience mode and he meekly walked back to Darling.

It is much better to speak quietly to a horse than shout at it as if it were a foreigner, and much better to talk to it than remain silent. A horse uses its ears from birth; one of the first things a new-born foal is aware of is the gentle nickering of its mother.

Many horsemen feel that it is wrong to chat to horses, and that all commands should be given by physical means. But horses, like dogs, can be taught the difference between 'yes' and 'no' without the human part of the partnership having to resort to yelling or brute force, although, obviously, there will always be moments, in the heat of action or due to outside distractions, when verbal commands will be useless. The fact that a loud noise is startling to a horse can be used in racing to the rider's advantage. A horse can be galvanised into extra effort by the jockey yelling; after all, a horse's flat-out gallop is a fear response and a sudden shout from behind his head can frighten him that little bit more.

Fashions in ears have changed over the centuries. Thankfully, we no longer crop ears to half their length, a barbaric practice carried out on carriage horses until the middle of the 18th century to achieve a 'smart' look. Nowadays, we admire big, bold ears on a horse, shunning one with small, 'pony' ears.

15 November 1989

Dick Francis is sure noise was the downfall of Devon Loch in the 1956 National (pictures above), when his mount collapsed 50 yards from the post.

THE GLORY

Honour and eminence spread far and wide in racing. A meeting that takes place each summer on the estate of the Duke of Richmond is even accorded the sobriquet of Glorious Goodwood. Glorious too are those who hurtle round Tattenham Corner in the Derby and the ones that line up for the Grand National. Even Becher's Brook shines with historic fame, for children are told about it as soon as they are old enough to learn that it is the most legendary jump in the whole world. But in the end, racing is no different from other sports and the ultimate accolade belongs to the winner, whether it is horse or man

Going hell for leather, the competitors in the 1989 King George Stakes at Goodwood fight out a thrilling finish to this five-furlong sprint.

Setting a record to stand for ever

When Martin Pipe first trained the winners of 200 races in a season it was deemed so remarkable a record that one Racing Post writer thought it might never be beaten

by PAUL HAIGH

MARTIN PIPE'S achievement in training the winners of 200 races in a jump season is so stupendous that it surpasses even Peter Scudamore's in riding that number to victory. To an extent Scudamore's triumph has been a function of Pipe's: two-thirds of his double century of winners have come from the Pipe yard and even if he has had to be responsible for the occasional miracle, a good proportion of those winners did not require the services of the best jump jockey. Frank Spencer could have won on some of them.

This isn't intended to belittle Scudamore. It's intended to emphasise the enormity of what the trainer has done. Although last season Pipe had beaten Michael Dickinson's supposedly unchallengeable total of 120, no-one, when this season began, could have predicted what has happened.

Pipe is not what you might call an establishment figure and that might be one reason why some have found it all just too hard to swallow.

His father Dave, still the main business brain behind the outfit, is a bookmaker who financed his son's idea of becoming a trainer out of the proceeds of the sale of his Somerset chain of shops to William Hill.

Martin Pipe met his wife Carol when they were both working in the head office. They are not Home Counties tweeds and green wellies types at all, and their success hasn't changed them either.

Martin may be much more hyped up but he still has the common touch. At Newton Abbot a couple of weeks ago he assembled the Nicholashayne stable staff for a night out, and when one of his runners turned up at 16-1, the winner's enclosure was surrounded by young girls shouting his Christian name.

To their delight he went over to them and accepted numerous kisses on both cheeks.

All sorts of rumours and allegations have been circulated about him. No evidence has been found to support them. As with Henry Cecil, whose total of 180 Flat wins in 1987 is perhaps the only British training record which bears comparison, his critics are now reduced to claiming rather feebly that, however good his record may look on paper, we only hear about the successes, not about the stable's wastage rate.

It is a claim that has a strong whiff of the last

resort about it. Gradually even the "he must be up to something" school is being forced to recognise that what we are witnessing is greatness.

It's hard to say where Pipe, the self-taught trainer who was once on his own admission "the worst point-to-point rider in the West", goes from here. If only one thing is sure – and he agrees – it is that he can't possibly continue the extraordinary progression which has seen him improve his total of winners in every one of the 12 years since he heard about the first one on his car radio on the way back from having his transfer from permit holder to public trainer granted.

It is quite possible that there never will be another combination of circumstances like this season's –

the dominance he has held over his rivals, the help he's received from a great jockey, the freedom his stable has enjoyed from epidemics, and the mild weather.

This really might be a record which will last forever.

20 May 1989

PS. Martin Pipe has achieved 200 winners in every jumps season since he first set his remarkable record in 1989.

Held in awe, Martin Pipe is unaffected by his incomparable record. His eye, instead, is constantly on fresh fields of glory.

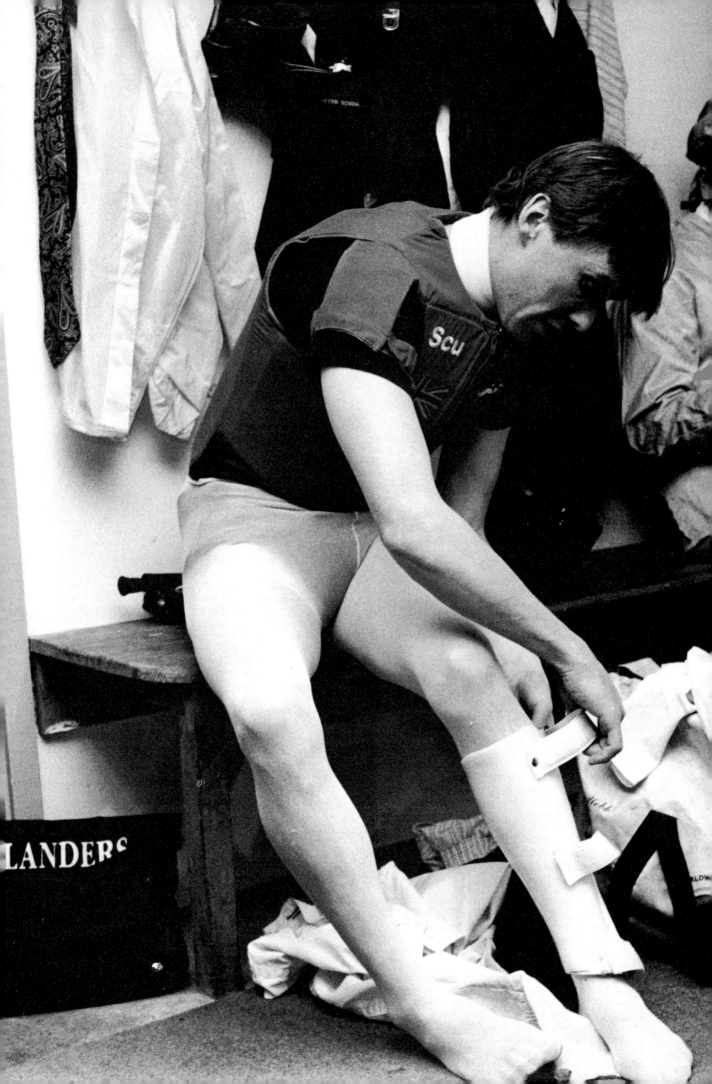

Scu comes back and shows he's still tops

When the champion jump jockey broke his left leg, it took him only 10 weeks to get back into the race. His return at Newton Abbot disappointed nobody

by GEORGE ENNOR

PETER SCUDAMORE is back. After 10 weeks out of action with a broken left leg, normal service was restored at Newton Abbot yesterday when the champion jockey rode a winner on his third come-back ride.

Not surprisingly, there were smiles all round when Scudamore – wearing a protective cast on the injured leg – returned to the winner's enclosure after steering Outside Edge to victory for Martin Pipe in the Torquay Hotels Association Handicap Chase over an extended three and a quarter miles.

"I was delighted to have a winner on my first day back, to satisfy myself and the people watching me," the champion said afterwards. "I didn't want to go three days without a winner and for people then to start saying 'Oh, he's gone'. I could not be more happy with the way things went.

"As far as the leg is concerned, sometimes I feel something before a race and sometimes I don't, but once the race has started there is nothing there to worry about. I've had problems getting the protective cast comfortable and I've had to cut bits of it away so that it now stops at my ankle, but it seems fine now."

Scudamore admitted that riding three and a quarter miles over fences had tested his reserves of stamina. "In the first two races (both two-mile hurdles) there was no problem, but I was breathing a bit

☐ *Continued overleaf*

Like a medieval knight, Peter Scudamore prepares himself for battle once more, attaching a protective case to his left leg before riding at Newton Abbot.

☐ *Continued from previous page*

after that," he explained. "I could have ridden Tree Poppy in the Novice Chase, but decided against it. When she won, I felt sick as a pig and I was glad about that – I would have been disappointed in myself if I hadn't been annoyed about missing a winner."

Typically, he played his own role in Outside Edge's victory.

The win put Scudamore on the 55 winner mark – 19 behind Richard Dunwoody – although for a long time Outside Edge looked like having to work very hard to give his jockey the comeback winner. For well over two miles, he was persistently pressed by Envopak Token with Flemish Fudge and Birling Jack in close attendance. Envopak Token led from the fourth to the tenth and Outside Edge made his only mistake at the eighth but it wasn't a serious error.

The Pipe runner regained the advantage from Envopak Token at halfway only to lose it briefly to Flemish Fudge at the 14th. But he was back in front at the next and from then on steadily asserted his authority as Scudamore set sail for home. The other three finally had their hopes dashed when Outside Edge put in a splendid leap at the last ditch, four from home, and as he came back to the final fence only a fall could beat him.

That thought was well to the front of his rider's mind. "I've said a few prayers in my time," Scudamore related afterwards, "and now I said 'please let me see a stride' and he came up long for me and jumped it well."

Outside Edge was now uncatchable and although he slowed down to an alarming extent – his decision and not his jockey's – as he neared the line, the gelding still had six lengths in hand of Envopak Token with four back to Flemish Fudge. "He'd been in front a long time and was probably getting a bit tired," said Scudamore before asking by how far the horse had won.

On learning the winning distance he replied: "Good, he won't go up much for that."

Scudamore has just two rides at Wincanton today, Tom Clapton and Fu's Lady for Martin Pipe, but is confident that he will soon be able to ride in six races a day and wouldn't be averse to doing so tomorrow.

The champion very nearly made a fairy-tale comeback when his first ride, Viking Flagship, was beaten only a head in the opening novice hurdle, and though he did not win, it was clear that the 10-week absence since that fall at Market Rasen had had no adverse effect on his dash and determination.

Viking Flagship was never out of the first two and never an inch away from the inside but he looked certain to be beaten by market rival Requested, who

was going much the better on the home turn. But when Requested's rather clumsy jump at the final flight let Viking Flagship in with a chance, Scudamore needed no second bidding to get into the drive position and go for glory; they only just failed.

Scudamore's other mount, Coolulah, was a dismal flop in the seller, but Martin Pipe had seen enough in that opening race despite the fact that even all of Scudamore's considerable talents coudn't force Viking Flagship home.

"It's great to see him back, he's a dedicated professional and he showed all his old dash. He nearly pulled the race out of the fire," said Pipe.

25 January 1991

In his first race, on his return, Scudamore rode Viking Flagship. It was nearly a fairy-tale comeback – his mount was only beaten a head.

Stripped of all but naked bravery

When the battle is over, behind the scenes at Cheltenham the equine athletes and their handlers are rid for a while of the heavy burden of winning expectations

by BROUGH SCOTT

IT'S more intimate afterwards. It always is. Royal Gait stands square-legged with fatigue in Cheltenham's 'dope box' on Tuesday. The vet checks his heart. Jason Ward finishes sponging off the sweat marks and tries to check he isn't dreaming. It has happened. He's handling the bridle of his own trace-clipped hold on history.

It's a little eddy of quiet amidst the pressing throng of the Cheltenham thousands. Hardly anyone ever gives a second glance to the neat, timber-built, four-box unit tucked away on the edge of the car park as you walk down to the members' entrance. But that's where all the stars have to come.

Back down the slope, the stewards ponder over the video and James Fanshawe charms everyone with his unaffected delight. Down there amongst the hacks and the hustlers it's possible that Royal Gait might be demoted. Up here it isn't.

Jason Ward was once a mini apprentice at Lester Piggott's. He's nearly six foot now and his smile is a couple of metres higher as he leads his hero round to ready him for the necessary indignity of the urine sample.

"He's always done everything we asked," says Jason, son of former trainer Bob Ward with whom L. Piggott shared several triumphs and one unhappily chronicled suspension.

Another rehabilitation act walks by. Oh So Risky, so freely derided as a horse living up to its name, had run a blinder to be second. His lad David Crofts has pulled 'Risky's' brow-band up over his ears for comfort. You would swear the horse was smiling with satisfaction.

Janice certainly was. Janice Coyle, forever associated with her beloved Dessie, is also Paul Holley's girlfriend. Paul had been jocked off Fragrant Dawn in the Arkle but had now come within half a length of Champion Hurdle immortality. Janice got hold of 'Risky's' narrow Flat-race neck in a simple hug of gratitude.

Up there by the dope box you have the beauty of nakedness. Calm down, chaps, we are talking horses. The athletes back in from the arena, stripped now not just of rugs, bandages and paddock parade shine, but of all the heavy entourage of expectation.

Jason Ward takes Royal Gait back into the box to give his sample. One of the assistants looks familiar. It's Stuart Shilston, who twice tasted Cheltenham fame on Crimson Embers. Neat and besweatered, he busies around the horses. Above all the straw the atmosphere hangs heady with success.

But not for all. Anthony Stroud walks up with troubled brow. On the TV we mistakenly tune into Lamont at Westminster. He is saying "utterly disgraceful". Have the stewards changed the result?

No, Anthony is looking for Kribensis. The former champion cut himself so badly inside his off-hind that the skin hung over his fetlock like a rugby stocking with the flesh and bone raw to the Cheltenham air.

Royal Gait has finished. Jason Ward leads him back along the sandpath towards the stables. He has to skirt a file of lads and manicured smart horses en route to the Kim Muir. Jason talks of his horse, of racing that has filled so much of his 22 years, of his unforgettable day at Warwick, a winner for Piggott on Vague Melody.

By the side of the gateway is a horse-box with the ramp down. It has a sign saying 'M. R. Stoute – Racehorses'. It is to be an ambulance for Kribensis.

His trainer comes hurrying out with that old brown overcoat we know so well. He goes to the edge of the ramp and ponders its steepness.

The horse appears looking reassuringly healthy. Both hind legs are heavily bandaged and only a trace of blood on the near-hind heel shows where the vet has had to work. Kribensis pauses and then potters up gamely. That will have to be his victory today.

Dave Baxter heaves up the ramp and prepares to drive the 160-mile slog to Newmarket. In the next few months he will be shipping all sorts of unpronounceable would-be wonder horses to the great competitions on the Flat. But before he swings up into the cab he looks a last time at the four-legged images of hope and failure clopping past, and adds a tribute for all of us.

"You know," says Dave, "I love 'em. Those jumping horses."

12 March 1992

Eddery's 200: relief came with the victory

With typical single-mindedness, Pat Eddery said early in the 1990 season that he wanted to climb the 200-winner 'mountain'. Typically, he did just that and his feat was reported on from Chepstow and marked by an appreciation, reprinted overleaf, of the great jockey

by J. A. McGRATH

PAT EDDERY rode into the record books at Chepstow yesterday, gaining the elusive winner he required to enter racing's exclusive '200 Club'. He became the first Flat jockey to complete a double-century since Sir Gordon Richards, who achieved the feat for the 12th and last time in 1952, the year the Irishman was born.

The 200 was as good as in the bag when Eddery made his final move on the Michael Jarvis-trained Miranda Jay just over two furlongs out in the Offa's Dyke Maiden Fillies' Stakes. Moving up on the outside, Miranda Jay gained the upper hand below the distance and kept going to the line to score by a length from Lara's Baby, with Sharp Dream one and a half lengths back in third.

Cheers erupted from a good-sized Chepstow crowd as Eddery crossed the line in front, and then they dashed to the unsaddling enclosure to welcome back the jockey who had just joined greats such as Fred Archer and Gordon Richards with this remarkable achievement. After acknowledging the crowd, photographers and television cameramen, Eddery turned to reporters and admitted: "It's a great relief to get the 200. I'm really chuffed."

Eddery, who has been in cracking form right throughout a memorable season, loomed into the 200 reckoning with a brilliant five-timer at York two weeks ago, but, apart from a treble at Redcar last week, the winners had come in dribs and drabs.

Clearly the task of getting the requisite winners had never worried the Irishman, who before racing had been more concerned with travel plans to Japan and Hong Kong during the winter than gaining the one winner he needed for a place in racing history.

"I first gave myself a chance of getting the 200 when I found myself 28 ahead of schedule at the Goodwood meeting," Eddery recalled, "but you've got to get through the second half of the season."

This he did with ruthless efficiency, in a season thankfully free from injury and minimal interference due to suspension. "You've got to work hard, doing two a day, and you've got to keep going right to the end," was the way Eddery summed up the path to the 200.

There has been an optimistic undercurrent running through the Eddery camp this season, but the confidence of reaching the double-century, achieved at a strike-rate of 24 per cent, has never become obvious until the past six weeks. The bookmakers stopped taking bets on his achieving the milestone after he completed a four-timer at Sandown in mid-September. For Eddery, though, there was a different marker. "I thought I had a real chance when I got that five-timer at York two weeks ago," he said.

Eddery's achievement is a great triumph for himself and his family, but could also be viewed as a wonderful triumph for the late Frenchie Nicholson, Eddery's boss in Britain after he crossed the Irish Sea after starting in racing with Seamus McGrath. "The guv'nor would have been proud," Eddery said. "Mrs Nicholson is here today."

Eddery is now heading for his eighth jockeys' title and vows that he will continue to the very end of the turf season. Asked how many he thought he might end up with, Eddery replied: "We haven't got much left now, I'll just keep going."

The reaction in the weighing room was enthusiastic and seemed to cap what has been a memorable season for jockeys in the limelight.

Brian Rouse, a long-time weighing room colleague, said: "I think it's great for Pat, and it's great for racing that he's ridden the 200. He's worked terribly hard and he thoroughly deserves the success." Richard Quinn was equally warm in offering his congratulations. "I think it's great that he's done it. Above all, it shows that it can be done in this day and age."

Rodger Farrant, clerk of the course at Chepstow, which has staged two events to attract national media attention in the past eight days, the other being Lester Piggott's first winners since his comeback, said: "I think it's marvellous that these sort of occasions keep occurring at our racecourse. Perhaps we should get a car bumper sticker printed with the slogan: 'Jockeys do it at Chepstow'!"

□ *Continued overleaf*

Pat set himself a target and went for it

by J. A. McGRATH

PAT EDDERY'S remarkable achievement in riding 200 winners in a British season is unlikely to extinguish the fires of ambition that rage deep within one of racing's most persistent and durable competitors.

The 200-barrier was there to be broken, and 38-year-old Eddery let his friends know very early in the year that this was another 'mountain' he was determined to conquer. All he needed, so he believed, was a season free of injury and suspension, and for the winners to keep flowing regularly. A winner a day was always the target. A double, a treble or four-timer were all treated as welcome bonuses along the way.

No-one since Gordon Richards in 1952 had ridden 200 winners in a domestic Flat season and, frankly, it should be acknowledged that achieving such a total is no pushover, no matter how brilliant the rider, or the stables for which he is riding.

The year 1990 will long be looked back on by Eddery with supreme satisfaction. Not only did he see his dream of the 200 come to fruition, he also won the Derby on Quest For Fame, and the French equivalent on Sanglamore, both colts sent out by first-season trainer Roger Charlton and carrying the colours of Prince Khalid Abdullah.

It must be remembered that Abdullah has become the trend-setter in jockey arrangements. Quickly realising that the services of the best jockey available are imperative when the Classics and major races come around, he sought and secured Eddery's services on contract for an undisclosed figure. It does not take much imagination to come to the conclusion that Eddery is among the highest-paid sportsmen in Britain. And when he wins a Classic on an Abdullah-owned horse, he is merely vindicating the owner's decision to retain him. Now it has become commonplace for the leading owners to retain jockeys.

Although Eddery's eyes have always been on the 200, his determination was doubled when he recorded his fastest 100 in a season on Singing on 27 June at Kempton Park. "I'm all out to get the 200 this time, and I don't care if I have to keep going to the very last day."

It is to his credit that he has reached the figure with time to spare, although he says he will ride at Folkestone on the last day of the turf programme.

Always destined to be a jockey, Eddery started in racing at the stables of Seamus McGrath in Ireland before joining Frenchie Nicholson, the renowned tutor of top-class riders, at Cheltenham in 1967. Even in those days all he wanted was to ride winners, which he did for the first time on Alvaro at Epsom in 1969.

His first major job in racing came when, fresh from his highly-successful days as an apprentice, he was snapped up by Peter Walwyn, thus adding impetus to the yard's domination during the golden era of Seven Barrows in the 1970s. These were days of Grundy, winner of the Derby and the race many still believe to be the 'Race of the Century', the 1975 King George VI and Queen Elizabeth Stakes, in which the Walwyn colt defeated Bustino after an epic battle.

Next for Eddery came the Ballydoyle years, during which the Irishman joined Vincent O'Brien, and the then leading owner, Robert Sangster, for an attack on the major races that made them the most formidable combination of their time. El Gran Senor, Lomond, Sadler's Wells and Law Society were just four stars during a magical era for Ballydoyle and its followers.

If El Gran Senor is considered an equine symbol for Eddery's association with Ballydoyle, Dancing Brave held the same status with the Abdullah outfit. The son of Lyphard, on whom Eddery won both the King George and the Prix de l'Arc de Triomphe, is the best colt so far to carry the Abdullah colours.

Eddery's retainer with Abdullah commenced in 1987, the year following the 'Dancing Brave season' and the winners have continued rolling since. The retainer is now well into a second three-year period.

Eddery, fit and determined, is as tough an opponent – and as skilful – as any jockey could ever come up against. Although he does not envisage a career lasting as long as Lester Piggott's, Pat Eddery is certain to be at the top for many years to come.

24 October 1990

PS. Pat Eddery finished the 1990 season with 209 winners.

Pat Eddery's eyes were always on the 200 and, at Chepstow, his toughess and his skill finally brought him to the coveted jockeys' goal.

The man who knew glory more than most

The Flat-race triumphs of Vincent O'Brien are legendary, but his career as a trainer of jumpers in his earlier days was equally amazing and successful

by PAUL HAIGH

VINCENT O'BRIEN has been nervous this week. We had his word for it at Ballydoyle on Tuesday. For those who have spent some or all of the past 40 years admiring his apparent sang-froid, through victory and the occasional defeat, it may be disconcerting to hear that the thought of having to say a few words in public makes him close his eyes with fear.

This time he knows he'll have to say something when today at Leopardstown he presents the trophy for the Vincent O'Brien Irish Gold Cup, Ireland's most valuable steeplechase. And it doesn't make any difference to him that the race bears his name or that he's contributed £25,000 himself towards its £75,000 prize money. It doesn't make any difference

that his audience will be entirely sympathetic. At 71 he is still the very private man he was when he began to train after briefly considering opening a butcher's shop in Buttevant, and the idea of making even a short speech appals him. Those of us who think we can imagine what it would be like to be a national hero – a role O'Brien fulfils – find it a bit harder to work out what it would be like to be a hero embarrassed by public attention.

In 1953 Early Mist became the first of O'Brien's three consecutive Grand National winners – no, of course no-one else has done it before or since. And it provides an appropriate reminder, as the day of the second running of 'his' race at Leopardstown approaches, that before he became the world's greatest trainer on the Flat he was the world's greatest trainer over jumps.

It is a truth that six Derbys, three Arcs, three King Georges and every English and Irish Classic might have obscured the fact that no-one, not even Michael Dickinson, has a record to touch the one O'Brien built between 1948 and his withdrawal to the Flat at the end of the 1950s. O'Brien remembers those days now as though they were part of another world, although he isn't one of those who believe jumping and the Flat are two different sports. Nor is there any sentimental nostalgia about the days before he made his business-like transition.

"After the war," he recalled quietly as the wind raged silently on the other side of his windows, "Irish farming was very seriously depressed. My father, who was a farmer and also trained, died in 1943. He'd had two families. I was part of his second and there was no way in which the farm could have supported us all. Fortunately for me, my eldest half-brother, who inherited it, had no interest in horses and so I was able to rent the yard and the gallops which my father had used."

It was another world. He started off with £4 he got from the sale of a greyhound bitch he'd bred, which he put on a 10-1 winner. "And," he says, "in those days because the market was so depressed you could buy five good horses for £100."

He explains that "betting was entirely responsible" for the development of his enterprise. "Because the people I began to train for were betting people. Fortunately I was successful," he says with the sort of careful understatement for which he is also famous. In fact, by the end of the 1940s he was winning, as his betting book proves, around £5,000 a year which was then worth about 20 times what it is now.

One prodigious bet in particular set him on the road. It was made not by him but by his first owner, Frank Vickerman, on the Irish Cambridgeshire/Irish Cesarewitch double. Vickerman bet £10 each-way and had £2 each-way for his trainer at 800-1. O'Brien produced one of the horses, Drybob, to dead-heat in the Cambridgeshire and the other, Good Days, to win.

"Oh, I did enjoy the gambling," he agrees now, "but it was a great strain you know. My career depended on it absolutely." Racing history depended on it. The money Frank Vickerman won on that momentous double bought Cottage Rake, one of O'Brien's first intake of half a dozen jumpers and the horse who was to win him three consecutive Gold Cups.

Cottage Rake who, as a six-year-old in 1945, was running wild in a bog having had only one bumper race, was one of the greatest, though not the first, example of O'Brien's staggering ability as a trainer and a judge. Hatton's Grace, who came to him as an eight-year-old and whom he improved out of all recognition to win three consecutive Champion Hurdles, was another.

By the time Early Mist got his civic reception in Dublin after his Aintree excursion, O'Brien had won four Gold Cups, three Champion Hurdles, the Grand National and the Irish Grand National besides various big Flat handicaps, many of them with his jumping horses. That summer he would also win his first Irish Derby with Chamier, the beginning of the process which would convert him from jump racing's most important participant into "just a fan and a follower of form".

What is his own explanation for what he was able to do then and has been able to do since? It's evidently not the first time he's been asked the question but, not surprisingly perhaps, he has no pat answer to satisfy the curiosity. "I would say hard work and attention to what I was doing. Making no mistakes in any direction. And I suppose I must have had a flair for it, too." Like Mozart "had a flair" for the piano.

There have been many results of that flair: like the emergence of Northern Dancer, like Ballydoyle itself and the shift in the whole balance of Flat racing back towards Europe, which Ballydoyle more than any other stable has done most to promote. Huge wealth and fame for O'Brien have been other results. And another – less direct – has been that for the past week he's been sitting at Ballydoyle worrying that somehow he's going to commit a faux pas when he presents his trophy.

13 February 1988

Opposite page, left: O'Brien, in 1977, a trainer who proved to be a genius both at the jumps and the Flat.

Opposite page, right: Hatton's Grace, the winner of the Champion Hurdle in 1949, 1950 and 1951.

Above: Cottage Rake won the Cheltenham Gold Cup in 1948, 1949 and 1950.

Bonanza Boy's run to glory in the mud

The 1989 Racing Post Chase produced one of the sport's most memorable moments, a victory fashioned out of will and heart by Peter Scudamore and a courageous horse

by DUDLEY DOUST

WHENEVER I think of Scudamore's sensational win on Bonanza Boy in the Racing Post Chase, achieved in what appeared to be sucking mud around the tight corners of Kempton Park, I think of an American basketball player named Bill Bradley. Bradley, a former Rhodes Scholar at Oxford, now a US Senator, and quite possibly the next President of the United States, once spoke of his game in The New Yorker.

"When you have played basketball for a while, you don't need to look at the basket," said Bradley, who for years shone first for Princeton and later for the New York Knicks professional team. "You know where it is. You develop a sense of where you are."

On 25 February 1989, Scudamore knew where he was for every one of the 386 seconds of what, by common consent, was his most memorable and dogged riding performance of the 1988-89 season. Later, Scudamore was quick to point out that his victory that day was more a tribute to workmanlike slogging than to finesse but, apart from that, he agreed with the American basketball player.

"I can see exactly what he means and, like he says, it comes with practice," Scudamore said. "Horseracing is different from basketball, obviously, in that every course I ride is slightly different from the next. Yet there are certain points, differing from course to course, where you can sense your position and know if you can still win."

Kempton Park is flat, the turns sharp. "It's a difficult track to come from behind on," said Peter, "you can't easily make up the ground. There are two points in a three-mile chase at Kempton where I can sense my position. You've got to be in some sort of

reasonable spot as you pass the two-and-a-half-mile gate at the beginning of the back straight. Again at the fourth last, because it's not a very long straight and the horses don't come back to you a lot."

Scudamore laughed, considering his much-acclaimed ride: "Things went wrong. I didn't ride a brilliant race because I was meant to be up there in front and I couldn't be. So I had to make the best of a bad situation."

What happened was this:

Heavy rain had fallen the previous day, presumably enhancing the strong little gelding's chances, but there were other factors that unsettled the jockey. Walking the track, Scudamore felt the soft ground would still be too fast for the horse. There Is soft and soft on racetracks.

"Soft around Kempton," Scudamore said, "isn't the same as soft around Chepstow." The going had been soft at Chepstow on 27 December, when Bonanza Boy, responding to extensive schooling from Scudamore, smashed some classy opposition to win the Welsh Grand National, a three-miles-six-furlongs haul, by a dozen lengths. Scu would have liked a longer distance than the mere three miles presented at Kempton.

More worryingly, Bonanza Boy had fallen heavily at Ascot 17 days earlier, and Scudamore had assumed much of the blame. "I was rushing him along at a downhill fence," said Peter, "and he hit the top and really bowled over himself. I was afraid the fall might have frightened him because last year, when he hit fences, it all became too much for him. We had to school him back over hurdles."

And finally, Scudamore felt there were too many front-runners in the 12-horse Kempton field for his liking. If he lined up on the inside, horses like Seagram and Cuddy Dale would squeeze out Bonanza Boy – no speed merchant – and Scu would have to hitch up and drop in behind them. Straightaway he'd lose a half-dozen lengths.

"It would be like coming down the M5 and hitting a traffic jam," was the way he put it much later, watching videotapes of the race. "So I decided it was better going down the A40, which is farther, but a smoother, uncluttered run."

So, his thinking was made up of a complex set of components. Scudamore lined up on the middle-inner and set off hoping to go wider before dropping on to the inside rail. Bonanza Boy jumped the first fence well: one problem met. Scudamore kept him in the middle, but at considerable cost for, when he cleared the next obstacle, the first open ditch, he had fallen far behind. In fact, Scudamore was dead last and as he swung through the immediate right-hander towards the back straight he felt briefly: "No chance, I'm going backwards.

☐ *Continued overleaf*

□ Continued from previous page

"What worried me was that I was behind the joint-favourite, Bishops Yarn," he said, referring to a good heavy-weather horse with a reputed finishing pace. "I wouldn't be able to accelerate around him. I was not having the clearest, easiest run. I was going to get chopped off."

Deep down, Peter none the less enjoyed a glimmer of hope. The field was going at too quick a gallop for the ground. The quick pace would, he knew, allow his durable stayer to stick with it in the end. "If we'd got off at a slow pace," he said later, "I'd have had no chance whatever. Not from out at the back. As it was, the others were going to stop at some stage. The question was whether I could hang in there long enough to take advantage of it. I didn't want to leave too much to do."

Going past the stands, about halfway through the race, Scudamore was off the television screen: his exact place in the field was open to debate. Was he 20 or 30 lengths off the pace being set by the young Irishman, Conor O'Dwyer, on Cuddy Dale? "At that point I'm still thinking negative," Scudamore said, and added illogically: "But I'm still very hopeful." Bonanza Boy's trainer, Martin Pipe, said he'd given up hope, back in the stands, at that stage: "I wouldn't have been at all surprised if Peter had pulled him up."

Scudamore had no such notion: "I've been farther back than that and won. I've fallen off and won." Furthermore he, like Bradley the basketball player, was experienced enough to have a sense of where he was. He was, in fact, now moving for the second time towards the open ditch and the sharp right-hander into the back straight. "I wasn't watching the whole field. My eye was on Bishops Yarn. He had a good chance. He was my marker. I could sense the other horses getting tired."

Bonanza Boy passed a clump of four or five horses as they went under the two-and-a-half-mile gate the second time. This, as Scudamore had said, was the first crucial point to take stock of where you are at Kempton. His heart leapt. "Four are in front of me," he said to himself. "Way out in front. But they can be taken. They're back-pedalling."

Scudamore now knew the horses ahead of him: Cuddy Dale, Gainsay, Ballyhane and, nearest to him, Seagram. "I know Gainsay," he thought. "I can have him." He reckoned that at least one of the other three would tire; they had started to race too early. That left him to drive for the third spot. Bonanza Boy, supremely economical, stayed on the rail and, as the horses passed the fifth from home, Gainsay took over the lead from Cuddy Dale.

Ten lengths adrift, Bonanza Boy pounded down towards that crucial fourth-from-home fence. "I remember thinking, if I jump the last fence on the back straight well, really well, I'll win this race." He didn't jump it well. Shit! "Then I looked up, and I hadn't lost any ground." Seagram, in fact, was coming back to him.

Scudamore swung off the rail to overtake Seagram and immediately went back to the rail. On the bend, the other three horses swung wide, but not Bonanza Boy ("They're not as handy as my little horse") and, hugging the rail, the bay gelding hit a good patch of ground and, in a few bounds, made up three or four lengths on Gainsay, Cuddy Dale and Ballyhane. "I knew I could beat Ballyhane. That kept me going."

Bonanza Boy's head was by now stuck out. Scudamore was aware of it: "What a fighting horse. He was determined to get up that rail. It was his guide. He was tired and it was keeping him straight. All he had to do was concentrate on keeping his legs going. He was really trying for me, but he wasn't getting anywhere."

Bonanza Boy was still in fourth spot at the second last. "He has a job to stand off," Scudamore remembered, in his excitement switching the tense of his narrative to the present. "All he can do is get popping and running, and every time he gets running a fence comes in his way and it slows him down. He's still third, still third over the last, still third."

Ballyhane came back, apparently beaten.

Into the last, Cuddy Dale was toiling hard and, from either side Gainsay and Bonanza Boy mounted their attacks. Over the fence, and Scudamore's horse, wobbling, battled for the lead. His head was out, the rail by his side. It now was a two-horse race. "When he gets to Gainsay he runs more because he's got even more hope," said Scudamore, picking up the story. "He's got this surge of confidence which is inexplicable. He's quickened up again when he's got no more to give."

He gave it. Bonanza Boy, gathering his last gasps of willpower, driven on under Scudamore's stick, got his nose in front some 60 yards from home. Stretching, heaving, he was there to stay. A stride back, Gainsay fought off a final challenge from Ballyhane. The race, though, was over. Bonanza Boy had swept past the post.

In the winner's enclosure, the gallant, mud-spattered gelding appeared to waver on his legs, exhausted. Then his head went up, his ears forward, responding to the cheers ringing round him. Within the hour, according to his stable lass, Donna Cornforth, he was ready to run again. Scudamore, reflecting much later on the famous run, picked the key moment of the race: "The sharpest point of that bend was the crucial point. That's where we won."

"That," said Pipe, "was the best race I've seen for a long, long time."

24 February 1990

Tales of derring-do in racing's back row

Racing focuses, naturally, on the great but hidden in little corners are some equally inspiring stories, like Lord Lickspittle's of The Charge of The Light Brigade

by BROUGH SCOTT

LET us now praise famous men. No doubt there were plenty at Ascot but the only time this one has ever worn a top hat was when he played Lord Lickspittle in The Charge of The Light Brigade. He's called Michael Dillon.

Mick Dillon has been jump jockey, stunt man, film extra, and is now the oldest operating stalls handler. He was 65 on Saturday but was working at Ascot every day. He loaded up Lester before The Maestro won the King Edward VII on Saddlers' Hall. Their combined ages were 122. It keeps you young.

In Mick's case only until Lingfield on 29 June. For reasons of insurance and creaking arthritis, Dillon will hang up his helmet and something new will have to be found for one of the most cheerful spirits in the game. At a time when racing is into paroxysms of self-doubt, it's worth wandering down to the stalls and remembering how a real survivor works.

Young Mick first rode out at Epsom when his father was head lad to Bobby Dick in 1936; the stables are now a police academy. He did 5st 11lb on the Flat at Nottingham in 1941. He joined the Air Force with Fred Winter but was never any threat to him in a jumping career which drifted on to 1961. "I was a very poor pilot," he says with that strong South London laugh, "just a few winners."

Not moderate in life, though. Starting with a Norman Wisdom film called Just My Luck, Mick got an Equity card and began other games. An Oscar never threatened, but if a director needed somebody to play an authentic equestrian scene, as likely as not it would be Mick who would be togged up for action. The dialogue rarely stretched further than

"whoa there my beauty" but you knew that they knew that he knew what he was doing.

If you go down to the video library you can find him in all sorts of things from Tom Jones to The Belstone Fox. More surprisingly, doubling for an ailing Buster Keaton in A Funny Thing Happened On The Way To The Forum, and more painfully as an Italian motor mechanic in Chitty Chitty Bang Bang. His car capsized in a stunt down the side of Box Hill. "Broke my skull," recalls Mick.

But for the past 15 years it has been the starting stalls, and in particular Peter Hickling's wonderfully well run southern team, which has been Dillon's permanent casting. A splendid lady called Dorothy Brandon is now organising a presentation to mark Mick's going.

If she wasn't of a certain age and so obviously respectable, you would call Dorothy a starting stalls groupie, organising picnics at Goodwood, talking about "my boys", sending cards at Christmas. But while we can all get a bit dewy-eyed about these things there is still something magnificently old-school English about Mrs Brandon's insistence that it's the unsung loaders who deserve our attention.

At Sandown on Saturday the other end of the races belonged to Darryll Holland. He had been 19 on Friday. The winners are coming thick and fast. He has got the winning feeling and it shows. He was happy to tell us so for the TV interview.

At this stage the very top of the mountain is possible for the carpenter's son from Manchester. But Monday's news that Darryll was taken faint from wasting was a reminder of just one of the hazards.

Whatever happens, he should vow never to lose the good humour of the men who link arms behind his horses' backsides today. It's a grand life while it's lasting but one wrong move can threaten it.

Ten years ago this April, Mick Dillon led a sprinter of Bob Turnell's called Winsor Boy into the stalls at Epsom. "Lester was on it," said Mick, "he was second last to go in. The thing that Greville Starkey was riding came in, then backed out again. Then, *whoosh*, Lester's horse had gone down underneath, with him on it. His skull was pinned, I thought he was a goner."

You will remember that it was just one week later that a temple-swathed, pain-killed Piggott won the 1,000 Guineas on Fairy Footsteps and all but expired in the weighing room afterwards. The 'Legend of Lester's Ear' was added to all the rest.

A decade on, The Long Man's saga goes into ever more extraordinary chapters. At Lingfield next Saturday evening another, rather less trumpeted, story will be over. No top hats maybe but Mick Dillon and his mates deserve a re-write of Milton:

"They also serve who only stand and shove."

20 June 1991

Mr Frisk makes a dream come true

In 1990, the Grand National produced an amazing coup for Racing Post. The winning jockey was one of its own writers, who since childhood had merely dreamed

by MARCUS ARMYTAGE

AM I dreaming, only to wake up in the morning? Other people win the Grand National, don't they?

A journalist never had a more inspiring experience about which to write and yet I can't find the words to describe how I felt as I crossed the line three-quarters of a length in front, how I felt going back to the winner's enclosure escorted by four police horses between cheering crowds, how I felt being carried by two burly policemen to weigh in. I swear my feet never touched the ground.

By the time I left Aintree at six o'clock it was only the hurt in my cheeks from the constant broad smile that convinced me this dream I had had since I was a child has indeed come true. And stuck in the traffic jam, I remembered the days when, as a little boy, I used to watch the race on television and practised falling off the arm of the sofa as if I had landed too steep over Becher's.

But Saturday was one of the rare days when nothing went wrong, one day when, for a change, everything went according to plan. If we were ever going to win a National with Mr Frisk, it was on Saturday. He had the ground and the weight, he was fresh and well. I had known for some time that this would be my greatest chance of achieving what I was convinced was only a dream.

There were three things we reckoned we had to overcome to win this National, provided Mr Frisk enjoyed himself. First, there was the parade. It was quite on the cards he would boil over, find the whole thing too exciting and, by the time we were running to the first, his eyes would be popping out of his head.

The next mountain to overcome was going to be that first jump. Too many of his flamboyant type have given this fence too much air and knuckled over on landing.

Third, the long run-in. I had had visions all week of it being a repeat of the Hennessy, doing all the donkey work only to be overtaken for lack of pace at the elbow. I wouldn't have been the first to have encountered the disappointment of that cruel long run-in.

The main plan therefore hinged on the successful negotiation of the first, somewhere towards the middle-to-outer, and to settle into a good rhythm. He always likes to run handy in his races although actually making the running is not essential.

The parade went well. Mr Frisk was black with

sweat, but once we were in racecard order and walking down past the stands, I could tell he was enjoying himself. Rachel, his girl, has a soporific effect on this horse, and I think it was probably her being there at his head that kept him calm. I said to her I thought he was beginning to enjoy the parade. She agreed, but I'm not sure we weren't just trying to calm and con ourselves about him.

We turned to canter to the start and Mr Frisk lobbed off on a loose rein, another good sign.

My own nerves at this stage were all right. I was almost disappointed that it was all to be over so soon, so convinced was I of being claimed a victim at the first fence.

We met Rachel back at the start and she again took charge. A quick girth check, Polyfemus reshod,

Lorcan Wyer's tack reassembled – he had arrived upsides me to look at the first with his girth undone. Much quicker than I thought, it was time to be called in.

Kim had told me not to line up next to Pukka Major and I found myself next to a grey. It was actually Star's Delight but with so much else to think about I just assumed it was Pukka Major. That would warrant a bollocking before we had even started, I thought. But it was too late to alter our position.

We were off, Mr Frisk just standing for half a sec-

□ *Continued overleaf*

Mr Frisk and Marcus Armytage (right) just have the edge over the hard-at-work Chris Grant and Durham Edition in the run-in for the 1990 National.

□ *Continued from previous page*

ond as the tapes went up. When I rode in the National before, I remember the roar of the crowd. I was on a no-hoper then, out to enjoy myself and take it all in. On Saturday my mind was focused on other things. I heard no roar, just the rushing of the wind and sound of galloping hooves.

The two horses either side of me were both about a length in front crossing the Melling Road. There was enough of a gap between them but not too much daylight. An ideal situation.

We went in on a long stride to the first. Not really the plan, I had hoped we would get close to the boards. It is in my nature to kick if I have a good, inviting long stride at a fence. So, somewhat recklessly, I agreed with Mr Frisk about meeting this fence on a long one and asked him up. It was advice I had been given just before the race by Graham Thorner. Treat every fence you're worried about as if it was normal, he had said, and that is what I had done.

Mr Frisk landed way out the other side, I sat back, legs locked, let him have about a yard of rein and prayed. His head came up and we kept running. In the relief of the moment, I dropped the reins but we were on our way. The slight drop had not bothered him and I knew now he had the scope to attack the fences and not just pop away at them. It was going to be a handy fact to know later on.

The second came and went, no problem although again my reins got in a tangle when I went to gather them up. I had not quite got into my own rhythm over a fence yet. The first ditch we met spot on. I had wanted to jump this well to give Mr Frisk an ounce more confidence and, by now, I had the reins sorted on landing.

Having got this far and settled down I began to take in more of what was going on about me. I think by this stage we had outjumped my two leads. I was in front of those around me. To my inside I could recognise Hywel Davies's style on Uncle Merlin. Mr Frisk was going well within himself now. I hadn't thought we were going that fast, a normal National gallop. At either the fourth or fifth we got a little close and Mr Frisk rapped himself behind. I hadn't wanted him to do it but in hindsight it was probably a good thing.

We were now on our way to Becher's, still steering towards the outside, I had only Uncle Merlin within my sights. Having swung wider to the right we followed him to the left meeting the fence about right. This was the sixth time I had jumped the fence but never had I ridden anything to make less of it. I don't think Mr Frisk even nodded.

We were both beginning to enjoy ourselves now. The gallop being set by Hywel was sorting us out. Going to the trappy seventh I had just Uncle Merlin

and Polyfemus in front of me. Little did I know these would be the last two horses I was to see in the race until the elbow.

A good rhythm is hard to maintain over the small seventh and the Canal Turn. You're turning all the way from Becher's and concentrating more on that than the actual jumping. We got close to the Canal Turn, but were carried round by the two in front.

Now we had a good straight line of fences to get back into this all-important rhythm. One, two, three and up, over Valentine's and on. I lost count of which fence was which at this stage, but at one, Uncle Merlin jumped across us.

It was not a worry and at the next, Mr Frisk made his only mistake. This was our only disagreement about taking off. I wanted to go long. I thought I had seen a not unreasonable long one, but Mr Frisk disagreed, put down and hit the fence very hard. It was lucky that I had not put him on the deck. It did nothing to dent his confidence, but had virtually destroyed mine.

All had gone well until now and I had made a fundamental error of judgment. We had jumped quite left-handed when impeded at the fence before.

The rhythm had gone temporarily, and my mind was full of negative thoughts. When we fall, I was beginning to say to myself, I have at least enjoyed myself and shouldn't be disappointed.

We pinged the next ditch, though, and we were back in business. Positive thoughts again. Polyfemus was still with us here. I had no idea where or what was behind us. There was not a lot of noise. If you're in the bunch, you hear the rattle of the stakes inside the fences banging off each other. Out, gloriously, in front, it's quiet.

Mr Frisk was going like a dream again as we swung round the bend towards the next two and

□ Continued overleaf

Before Marcus Armytage "knew it", he had jumped the last ditch (picture, opposite page) and the third-last fence (picture, this page) with Mr Frisk. Now, for a few strides, Mr Frisk took a deep breath, and Armytage thought "I might have overdone it . . . I was waiting for a bunch of about four to join us and ruin our day. Soon after thoughts of victory began to cross his mind. "Where are the others?" he kept asking himself.

□ *Continued from previous page*

The Chair. I was full of confidence again, brimming with it, determined to make the best of it. If nothing else I would be able to dine off the fact that I had led the field to The Chair.

Jumping well we were landing upside Hywel. "Don't go any faster," he said. I had no intention. I wanted a lead off him and he wanted a lead too, and several times he mentioned it. When Mr Frisk did join him in front, both horses took hold of their bridles and started racing. Neither of us wanted that so I was happy taking a pull.

My blood was now up, the bit between my teeth. The Chair and the water came and went and I could now think about riding some sort of race although victory never crossed my mind.

Hywel, I could see, was in an inspired mood, riding with tremendous determination, and Uncle Merlin was travelling very sweetly. At one stage going towards Becher's, he had gone three lengths clear without moving on the horse. I just didn't want to lose touch of him.

When I walked the course on Friday I had said to someone that I would love a lead to Becher's second time, for my lead to fall, leaving me in front. I know you shouldn't wish horses to fall, but leading over the fence on the second circuit has undone so many potential winners and it did again. Approaching it I switched to his outside. I saw Hywel on Uncle Merlin's head as I passed him. He was at the point where getting back in the saddle might almost have been possible. I didn't actually see him go and for all I knew he could have survived.

I was now in front on my own for the first time. This was a new experience for Mr Frisk and going to Foinavon's fence he pricked his ears and began to look about. I had to ride him into the fence. For an awful moment I had visions of him refusing; he was just looking at the crowd. If he was going to be like this from here on in, he would be a hard ride.

We swung out wide to angle the Canal Turn. Here, where in 1982 I had stood and watched Dick Saunders lead over the fence on Grittar, I got the first inkling I might have a fair lead. No-one swore at me as I jumped it at an angle, so I couldn't have carved anyone up.

After the initial excitement of being in front, I was now relaxed, far more so than I could have expected. Mr Frisk was now back in a good rhythm going to Valentine's, switched off and not off the bridle as he had been over the last two. It was now that our rhythm was going to play an important part, just to get us a length over each fence all the way home.

We were both seeing a stride together. I simply had no doubts about jumping round now and nor did Mr Frisk. Before I knew it, I had jumped the last ditch and the third-last. For a few strides at this stage, Mr Frisk had taken a deep breath. I thought then I might have overdone it and I was waiting for a bunch of about four to join us and ruin our day.

I was still able to let him run along in his own time on the long run to the second-last. It didn't seem so long on Mr Frisk and I was able to save petrol all the time. I was never all out on him. We met the second-last well, landed running and, for the first time, thoughts of victory began to cross my mind. Where are the others? I kept asking myself.

Again, we met the last long and landed running. I could hear a horse getting nearer and out of the corner of my eye saw Durham Edition creeping ever closer. I don't think I have remained calmer up a run-in, not even in a selling hurdle.

Something kept telling me I was not in serious danger. Perhaps if I had known at the time it was Chris Grant I would have panicked. I had not planned to hit Mr Frisk at all but I still felt strong enough myself to give him a couple without unbalancing him. I had the rail from the elbow and I knew then that victory was safe. I still had 100 yards to run when I was already in a state of complete disbelief.

And crossing the line, I've never been happier. I wasn't tired – just in a state of shock and a bit out of breath. I still didn't know what I had beaten. It is a feeling that can't be put in words. I think my smile said it all.

Other people win the Grand National, don't they?

9 April 1990

Over the last Mr Frisk landed running. Grand National glory beckoned. Only the challenge from Chris Grant and Durham Edition had to be met.

VICTORY SPRINT: As Seagram clears the final jump, Garrison Savannah is four lengths ahead and . . .

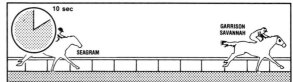

10 seconds later even further in front but . . .

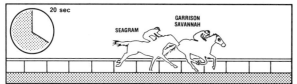

by the time 20 seconds have elapsed Seagram is virtually at the leader's quarters and . . .

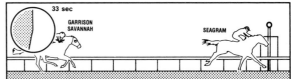

after 30 seconds is ahead, going away easily

The sprint that dashed a dream

SEAGRAM'S victory in the 1991 Grand National was snatched in the final dramatic act of the race, as he hauled back Garrison Savannah in a glorious spurt for the line.

Touching down over the last, four lengths to the good, and to all appearances going away, Graham Dench wrote, Garrison Savannah looked sure to complete the elusive Gold Cup/Grand National double for the first time since the great Golden Miller in 1934. But the final 494 yards takes more than half a minute and can seem an eternity when you have already covered well over four miles in stamina-sapping soft ground, and negotiated 30 of steeplechasing's most formidable obstacles.

Approaching the elbow Garrison Savannah was suddenly in trouble. Meeting the running rail again Garrison Savannah was perhaps still three lengths clear, but horse and rider were both sending out distress signals while the proven stayer, Seagram, was gaining hand over fist. As the race approached its climax Seagram was travelling so much faster that in no time at all he was upsides and going clear so quickly that his rider Nigel Hawke was punching the air in celebration and easing down with fully 60 yards still to go.

Yet Garrison Savannah, approaching the last, had still seemed full of running, and looked to have only to negotiate it safely to land the prize. But outstayed on the long run-in, he was eventually beaten five lengths by Seagram. Auntie Dot was another eight lengths back in third, a gallant effort from one who had never won over further than two and three-quarter miles, and the best placing from a mare since Eyecatcher in 1977. In all, 17 completed the course, slightly more than average for the previous 10 years.

Seagram's winning dash from the last had taken him to the line in just 33.8 seconds – fully 2.8 seconds faster than Garrison Savannah. Mr Frisk had done it in 30.7 seconds in 1990, but that was on fast ground.

8 April 1991

Nigel Hawke's victory salute on Seagram, the 1991 Grand National winner, came with 60 yards still to go, so devastating was his horse's surge.

A victory that lifted the roof for Hern

Never was a victory in the 2,000 Guineas greeted with more jubilation than that of Nashwan in 1989. It seemed as if fate had played a part in dealing out retribution

by PAUL HAYWARD

NASHWAN'S win in record time in the 2,000 Guineas at Newmarket on Saturday has intensified debate surrounding the decision not to renew Dick Hern's tenancy on the Queen's West Ilsley Stables next season. Backed as an outsider down to 3-1 favourite for this, his first race of the season, Nashwan is now firmly established as market leader for the Derby on 7 June. Hern says the horse will not run again before Epsom.

Wins on Friday for Prince Of Dance and Unfuwain, who is currently long-range favourite for the Prix de l'Arc de Triomphe, have increased the chance of Hern being champion trainer in his final year at West Ilsley.

During the winter, Hern, 69, was told by the Queen and her racing manager Lord Carnarvon that William Hastings-Bass would be taking over the yard in the autumn. No official explanation was given but it is widely believed that Hern's ill-health since his hunting accident, which committed him to a wheelchair five years ago, lay behind the move.

With the Derby just four weeks away, the public reception accorded to Hern on Saturday will have greatly increased pressure on the Queen and her advisers to delay the change in tenancy until Hern is ready to retire.

Among the questions raised by Nashwan's win, by a length and half a length over Exbourne and Danehill, was the future of the horse itself. If owner Sheikh Hamdan Al Maktoum should decide to race his Guineas winner as a four-year-old, as he has done with Nashwan's half-brother, Unfuwain, the colt would almost certainly remain with Hern. But at present it is impossible to say where.

What became clear as Hern was warmly greeted on Saturday is that private disquiet over the forthcoming change far exceeds any dissent that has so far been publicly voiced. This uneasiness is apparent among some of the sport's most prominent figures and would draw considerable attention from the outside world if Nashwan were to win the Derby.

Furthermore, it is significant that Hern's two best horses – Nashwan and Unfuwain – are out of Height Of Fashion, the mare sold by the Queen to Hamdan Al Maktoum to help finance the purchase of West Ilsley.

Nashwan provided Hern with his 15th Classic winner and his first in the 2,000 Guineas since Brigadier Gerard in 1971. News of Nashwan's impressive

home work had spread through the bush telegraph, causing his price to contract almost by the day from the 40-1 available a month ago.

Hern, reflecting yesterday on the supreme achievement of saddling a Classic winner without a previous run, said: "I'm pleased to say that he has taken the race very well. He's bright and well in himself and I doubt very much whether he'll run before the Derby."

Asked whether the evidence of the stopwatch had played a big part in assessing Nashwan's progress during the build-up, Hern replied: "It must be a good pointer."

Although bookmakers were bowled over with Derby bets after the race, they were surprisingly content with the result.

The major firms stayed ahead of punters in shortening Nashwan as the reports emerged. Corals' Wally Pyrah explained: "We knew plenty about this horse and, ante-post wise, it is not a bad result for us."

On the Derby front, he added: "There was a deluge of money for Nashwan throughout the rest of Saturday and we had to go 2-1. Pirate Army is 6-1 second-favourite."

Ladbrokes, William Hill and Swift Leisure also go 2-1. City Index are 7-4.

8 May 1989

A moment for racing to savour as Dick Hern welcomes Willie Carson and Nashwan to the winner's enclosure after their victory in the 2,000 Guineas.

'The greatest day in the year'

What the Derby means to people can vary. But even when you talk to such disparate people as the Epsom groundsman and a fan, the enthusiasm is unbounded

by NORMAN HARRIS

Groundsman: SEAMUS BUCKLEY

IF you look for it, you'll see a Land Rover on the course at Tattenham Corner as the big race streams by. It's from there that Seamus Buckley, the head groundsman, always watches anxiously over the Derby. If possible, he'd like to be everywhere – as he is throughout the rest of the day – but when the big race is run he can be only in one place, and he reasons that Tattenham Corner is the place where there's most likely to be a problem.

You might say that it really isn't his problem – not if you think that the head groundsman's job is just to cut the grass. But Buckley's job is much bigger, and it's the responsibility that seems to exercise him more than anything.

"If it's not my problem," he says, "whose problem is it then? Accidents can happen very, very quickly, and one has to be there on hand to make sure that the right people are contacted."

This will be the eighth Derby for former jump jockey Buckley (brother of Pat Buckley), and while they have all gone relatively smoothly, he remains alert to problems. Especially this year, with an exceptionally mild winter followed by the very warm early summer. He's pursued by a double-edged fear: the best three-year-olds in the world being subjected to a jarringly hard surface, or having to gallop on bottomless soft ground. The latter can happen if, having watered the course thoroughly, he is hit by a freak thunderstorm. The desired recipe, therefore, is "sunshine and showers".

"We do our utmost," he says, "to produce perfect Flat-racing ground. In life one is always looking for

perfection . . . But after the Derby you're inevitably looking back and thinking that if you'd cut the grass two days before instead of three it would have been just right, or perhaps you could have risked a bit more water. Or you might have seen a couple of people jumping over a bit of fencing and you wonder why you didn't fix it a bit higher. You always think that you'll get it right next year."

Today, controlling a quarter of a million people will be only one of his concerns.

As he buzzes here and there in his Land Rover he will be paying particular attention to the two-inch coconut matting which covers the four roads that the course crosses – 100 mats in all.

He will be also checking carefully on the gang who tread in the divots that have been cut loose by the early races. Already, three weeks have been spent in putting 60 tons of topsoil, a shovelful at a time, into the myriad of holes left by the Spring Meeting.

"Some people think that what we're talking about is a field with a few rails around it. It's not like that at all. It's 10 or 12 horses, 50 million quid, and the one who goes past the post first is going to be worth about 25 million quid. And if he broke his leg 10 yards from the post because I didn't have a hole filled in, think how that would be . . . "

Not surprisingly, Seamus Buckley says he looks forward to the Derby all year, but he doesn't enjoy Derby Day. He's on a knife edge.

"It psyches me up, I get very sharp. And I'm not normally like this. I'm quite a laid-back person – for 50 weeks of the year."

Enthusiast: JACK REYNOLDS

"FOR 200 years," says Jack Reynolds, "people have been tramping across London to get to the Surrey Downs on Derby Day." He still does his "tramping" by train, even though he now lives in the heart of Essex and goes everywhere else by car.

Every Derby Day he takes the train from London Bridge which gets to Tattenham Corner at 12.20. It is a journey which, in itself, marks the day out as being unique: "When you go to an ordinary race meeting the talk is always of the racing. When you go to the Derby the talk is always of past Derbys." On that train he "grips the atmosphere".

And each year he re-lives the thrill of the first time he emerged from Tattenham Corner station. "You can't see the course, and you almost wonder where all these people are going.

"Ahead of you is a sort of high-rise mound, and as you get to the top of that mound the spectacle suddenly unfolds. Everyone's on the move, the stands are filling up . . . You just gasp at all the colour and the movement."

Next Wednesday Jack Reynolds will be celebrating his 30th consecutive Derby. His first, in 1960, came after he had been going to race meetings for two years. His previous problem, of getting time off from work, ceased to be a problem, because at this time he had no job. He had a memorable first Derby. "The favourite was the French horse Angers," he recalls, "but Lester Piggott, who was on his way up, was the public's choice. He won it by three lengths on St Paddy, and it was magic. And there I was with all this money and thinking, 'This is the greatest day of my life'." Jack is somewhat coy in letting on how much he won that day, fearing it makes him seem mercenary. Persuaded to tell, he says it was "about a grand".

It was a goodly sum of money for a 21-year-old unemployed East Ender – and, moreover, one who had been partially disabled by rheumatism in his teens. His success led him to think he might be able to make a living out of betting.

He certainly made a good stab at it, not working again for several years. Curiously, he started following a trainer in the same way other people follow a football team or a cricketer. Initially he followed Walter Nightingall, who had had a Derby winner, Straight Deal, in 1943, but the stable did not survive the trainer's untimely death in 1968, and Jack Reynolds' luck seemed to go too. He found work with Remploy, who employ disabled people in their 96 factories. More importantly to Jack, Remploy allow him to use his holiday entitlement on various race days.

Almost all of the 29 Derbys Reynolds has seen since that first one have been memorable in some way. "You've got those where you've seen sheer domination, like Shergar in '81 and Slip Anchor in '85. Then you've got the titanic battles – Roberto and Rheingold in '72, Secreto and El Gran Senor in '84. Tremendous, short-head struggles. Then there's the element of gallantry, Henbit struggling home in '80 after cracking a cannon-bone."

But his own pick is, he thinks, "a bit controversial". It is Troy's win in 1979. "None of the other winners had the problems he did. He seemed to have no chance two a half furlongs out, when he was pinned on the rails. Even Carson said he'd given up. Then a chink of light opened and he produced a burst of speed that was breathless. It was like those brilliant football goals they keep showing, or Botham in full cry. Sheer brilliance."

On long winter nights Jack will watch videos of such Derbys. Yet it's not just to watch great horses that he keeps persuading friends and relatives to go with him to the Derby. And when they're there, he wants to know: "Can you feel the experience?"

"The greatest day in the year", as he calls it, ends with a walk to the Fair, for a turn on the helter-skelter and a bowl of jellied eels. Returning to Tattenham Corner station, he ritually stands on top of the high-rise mound and takes a "long-lasting" look down the course. "It's usually been a nice day, the sun's going down, and it's almost like a painting. And you think 'It's another year before I'll be back.' It isn't, in fact. You come back for the Oaks on the Saturday, but then Epsom is totally different. Gone are the great crowds and the atmosphere, and it's just another day's racing."

7 June 1989

Howard's way is the pursuit of a record

Being at the event can be of paramount importance, over-riding pain and perhaps closeness to death. The St Leger is just such a race bestowing glory on its devotees

by TONY MORRIS

"THE fittest horse wins the Guineas, the luckiest horse wins the Derby, but the best horse wins the St Leger." No, I'm not trotting out that old adage because I think it's applicable in 1991; I'm not that daft. In fact, I would go so far as to say that it hasn't been true since 1990.

Nevertheless, there certainly was a time when it had the ring of truth about it more often than not. That's why somebody coined it, around 150 years ago, and that's why it came to be handed down through the generations and to remain current still, though now "a custom more honoured in the breach than in the observance".

Just who it was who first made the remark we shall never know, but we can be sure that its author was a keen St Leger devotee. We also know that the adage dates from the time when the Leger had no keener devotee than the famous Yorkshire landowner and sportsman, Sir Tatton Sykes. If he was not the originator, you can bet your life he concurred with the bloke who was.

It was not that Sir Tatton had anything against the Derby. He went to it twice, on the first occasion (in 1791) actually walking from London to Epsom and back, setting out at four in the morning and reaching home an hour before midnight. But while he had no real objection to the Derby, he did seem to prefer the St Leger. In fact, he liked the race so much, he saw it run on 76 occasions.

He was there when Cowslip won in 1785 and he

At the Breeders' Cup one is corn-fed

Go to the Breeders' Cup and for a journalist it's like being put on the teat. You get food, drink and information until it's coming out of your ears!

by PAUL HAIGH

PEOPLE say you can get Americanised very quickly, but I don't believe it. One of the things you notice is the way people from the press get pampered. This is particularly true if you are a member of the press.

The people who run American racing see the press as the link between them and the customer, and in almost direct contradiction of the principles that guide British racing, they do everything with the customer in mind. So well is the press treated at the Breeders' Cup ("Hey you're not from round here are ya? I can tell. How're y'all likin' our city now?") that if such a thing as a lazy journalist existed, he'd never have to move from his seat; he could write his stories entirely from handouts.

These are provided for him by teams of industrious persons whose duty it is to bring the thoughts of every trainer on every conceivable (and inconceivable) issue and every bit of information about every horse, including some bits you didn't know you wanted. So that the journalist can get down to the important business of digesting the goodies that descend on him like gentle rain, and the even more important business of trying to find a chair big enough for his butt, which, for reasons that escape me, expands like Russia in the 1940s. Only those with iron wills keep drinking in the face of all the free alcohol.

A piece of paper arrives to tell you that Woody Stephens says: "Arazi's run some good races in France . . . but this isn't France," and you write it down, tap it in or shout it down the phone.

When a bulletin advises you that Richard Hannon

was there for Caller Ou's win in 1861. He missed The Marquis's victory in 1862 for the very good reason that he thought he was on his deathbed, but he rallied well and was looking forward to the meeting of '63 when he suffered a relapse and expired, 10 short of his century. The great mystery about Sir Tatton's sequence was how it came to be interrupted in 1839. History records that he missed the epic dead-heat (and re-run) between Charles the Twelfth and Euclid 'because of illness'.

To the best of my knowledge, Sir Tatton's record of 76 St Legers as a spectator still stands. Jack Fairfax-Blakeborough saw Sceptre win in 1902 and was there, I fancy, for Bruni in 1975, but even if he witnessed all the wartime substitute events, run elsewhere, the cancellation in 1939 would have restricted his score to a mere 73. He died in January 1976.

I know people with over 50 Legers to their credit now, but the best bet to overhaul the Sykes record has to be this paper's own Howard Wright. By dint of being Doncaster-born into a family fond of racing, the still-young (well, younger than me) Wright chalked up number 44 on Saturday. The word is, he got so excited when Black Tarquin beat Alycidon, he almost dropped his dummy. In another 20 years he'll be giving up cigarettes and getting down to some serious training for the record.

As for me, I'm still a comparative beginner, but I did have good cause to remember both Sir Tatton Sykes and that old adage last week. You see, the fittest horse (Privy Councillor) did win the Guineas, the luckiest horse (Larkspur) did win the Derby and the best horse (Hethersett) did win the Leger when last I failed to attend the final Classic. What's more, my own sequence was never more seriously threatened than it was last week, when a saner human being would probably have stayed at home.

I rather neatly fended off the suggestion that perhaps I would be better off in hospital, fearful that it might be hard to make my escape from there, so I readily accepted that a week of intensive physiotherapy was appropriate for my condition, while ensuring that 'week' meant Monday to Friday. They can do what they like to me now, put me back on the rack, tear me limb from limb, whatever. At the very least I shall get a right rollocking for doing what was obviously unwise, but at least I got my way over what really mattered.

I'll grant you it wasn't the best Leger I've ever seen, though it unquestionably was a cracking contest, and I've no doubt that the first two are very good horses. But that's not the point; I'd have settled for a duller race than the one I saw.

16 September 1991

---

will not be giving Lester Piggott riding instructions, because "I don't know anything about this [dirt] game, he probably knows more about it than me," you do not doubt. You pass it on to the public.

Some of the best quotes come to you by word of mouth. For example: "Pee-Wee Herman's got more chance of getting invited to the White House than Arazi's got of getting to the rail." (Mr Herman, for those unfamiliar with his work, is a children's entertainer of unusual appearance who was recently arrested for allegedly 'manipulating his genitalia' in a pornographic cinema.) "Mind you," the man adds grimly, "you never know with Bush."

But on the whole you're better off with the bits of paper. Sometimes though you come across one of these and it just makes you wonder. We got one yesterday that told us that John Dunlop, on hearing of Shadayid's No. 1 draw, had said: "I sure would prefer to be in the middle, but she's got plenty of speed, and she can come from behind."

Why did I doubt this? Oh, I don't know. A hunch. Call it a newsman's intuition if you like. So with a dedication to duty that rather surprised me, I finished my chili dog, clam chowder and root beer, and only spilling a few pumpkin fritters and hush puppies, prised myself out of my seat to get confirmation.

It was unorthodox maybe, but – what the hell? –

it paid off. As I thought, the quote was wrong. What Dunlop really said, he told me when I found him chewing gum at his barn with a baseball cap on the wrong way round, was: "No. 1? No sweat. This baby can do it from the front or sit in and burn their asses in the stretch. With Tight Spot and In Excess there ain't gonna be no easy rides, but we still got some gas left even if this is late fall.

"No. 1. Oh yeah. This is exceptionally exceptional. If Willy can break and grab paint I'm gonna be standin' in line at the payout window. If he's sittin' in three or four that'll be okay too. You copy? Orright. Whoo."

So now you read me? Sometimes there's no substitute for the personal touch. You want the stories, you gotta work for them. And you know what? I think the guy could be right. Put a few bucks on In Excess and Tight Spot with those bookies you got in England, then take Shadayid on the *pari mutuel*.

What else can win? Hey, how do I know? This is Breeders' Cup. Anything can take any race. There's no bums here. You want the rest of my Pick 7? Okay. The two and the nine in the first. The one in the second. The 10 in the third. The 10 in the Turf, and the 11 in the Classic.

Okay, happy now? So relax. Enjoy. Have some nachos.

2 November 1991

Munro zooms to Generous triumph

In the 1991 Derby, a streamlined jockey rode with an ice-cold calm and skilful precision to an impressive first victory in the historic Classic

by GRAHAM DENCH

THE instant Alan Munro sent Generous past front-runner Mystiko well over two furlongs from home the 212th Derby was all over bar the shouting. The chestnut quickened clear in a matter of strides and, hard though they tried, Hector Protector, Marju and the rest could do nothing about it.

Powering right away under his ice-cool partner – whose streamlined American riding style is capturing the imagination of both the public and would-be imitators – he scored in a manner reminiscent of the brilliant Nashwan two years ago.

The moment the stalls opened it was clear this was not going to be a Derby for any horse who was in the least bit faint of heart or short on stamina, the 2,000 Guineas winner Mystiko setting a gallop that even Toulon's pacemaker Arokat was never quite able to match.

Munro soon had Generous settled nicely about three lengths off the leaders, racing alongside Piggott on Hokusai, and throughout the race he seemed perfectly placed. Munro had spent time viewing Piggott's Derby videos, and this proved so well spent that one would never have guessed this was only his second ride in the race.

In truth, the pattern of the race changed little until the field straightened up for home, but the hopes of several of the principals were gone long before then. For neither Toulon nor Environment Friend was ever travelling particularly easily and Mystiko, who had handled the preliminaries better than many anticipated, would surely never maintain such a gallop for the full mile and a half.

Rounding Tattenham Corner it was Mystiko still, from Arokat, Generous, Hokusai, Hector Protector and Hailsham. Then came Marju on the rails, with Star of Gdansk and Corrupt to his outside, followed by Environment Friend, Hundra and Toulon. Mujaazif was starting to tail off already, something clearly amiss.

Mystiko started running out of petrol almost as soon as he had straightened up for home, and Generous went past him almost as though he was standing still. From there on it was one-way traffic. Hector Protector and Marju, who enjoyed a lovely run up the rails, tried to go with him. But Marju took a moment or two to get into top gear and Hector Protector's effort was short-lived, his marvellous unbeaten run coming to an end as his stamina ran out.

Generous, given four or five cracks in the last furlong to be sure, passed the post five lengths clear of Marju, who fully redeemed his reputation by pulling a further seven lengths clear of the rest. Star of Gdansk just pipped Hector Protector for third, and then came outsider Hundra, staying on well after being momentarily impeded, and Corrupt, who had no apparent excuse. Hokusai was seventh, the Italian Derby winner Hailsham eighth, Toulon ninth, and Mystiko, allowed to come home in his own time, tenth.

The winning time of 2min 34.00sec, a mere 0.16 outside Kahyasi's electrically-timed record for the race, was not, in itself, exceptional on a day when course records had been broken in both the afternoon's preceding races. But the devastating manner in which Generous dismissed a field which included nine other Group winners will leave a lasting memory and must have sent shivers down the spines of the connections of Suave Dancer, whose opponents in last Sunday's Prix du Jockey-Club paled in comparison.

What a race it will be when the two meet.

6 June 1991

HORSES NUMBERED IN RACECARD ORDER			
1	Arokat *Paul Eddery*	Hundra *Bruce Raymond*	8
2	Corrupt *Cash Asmussen*	Marju *Willie Carson*	9
3	Environment Friend *George Duffield*	Mujaazif *Walter Swinburn*	10
4	Generous *Alan Munro*	Mystiko *Michael Roberts*	11
5	Hailsham *Steve Cauthen*	Star Of Gdansk *Christy Roche*	12
6	Hector Protector *Freddie Head*	Toulon *Pat Eddery*	13
7	Hokusai *Lester Piggott*		

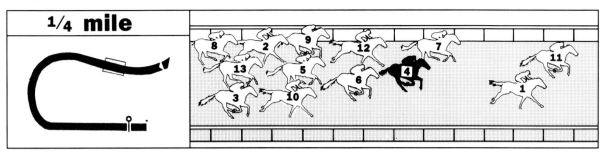

¼ mile

The 2,000 Guineas winner Mystiko (11) leads the intended pacemaker Arokat (1) at a scorching gallop, the pair racing several lengths clear of Lester Piggott's mount Hokusai (7) and the eventual winner Generous (4). The unbeaten Hector Protector (6) and Irish 2,000 Guineas winner Star of Gdansk are nicely placed in mid-field, but Pat Eddery has only Hundra (8) behind him on the Chester Vase winner Toulon (13)

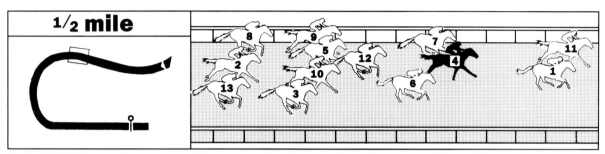

½ mile

Mystiko (11) still holds the call from Arokat (1), who has never quite been able to get to the front. Generous (4) and Hokusai (7) have them nicely in their sights, Munro keeping his mount more or less alongside the Epsom maestro Piggott, in perfect position

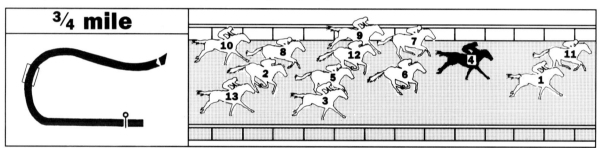

¾ mile

At the top of the hill Mystiko (11) still shades Arokat (1) for the lead, but Generous (4) is a bit closer and the field are starting to bunch up behind. But it is already emerging that neither Toulon (13) nor Environment Friend (3) is going well, and Mujaazif (10) is already back-pedalling.

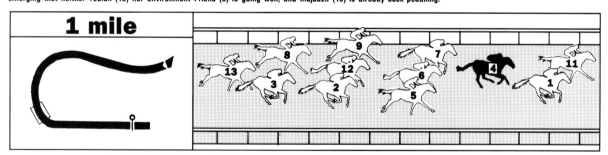

1 mile

It is still just Mystiko (11) from Arokat (1), but Generous (4) is travelling ominously well on their heels and Hokusai (7), Hector Protector (6) and the Italian Derby winner Hailsham (5) are all well placed. The Craven winner Marju (9), who has been tight against the rails throughout, is close enough too

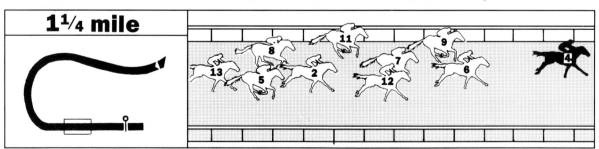

1¼ mile

The pattern has changed completely. Arokat (1) has dropped right out, Mystiko (11) has also run out of petrol and is fast on the retreat, and Generous (4) is now well in command, having quickened clear with an impressive burst of acceleration. Hector Protector (6) is trying hard to go with him, and so is Marju (9), but Generous is fast disappearing beyond recall. The eventual third, Star of Gdansk (12), is sticking on well, but joint-favourite Corrupt (2) is not going to get in a blow and Hailsham (5) and Hokusai (7) are all but done with; Hundra (8) is improving on the rails but is shortly impeded by Hokusai. Toulon (13) is right out of it

Battle for the throne of Europe

After Generous won the 1991 Derby the season was adorned with the subsequent clashes between him and Suave Dancer. Which was Europe's Classic king?

by TONY O'HEHIR

NOW for the older horses. That was the emphatic message Generous delivered at The Curragh yesterday when he swept aside French star Suave Dancer with a convincing three-length win in an Irish Derby which fully lived up to its billing as a clash of champions.

After his brilliant chestnut had become the 11th horse to complete the English-Irish Derby double, trainer Paul Cole hinted strongly that a clash with the older brigade, including stablemate Snurge and yesterday's Grand Prix de Saint-Cloud winner Epervier Bleu, in the King George VI and Queen Elizabeth Diamond Stakes at Ascot, was very much on the cards.

"Such decisions are never made in the winner's enclosure but the plan on paper is to go for the King George," Cole said. Cole was quick to praise Alan Munro's splendid handling of the winner. "Tactically he rode the perfect race. We were afraid the others would want to slow it down to try and beat us, and when there was no pace on he had the intelligence to go on," he said.

After Barry's Run and Nordic Admirer had made the running, Munro decided to step up the tempo over a mile from home and Generous still looked vulnerable as first Sportsworld and then Suave Dancer, who had been tucked in behind, began to close on the downhill run to the straight.

A roar from the stands greeted Sportsworld and Lester Piggott when they moved into second spot five furlongs out, but Vincent O'Brien's colt was done with once they had straightened up and hopes of a home win were denied. Instead the race

worked to script with Suave Dancer, who appeared to be full of running, poised on the outside to tackle Generous as they stretched into the last quarter-mile. Walter Swinburn got Suave Dancer to within three-quarters of a length, but he could then give no more and Generous had all the answers when Munro asked for a greater effort. A further surge of power saw him increase his advantage in the last 100 yards. Star Of Gdansk, 12 lengths behind Generous at Epsom, again finished third, 11 lengths off the winner.

Munro, who has ridden Derby winners in England, Spain and Ireland this year, commented: "That was a better effort than Epsom. He had to do most of it himself today. He acted on the yielding ground but he's better on faster ground. I expected Suave Dancer would get closer to me than he did," he added, "but Mr Cole told me that our horse was in better shape than he was at Epsom and that did a lot for my confidence."

Cole revealed that Generous had done no serious work since his Epsom win and added: "Tommy Jen-

So slick and so very, very Suave

After winning the King George VI and Queen Elizabeth Diamond Stakes Generous went to compete once more with Suave Dancer, in the Arc

by TIM RICHARDS

BRITAIN'S hero Generous curled up like a timid kitten behind Suave Dancer in the Prix de l'Arc de Triomphe at Longchamp. The instant the dual Derby winner faded, John Hammond, Suave Dancer's trainer, knew that his horse was going to produce a famous turbo-charged victory run up the straight. And that is exactly what happened. Suave Dancer, described by his fast-talking Texan jockey Cash Asmussen as a "super-champion", murdered the opposition.

The partnership came home two lengths ahead of the Prix Vermeille winner Magic Night, with Generous only eighth, over nine lengths behind Suave Dancer, whom he had beaten by three lengths in the Irish Derby. Third-placed Pistolet Bleu and St Leger winner Toulon in fourth, completed a clean sweep for French-trained horses.

First home for the British in a bitterly disappointing race was David Elsworth's game filly, In The Groove, who was sixth.

Generous's trainer, Paul Cole, drinking champagne in the gathering gloom of an autumn Paris evening, said: "Alan Munro was swinging off Generous coming into the straight and I thought that's great, they're going to win. But no sooner had the thought crossed my mind than Generous was beaten. It happened in a split-second. He went from winning to running a bad race."

□ *Continued overleaf*

Alan Munro on Generous reacts to the challenge of Walter Swinburn on Suave Dancer in the Irish Derby, and the English-trained colt begins to surge clear.

nings, who rides him at home, deserves a lot of the credit for having the horse the way he is today."

Cole, whose Insan was beaten in a photo-finish by Kahyasi in this race three years ago, was winning his third Classic in Ireland, following Knight's Baroness's Oaks and Ibn Bey's St Leger last year. "What makes Generous so nice to train is that he's a very sound horse. We can keep going forward with him."

Munro, clearly more comfortable at the post-race press conference than he had been at Epsom, again stressed how important his American visits have been in his success story.

"Without going to America I wouldn't have had any of this," he said. "I want to get as much out of the game as I can. And if that sounds greedy I'm sorry." When asked if his ambitions included becoming champion jockey he answered an emphatic "yes".

The time of 2min 33.3sec was the slowest recorded in the race since Tyrnavos won on testing ground in 1980.

1 July 1991

□ *Continued from previous page*

Generous's eclipse was a sad end to what had seemed a perfectly executed plan. The colt had returned fresh and well from a mid-season break and worries about his trip to France had evaporated on Saturday evening after a smooth flight to Paris, after which Generous had settled perfectly happily into his Longchamp stall.

All had seemed well as the horses went to the start, but it was a very different story for Generous as they came back. Pressed for the cause of Generous's defeat, Cole could not be specific. But he reasoned: "Perhaps the ground was softer than he likes, but he was cantering on it until they got to the straight. He does prefer fast going. Maybe it's France. I've brought him here twice and he's run badly both times. I don't know."

Cole's vet James Maine gave the chestnut a thorough check-up after racing and although Maine was blood-testing the colt, connections were playing down any suggestion that the dual Derby winner might have been 'got at'. Cole confirmed that Generous, who has been syndicated for £7.875m, will now be retired to stand at Khalid Abdullah's Banstead Manor Stud in Newmarket.

London-born John Hammond, who with his jockey Cash Asmussen was the hero of the hour, was to be found an hour after the race in the racecourse stables mulling over the greatest moment of his short training career. "Suave Dancer has 150 metres of great, great speed. And I mean great because it really is terrific," said Hammond, 31, who trains at Chantilly. "It all happened very quickly. As Generous appeared to be in trouble I could see that Cash would produce Suave Dancer's great burst. He actually hit the front too soon and Suave Dancer made hard work of it inside the final furlong."

With the signs of Generous's greatness fading, Suave Dancer's stature began to grow with every flowing stride yesterday. As the field hurtled into the straight and Munro started to flex his young arms the distress signals flashed back to the packed stands, the writing was on the wall. A sigh of disbelief went up from the British contingent as it became obvious that Generous was a spent force. The message from Asmussen's motionless poise could not have been more of a contrast; the long-legged Texan oozed confidence.

□ *Continued overleaf*

Top picture: Cash Asmussen rides Suave Dancer imperiously away from Magic Night (noseband) and Pistolet Bleu to land the Prix de l'Arc de Triomphe.

Bottom picture: Suave Dancer and an expansive Cash Asmussen are swamped as they return to the winner's enclosure at Longchamp.

☐ *Continued from previous page*

Five times champion of France, Asmussen had executed his Arc plan with professional precision, even if the race did not turn out exactly as he had anticipated. It was a real family triumph, for his father Keith bought Suave Dancer as a yearling for owner Henri Chalhoub.

The rider said: "I was tracking Snurge, who was not going as well as I had expected, and I found myself further back than I wanted. When we left the false straight I pulled out to have a look at the horses ahead and when I saw they were all struggling I fiddled about on him and gave him 150 metres of fresh air so he could catch his breath. Then when I went to work on him he left them for dead. That must confirm he likes the soft ground and does stay a mile and a half."

Asmussen, who has partnered a host of top-class horses, added with a note of passion in his American tones: "This is the best horse I have ridden."

Munro said: "Turning for home Generous was going as well as in any of his previous races. Then he went as weak as a kitten. It was very disappointing. He had been a bit keen early on but then just fell away to pieces. There should have been more there."

Generous's owner Fahd Salman was most gracious in defeat. "You simply cannot win them all," he said, before dashing off to congratulate Henri Chalhoub. Salman brushed through the big security men around the winner's spot to kiss Chalhoub on both cheeks. After freeing himself from the celebrating winning connections Salman said with pride: "Generous has had a wonderful season and you cannot take that away from him."

7 October 1991

London-born Trainer John Hammond (left) and owner Henri Chalhoub share the satisfaction of Suave Dancer's victory in the Prix de l'Arc de Triomphe.

Taking stock in the glare of Camy's

It may be scruffy but as a place to meet after the Arc and celebrate victory or ruminate on defeat it cannot be beaten, even for the trainer of Suave Dancer

by PAUL HAIGH

JUST across from the main gate at Longchamp there's a sort of lean-to caff made of canvas and a few struts. It's known as Camy's, not because it calls itself anything but just because that's the name of the bloke who runs it.

It sells cheap wine, sausage and chips, and it's lit, after racing, by a single blazing spotlight that makes all its customers who haven't had the luck to get a seat with their back to it blink like suspects under the third degree. It only appears on race days. Its chairs are either foldaways or cold metal stools. Its conveniences are the trees of the Bois de Boulogne. Its few staff are run off their feet and don't mind showing it. It's about as different as you can get from the glittering chic on the other side of the road, and it's become a bit of a post-Arc tradition for those who know about it.

John Hammond came over for a drink there after racing on Sunday. He seemed in a pretty good mood. Understandable, really. I can't think of any other trainer who's gone straight into the top bracket in a year the way he has, or one who's come back so fast from what looked at the time like an almost insuperable setback. When he lost the Wildenstein horses and his (Wildenstein-owned) yard a couple of years ago, not many would have taken a price about this young man, without a silver spoon, getting back on the ladder so quickly.

Even those who hadn't backed Suave Dancer were still exhilarated as they sat there swigging their *vin ordinaire*. What it felt like to have trained him is something we can only guess at. Trainers wait all their lives for a horse like this and never get a sniff

of one. Although he had quite a teacher to learn from in André Fabre, John must have bought some heather off the right gypsy sometime or other.

It isn't just luck, though. This is no one-horse wonder. He's now got a yard which, apart from the presence in it of the new heavyweight champ, is beginning to look a bit like the equivalent of Kronk's gym. Polar Falcon may or may not be the best horse around at six or seven furlongs, but if he isn't he's not far off it. Goofalik, who only just failed to get up in the Prix Rond Point, looks a very high second-division performer.

On Sunday evening the trainer was already thinking about Dear Doctor, who was due off in the Turf Classic at Belmont at about the time he was meeting his, no doubt, fairly proud mother in a restaurant. (No, he's not a mummy's boy, in case that's what you're thinking, and Dear Doctor only ran second, thereby proving that no-one's allowed to have the lot.) There are other good ones too.

Suave Dancer will not, if his trainer has his way – and it seems unlikely that Henri Chalhoub will want to disagree – be going to the Breeders' Cup this year. Hammond thought he'd had to work quite hard for his victory on Sunday's softish ground and when you've got another year to think about, there's no point in asking too much. Besides, European trainers are not, after the 1988 experience, exactly united in admiration of the Churchill Downs turf track, which is too tight for most tastes. And, moreover, we shouldn't let ourselves get carried away by the fact that most newspapers seemed to report the Arc in terms of the defeat of Generous.

Suave Dancer is something terrific in his own right. He's nearly as good as Cash Asmussen says he is. The main thing must be to keep this horse sound and still thinking racing's good fun. We can take it that anything that even hints at jeopardising these objectives is going to be ruled out at once, for J. Hammond still thinks racing's pretty good fun, or at least he seemed to on Sunday night.

He's not the sort of man you grudge victory to. In fact we felt just about as pleased for him as we did for the horse. "Just wait till he starts reading in the papers that he's brilliant," said someone in the press room earlier, in reply to the observation that he makes a very unassuming winner.

Well, it might happen. Plenty of people have suddenly turned pompous and self-important when it's dawned on them that they're actually not nobody any more. I just don't think it's going to happen to this one. Hammond has a sense of humour that's always going to protect him from pomposity. And anyway, the people who suffer this tragic fate probably aren't the sort who'd come across to Camy's for a drink when they've just won the Arc.

8 October 1991

Pleasure and pain of living a vision

Few who love racing fail to cherish the idea of a horse of their own. Here, the author, an actor by profession, movingly records a story that touches the heart

by PHILIP BOWEN

"I GOTTA HORSE!" racegoers at Epsom would hear between the wars as Prince Monolulu proudly showed photographs of his previous successes, and encouraged them to buy a future success of their own.

Well, I had a horse, and I encouraged my friends to participate in my own future success.

My friends' suspicion was fuelled with mystification when they learned that my beast was not a financial investment but 'fun'. Indeed, a more accurate description would be a lot of fun.

I've adored the shape, speed and smell of horses for as long as I can remember. It's been a masochistic relationship on my part, because I'm frightened when I ride and I tend to lose when I bet. By a series of coincidences and chance, however, I ended up with enough money to spend on a 'leg' when I was told that there was a six-year-old gelding in Littleton which was worth a look.

I travelled down via Lambourn, where I picked up my only famous contact in the racing world, a lady who runs an equine psychiatric hospital that is patronised by some of the biggest trainers in Berkshire. She'd agreed to join us for the 'jolly' and give us an evaluation.

When we arrived at the yard we saw that our trainer knew my friend by reputation. The respect he showed her demonstrated that her reputation was high. He wasn't going to be able to blag us while Mary was in the yard. She walked around the horse and looked at his legs and teeth before getting him out of his box to walk, then trot. At last she gave us her verdict. She didn't say he'd win or he'd even run

quickly. She just asked us the price he was going for and said: "That's fair enough and you should have some fun." The deal was done.

We were now part-owners of a racehorse called Tenpercent! There was insurance to pay and a regular standing order to the trainer each month. There was the furious riffling through the yellowing pages of the formbook, since he hadn't run for two years. And there was the choosing of the colours.

As a jumper, he'd be running on dark wintry afternoons. We wanted something light and bright that we could see as the mud flew on the far side. We also wanted something simple in design; no diabolos or armlets for us. The colours would be light blue and yellow, we thought, and after a call to Weatherbys we discovered that yellow and light blue quarters with light blue sleeves and a light blue cap were free and could be ours. We booked them.

Oh! Those long weeks in the autumn when jumping owners look up at the sky and do their rain dances. We were stuck in the tail-end of the hottest and driest year since records began, the ground was rock hard and we couldn't train even on the harrowed, all-weather gallop. Tenpercent could eat but we didn't know whether he could run. His history had been mysteriously romantic; he'd spent the previous season in a field in Ireland as a result of some ownership dispute. This had given him not only an element of the glorious uncertain but also a very fat tummy. It was called 'condition', as I understood, and would be 'worked on' when we had some rain. The vocabulary was beginning to roll off the tongue almost as quickly as the monthly payments.

Eventually we went to see him. The trainer told us that he would be cantering with another horse at about 7.30 one particular morning and we'd get an idea of his worth. I travelled to Winchester the day before to stay with one of the co-owners. I was already thinking of him winning his very first novices' hurdle but by long past midnight and well into a bottle of brandy we were talking in terms of the Queen Mother Chase at Cheltenham in 1991.

Dawn carried its own retribution for the stupidity of the night before. If I drank brandy regularly and to excess I think I'd end up as cranially distorted as an African tribeswoman, my skull elongated with the constant pressure of the bands of iron that always seemed to be strapped around my head the following morning.

This pressure seems to have a rather surprising effect on the process of normal thought. Let me give you an example. On arrival at the yard we went straight to Tenpercent's box. Now I was told later that he was standing there and that he even looked at us but I couldn't see him. I wandered off to another part of the yard and found some activity. I could see the trainer standing behind a horse whose head was being held by Tenpercent's girl.

Most people, when they don't know much about a particular subject, keep their mouths shut; I tend to open mine wider. "Hey!" I said. "He's looking great!"

The trainer pulled his arm out from the animal's bum, shook the thermometer that he was holding, and said: "Mr Bowen, I sold you a six-year-old gelding. This is a two-year-old filly. You're exactly the kind of owner I'm looking for."

The lass holding the bridle sniggered. I felt a complete prat.

I got back to Tenpercent's box seeing quite clearly. Unfortunately he was as tubby as ever and looking just as hungry. He was led out into the yard and I was put into the back of a Land Rover.

Soon, standing in a field of cabbages, our breath was clearly visible in the pale grey light. This, I thought, is being an owner.

"Your fellow is galloping with Bold Spirit," the trainer said. I was pretty confident that he was talking about another horse rather than the manner in which he was galloping but, after my contribution to the annals of the stable's folklore only half an hour before, I wasn't going to ask.

"They'll come steadily up the hill and then yours should accelerate away from the other." We were going to be given a show, the cynical side of me thought.

"Here they come." Our binoculars went up.

"This is where yours will go on," said the trainer. We gripped our glasses tightly. I was in the stands at the Festival meeting.

I'd mistaken our horse once already that morning and maybe I was mistaking him again but, no, as Bold Spirit quickened away from our chap I lowered my glasses to see the trainer's jaw tighten.

"Well," was all he could say. "He needs a bit more work."

Back at the yard we were given coffee in the kitchen and the disappointment of the morning gallop slipped away as the dreams started to be rewritten. It would be a definite run before Christmas rather than in a week or two; there was, after all, a lot to work on but his heart was good and he'd eventually make a chaser.

Another month of training fees and then the moment that all owners wait for: he was entered up. It was either a two-mile race at Worcester or a two-and-a-half-mile novices' hurdle at Bangor. Worcester was dispensed with because of the going so everything was set for Bangor on the Friday.

Friday morning was beautiful. We were off to see our horse run. But round about Birmingham the fog came down.

"It's the industrial Midlands," we said. "Just wait till we get further north; it'll be clear then." We got

further north and it didn't. We trailed nose-to-tail, but at last, five hours after leaving London, we turned into a field marked Bangor Racecourse and stopped the car. "We're in touch with God," said the attendant. "It'll clear half an hour before the first."

"Owners," we said at the turnstile but it didn't have quite the impact we were expecting. There was no query, just a dull resignation and, if anything, a relief from the man at the gate that he could get rid of another two pieces of useless cardboard.

Once on to the course it was clear that even the basic requirement that you should be able to see the next hurdle as you jump the one before would not be satisfied. Racing would definitely be 'Off'.

It's a long drive from Bangor in the fog and the dark. We'd gone round to the stables to look at our baby before setting off for home and he'd looked great. "Jumping out of his skin," the lass had said.

"But is he getting away from his hurdles?"

"Oh yes."

There was another month's training fees, followed by another two entries, this time Warwick and Fakenham. It had to be Fakenham, really. The principle was rapidly becoming clear: that the more difficult of any two options was the one we'd choose.

☐ *Continued overleaf*

☐ *Continued from previous page*
Why travel a hundred miles when you can travel two hundred? So, off we went again, checking the weather reports for fog, but so confident, not just of racing but of success, that we stayed with friends the night before the race and talked of winning throughout the evening meal. By midnight the only thing in doubt was by how many lengths.

Once more the day started bright and we phoned bookmakers, taking a little 20-1. Our idea was to back small amounts with several bookies but by 10 o'clock we had the disturbing feeling that the price was slipping. By quarter past it seemed a major gamble was going on and it was on our horse. We hadn't got all we wanted and someone was taking our price. It fell rapidly until a call to a bookmaker in Dublin told us that Tenpercent stood at 10-1! Who was getting on and how had the information, tenuous as we knew it to be, got out?

In the parade ring we met the jockey. He who was wearing our silks! They did what we hoped and shone in the winter afternoon light. Our trainer introduced us and then we heard him being instructed. "He'll make the pace; we've got a bit each way on him but don't be too hard on him. Let him run his own race."

We saw them out of the paddock and ran to the rail to see Tenpercent cantering to the start. His head held low, he acted perfectly on the ground. It had been raining all night but Fakenham drains well and there was no doubt that conditions were ideal for him.

Into the ring to check the price. The thrill of pride as punters quite unknown and not a few of them, too, could be heard saying "Tenpercent". He was steady on tens but it was still too short for any further involvement.

We found the little Owners and Trainers box. It sounds quite grand but is only a cordoned-off area in the Members stand. "They're over on the far side," said someone and I trained my glasses on the field.

"They're under orders!"

That was it. This was the moment that throughout 30 years of backing horses I'd been waiting for.

"And they're off!"

He was lying in second place as they came to the first. How would he jump? I only had the stable lass's word for it that he was a natural. He came up to the hurdle and sailed over like a bird. His front legs neatly together, he landed galloping.

So fast did he jump that he took the lead, the jockey's hands well down and not moving. Two more and they came up to the stands for the first time. He was not just running his own race. He was determining the pace of the whole field. He was doing what he and a hundred thousand horses before him had been bred to do; he was doing something that was in his blood; he was galloping and he was racing.

Down the back straight and he was still carrying them along. With a beautiful action, he cleared his hurdles while the others tried to keep with him. Twelve lengths covered the field but I could only look at one horse: our horse; my horse; me.

Round the top bend they swung again and back up towards the stand with just a circuit to go.

The few friends who knew he was running were in betting shops around the country watching the race on television screens. Perhaps they'd backed a little each way; they weren't the ones who'd taken our price in the early morning. We'd done that ourselves by backing a horse from a gambling stable. They too were willing that horse to jump and willing him to win.

They saw him leading the field along and they would probably have seen him being overtaken on the final bend. What they didn't see, because the television cameras stayed with the winner, was Tenpercent's fall.

It happened at the last. He was tired and reverted to jumping like a chaser rather than a hurdler. He took off and leapt high into the air, coming down vertically on his neck.

The vet said later that the moment he saw the fall he rang for the knacker's van. It's seldom a horse survives a fall like that. We ran from the stands. I could hear someone shout "Owner" as I pressed through the gate on to the course.

We got the saddle off as fast as we could and the trainer began slapping his mouth to make him breathe again but this huge, gorgeous, noble beast lay in the mud, his eyes still open and bright, those powerful legs twitching but all life gone. As we stood helplessly, watching him, the eyes gradually clouded. The jockey got up from the ground, our proud blue and yellow colours now torn and muddy, while the racecourse's groundstaff pegged out a green tarpaulin around Tenpercent's body.

I'd owned him for a few months and only seen him four times. I felt a bond of ridiculous closeness. The rest of the afternoon passed in a daze. We were invited into the stewards' private room where a gentleman told me that he'd lost a son on the course. He then added: "Tames lions, racing does, you know. Tames lions."

"I gotta a horse!" said Prince Monolulu. "I gotta a horse!"

Well, I've got a horse. He's a six-year-old gelding and his photograph is on my desk. He'll never be a seven-year-old nor will he ever run again but whenever I go racing there'll always be a suspicion of that wonderful might-have-been.

10 February 1990

Champions who made a decade memorable

Towards the end of 1989, the year Desert Orchid won the Gold Cup, Racing Post asked its readers to nominate the Flat and jumps horse of the decade. Nominations flooded in, but when the arguing stopped and the votes were counted there was no doubt about it: Dancing Brave and Desert Orchid were well ahead of any other horses nominated. Two readers, one for each category, sent in outstanding letters that were printed in the paper. They are republished on the following pages

Top picture: Desert Orchid, jumps horse of the decade, with owner Richard Burridge and members of his adoring fan club.

Bottom picture: Dancing Brave, Flat horse of the decade, who secured his place in the public's affection by the style of his Arc victory.

At Ascot the fans saluted the Brave

In the 1986 King George VI and Queen Elizabeth Stakes, Dancing Brave shone like a jewel in the sun and gained revenge on the horse that beat him in the Derby

by GEORGE ENNOR

THIS time there is absolutely no room for argument. Dancing Brave won the King George VI and Queen Elizabeth Diamond Stakes at Ascot on Saturday in the style of an outstanding colt.

Ridden by Pat Eddery, he effectively ridiculed the theory he lacks stamina by covering the mile and a half in 2min 29.49 sec, and on what developed into a glorious summer's day he gained handsome revenge on his Derby conqueror Shahrastani.

It may seem cruel to say it, but if you had gone to Ascot to decide between Dancing Brave and Shahrastani there was only one conclusion to be reached. Dancing Brave looked magnificent and totally relaxed. Shahrastani, while obviously superbly fit, seemed edgy and was beginning to sweat up as the jockeys came in. From the moment the stalls opened, the race was going to be a test of stamina, as Boldden and Vouchsafe went hammer and tongs in front. By Swinley Bottom they must have been 10 lengths clear of Dihistan, Shardari and Shahrastani. Then came Petoski, for whom the leaders were making it, Supreme Leader and Dancing Brave.

As the field closed up on the new leader Dihistan with half a mile to go, Dancing Brave was right with the pack. And here came the moment which could have made the vital difference to the race, but in the end served only to illustrate the pace the winner possesses.

As Boldden and Vouchsafe dropped back, Eddery had to negotiate them and avoid being chopped off by Petoski, as last year's winner went in pursuit of Shahrastani. For two or three strides Dancing Brave looked like having nowhere to go and Eddery was

sitting down in the saddle as if having to ride a flat-out finish. But almost as soon as the problem arose, it disappeared.

Inside the last two furlongs Shardari, on whom Steve Cauthen was wearing the old Aga's colours, went for home.

At this point Shahrastani was clearly beaten, but Dancing Brave quite as clearly was not. As Eddery switched him off the rails towards the centre of the course, past the fading Petoski, the Guineas winner's supporters began to give full vent to their feelings. Dancing Brave was travelling so fast that he hit the front before the final furlong — a bit too soon, according to Eddery. As he went past Shardari, Dancing Brave went over to his right, back towards the rails, and Eddery had his whip out for more than just decorative purposes. Shardari, switched to the outside, ran on most courageously and Eddery had to drive Dancing Brave to make sure. At the line there was three-quarters of a length between them, with Triptych running on to take third place, four lengths away. It was then five to Shahrastani, two to Dihistan, who ran really well for a 100-1 shot, and another length and a half to the never-dangerous Petoski.

28 July 1986

Then he became king of Europe

LATER in the year Dancing Brave put the icing on the cake before an excited crowd of 31,000 at Longchamp. He won the Prix de l'Arc de Triomphe and, reported the Racing Post's Desmond Stoneham, evoked memories of the mighty Mill Reef in 1971. A headline proclaimed him as the 'magnificent flying machine'.

Dancing Brave outclassed his 14 rivals in a course record time to win one of the greatest races ever seen for the French prize. At the post the superb English-trained colt had a length and a half to spare over the French ace Bering, while Triptych made late progress to take third position from a trio of Aga Khan-owned horses in Shahrastani, Shardari and Darara. With Dihistan unable to play his intended pacemaking role for the Aga Khan, Baby Turk led the field until the straight, where he was attended by Nemain and Acatenango.

All three came under pressure two furlongs out, where the race warmed up with Shahrastani and Shardari among the leaders, and Bering beginning his run on the outside hotly pursued by Dancing Brave.

French voices began to roar at the furlong marker as Bering hit the front. But at the same moment Dancing Brave slipped into overdrive, and flew the last 100 yards. Dancing Brave and Pat Eddery covered the 12 furlongs in 2min 27.7sec, knocking 0.3sec off the race record set by Eddery and Detroit in 1980.

Eddery was winning his second consecutive Arc, but this time he did not need the intervention of the stewards, who the previous year awarded the race to Dancing Brave's owner Khalid Abdullah with Rainbow Quest on the disqualification of Sagace. Bering ran a perfect race but was simply beaten by a phenomenon, though things might have been different if the ground had been soft instead of firm.

Triptych ran her usual game race, making ground on the inside to snatch third place off Shahrastani near the line.

6 October 1986

When Dancing Brave won the Prix de l'Arc de Triomphe he outclassed his rivals and evoked memories of the mighty Mill Reef.

Dreams of Gold Cup splendour come true

Up to the last moment, it was not certain that Desert Orchid would run in the 1989 Gold Cup. Despite atrocious conditions he did run and history was made

by PAUL HAYWARD

HE did it. Desert Orchid did it. Amid tumultuous scenes at Cheltenham yesterday the nation's favourite horse landed the £100,000 Tote Gold Cup with a final flourish that will live on in legend.

But once again pure glory and pain were potently mixed. The race, which will have set the statue-makers to work on one of the great steeplechasers, also claimed the life of Fulke Walwyn's Ten Plus, who broke a leg and had to be put down.

The euphoria that greeted Desert Orchid was reminiscent of Dawn Run's reception here three years ago. David Elsworth pushed his way through the crowds to the winner's enclosure in a flood of tears and spent at least a minute and a half trying to persuade the policeman on the gate that he was the winning trainer.

The race reached its climax where it should – at the very end. Simon Sherwood, who rode a craftsman's race, had given his mount a break on the second circuit but came with a driving, gripping run again on ground that was testing the very spirit.

"He absolutely hated this going but still acted on it," said Sherwood. "He's two stones better on good ground. Yahoo jumped the last in front, but I'd given him a breather and knew I could get back at him. Dessie just kept digging and digging. Yahoo was still going well but I heard the roar of the crowd and just put my head down. I put my head down and kept kicking."

At the line the distance between the winner and Yahoo was just a length and a half, with last year's winner Charter Party eight lengths back in third. Desert Orchid had never won in five attempts at

---

JUMPS: THE WINNING LETTER
Desert Orchid: A symbol for his sport

EVERY so often, a sport will throw up a character who transcends the game itself and takes it to a wider audience. Moreover, he will have charisma, style and, in this modern day, he will probably have a fan club.

Yes, Desert Orchid has to be 'The Greatest' of the past decade. His deeds, over distances from two miles to three miles five furlongs, mark him out as our current champion. However, even Dessie's remarkable racing record is overshadowed by his incredible popularity and his personal ambassadorship for the sport of jump racing.

By the same token, in the wide context of 'Horse of the 1980s', questions as to whether Desert Orchid could have coped with the likes of Burrough Hill Lad and Dawn Run, or whether See You Then and Sea Pigeon had more class, are largely academic.

Desert Orchid has caught the public's imagination; he has put steeplechasing back on the map; he it is whom people flock to see perform heroic deeds at his beloved Sandown Park, Kempton Park, and (at long last) Cheltenham.

Desert Orchid is Jump Horse of the Decade. Like Coe, Maradona and Ballesteros, Dessie is the symbol for his sport in the 1980s.

Peter Hicks
Otham
Kent

Cheltenham and owner Richard Burridge was in a pessimistic mood when he arrived at the track after heavy snow and sleet had fallen in the morning. Burridge, however, played down rumours that he had implored his trainer to withdraw the horse.

"Absolutely not," he said. "When I got here I was worried because the ground was appalling, but I spoke to David and he said we would win. This horse produces a great emotional response in the public. He's brilliant."

Elsworth was surrounded by a swarm of bodies in the winner's enclosure and found words, so redundant after such a spectacle, hard to come by. "The ground didn't worry me," he said. "Next year, anything could have happened. I told Richard it would be all right."

The losers and the fallen were left in the mud, but this was the day all of racing wanted. The Gold Cup has a history whole nations would be envious of, but it may be decades before we see such a thing again.

17 March 1989

The hero, Desert Orchid, returns in triumph with owner Richard Burridge and lass Janice Coyle.

The day of the Wonder Horse

When Arazi won the Breeders' Cup Juvenile at Churchill Downs, the manner of the victory left Americans speechless and created a sense of pride among Europeans

by TIM RICHARDS

IT had to be seen to be believed.

It wasn't so much that Arazi overcame the disadvantages of a bad draw and a strange racing surface to demolish the best America could offer in the Breeders' Cup Juvenile. It was that he did it all with such contemptuous ease and blinding brilliance.

What happened at Churchill Downs on Saturday will live long in the memory of racing people around the globe. Now the François Boutin-trained colt is set to scoop honours galore after climaxing an historic day for European-trained horses in the Breeders' Cup.

Sheikh Albadou silenced the crowd, if not his trainer Alex Scott, by galloping away with the first race, the Sprint, and Miss Alleged, trained by Pascal Bary, followed up in the Turf as European-trained horses produced a further four prize-earning placings on the $10 million seven-race card.

The final total, accumulated in a pulsating period that lasted a little over three hours but will have much longer-term repercussions, was $2,436,000 or £1.34 million.

But Arazi stood out like a beacon of brilliance, cruising through the $1 million Juvenile on dirt for a spectacular success. Having been second last early on, Arazi who was declared for Butazolidin, cut through his rivals for a victory that was as easy as it was breath-taking. Having made up all of 15 lengths, he was still cantering on the bridle as he loomed upsides market rival Bertrando on the turn for home.

Shooting clear in tremendous style, he won officially by five lengths – a winning distance that could have been doubled if Pat Valenzuela wanted.

Now Arazi, named after an Arizona checkpoint in joint-owner Allen Paulson's record-breaking round-the-world jet flight three years ago, is poised to become:

● America's Horse of the Year.

● The first horse to top America's Experimental Handicap and the International Classification.

●The highest-rated two-year-old since the Classification began for this age group in 1978.

Horse of the Year in the States is a coveted prize the significance of which cannot be matched or perhaps even appreciated in Britain, and Arazi could follow All Along as only the second European-trained runner to receive this accolade. And Paulson, once Arazi's sole owner but now sharing the honour with Sheikh Mohammed, cannot see why the son of Blushing Groom shouldn't pick up the title.

"I don't know why he wouldn't be Horse of the Year. Does anyone else know?" he asked.

No-one could come up with an immediate answer. Only time, and the Eclipse Awards early next year, will tell. Before then, though, further proof of Arazi's star status, will be available.

It is only a question now of how far clear he will be of his rivals in the International Classification and unless something extraordinary happens in the United States, he will head the equivalent Experimental Free Handicap.

His ranking in Europe will be settled at a meeting of the Pattern-country handicappers next month. Geoffrey Gibbs, the senior Jockey Club official and responsible for the Juvenile Division, said yesterday: "Arazi breaks new territory"

The suggestion must be that he will be ranked above Tromos, who at 128 in 1978, the first year of the International Classification, is the highest-rated two-year-old on record.

Gibbs added: "It's the best performance I've ever seen from a two-year-old and one of the most amazing performances I've seen in 28 years as a handicapper.

"The totally exceptional speed he showed was staggering. He passed Bertrando on a long rein with his jockey looking at the other horse. Bertrando has to be the next best horse in the race on what he had done previously, and yet Arazi has laughed at him."

Not many Americans were laughing on Saturday; they were wondering what sort of a horse they may have to take on in next year's Kentucky Derby back at Churchill Downs, which has been put even more firmly on the agenda.

Paulson, who also won the Mile with Opening Verse, remarked: "I said if he ran well here, I'd want him to go for the Kentucky Derby; well he did!"

The shattering of the Arazi dream
After all the adulation, not to mention hype, Arazi proved a disappointment when he went back to Churchill Downs for the Kentucky Derby the following year. For one fleeting moment at the top of the back straight it looked as if the flying chestnut would pull off the miracle of November once more in May, but he folded tamely to finish eighth – Valenzuela's face says it all.

If all goes well over the winter, Arazi, who will eventually stand at Dalham Hall Stud at Newmarket, will soon be finding his way to race across the Atlantic more often. And so too will more and more European horses, as owners and trainers digest the implications of wins by Arazi and Sheikh Albadou on the dirt and Miss Alleged on Turf.

Saturday will be remembered as Arazi's day. But in terms of European raids on top US races, it could rank as the day that turned the stream into a flood.

4 November 1991

Arazi put up a breath-taking display under Pat Valenzuela to demolish the opposition in the Breeders' Cup Juvenile in November 1991.

A young man joins the Epsom pantheon

Before the 1992 Derby the prime question was whether Lester Piggott could ride the winner for the tenth time. The dream proved impossible but another came to life

by TIM RICHARDS

DR DEVIOUS, the gift-horse who romped to Epsom glory yesterday, will go down in the history books as the Derby winner who nearly got away – twice. It was a dream come true for the popular Ulster-born rider and for the winner's talented trainer, Peter Chapple-Hyam, who is only 29.

There were ecstatic scenes as John Reid rode Dr Devious back to unsaddle, punching the air with his right fist after emphatically beating St Jovite and Silver Wisp by two lengths and a short head. But it could all have been so very different. Chapple-Hyam, knowing how close he came to losing the horse, couldn't believe his luck yesterday.

Last summer, during Glorious Goodwood, Robert Sangster, whose 13-2 favourite Rodrigo de Triano finished only ninth behind his stable companion yesterday, sold Dr Devious to Italian owner Luciano Gaucci. When the deal was clinched, it was expected that Dr Devious would be moved to Italy. But he stayed with Chapple-Hyam to win the Dewhurst Stakes at Newmarket.

This spring, Jenny Craig bought the horse for her husband, Sidney, as a 60th birthday present. The plan was to try to win the Kentucky Derby with Dr Devious and then keep him in the US. Amazingly, Chapple-Hyam again contrived to hang on to the horse. But yesterday he admitted he feared the worst when he dispatched Dr Devious to Kentucky.

"I patted him as he went into the box, convinced that it would be the last time I would see him. I really thought it was goodbye," he said. "I have been very lucky and I have Ron McAnally to thank for Dr Devious coming back to me after the

The day the Lester dream collapsed

As Lester Piggott went to the Derby start on Rodrigo de Triano, he received the kind of reaction that left everyone wondering what would happen if he went and won. The question sadly remained unanswered. The worst fears of his supporters and the cold opinions of cynical pros alike were bluntly confirmed when the 56-year-old dismounted from ninth-placed Rodrigo de Triano. "Didn't handle it, didn't stay," muttered Lester in his usual fashion. The dream was over.

Kentucky Derby. It was after he had talked to Mr and Mrs Craig in the aftermath of Dr Devious's defeat that Ron suggested the horse should come back. And here we are."

California-based McAnally, who trains some 20 horses for the Craigs, was unhappy with Dr Devious after the Kentucky Derby. But Chapple-Hyam reported that the horse came back to him in good nick. "He had a long box drive from Louisville to New York and a night sleeping with gorillas in Frankfurt on his German stop-over, before arriving back here.

"But he's a tough horse. He lost five kilos in the States and came back dry in his skin and scratched down his throat. We gave him 10 days off and then started to build him up for Epsom. He is in the Irish Derby, the Eclipse Stakes . . . everything."

Craig, on his first visit to England from Del Mar, California, admitted that the $2.5 million present had finally become a "capital gain". For Reid, 36, who

had previously won the Prix de l'Arc de Triomphe on Tony Bin and the King George VI and Queen Elizabeth Stakes on Ile de Bourbon, this was the climax of a career of hard graft and dedication. One of the most articulate members of the jockeys' room, Reid said: "As we passed the post I threw my fist in the air and shouted: 'You beauty! I can't believe it.' I very nearly stayed in Hong Kong two years ago and, despite the temptation, I decided to come home. Simply, it has always been my ambition to win the Derby and I couldn't achieve it over there.

"Dr Devious is the best horse I have ridden – in a different league to Tony Bin. He popped out of the stalls quick and took a strong hold. I eased him back and then he settled. The pace was not that strong and I had a lovely position at Tattenham Corner. When Dr Devious hit the straight it was just a matter of when to go.

"I knew it was all down to him and me. I asked him at the two-furlong marker and away he went."

The first Sidney Craig heard of Dr Devious was at his 60th birthday party, which was held on 7 March in Palm Springs – two weeks early. His wife Jenny, who heads a business of 700 diet clinics across America, had invited 120 guests and held up entertainer Jack Jones for half an hour as she showed the film of the Dewhurst Stakes. "I announced," she said, "that I had bought Sidney a horse that would win the Kentucky Derby for him."

Yesterday, her husband added: "Nothing will beat this dream. Perhaps we will race him in the States, at the Breeders' Cup on turf. But first, I shall discuss it with Peter Chapple-Hyam – he's my new hero."

4 June 1992

Dr Devious has won the 1992 Derby and the colt's trainer, Peter Chapple-Hyam, steps forward to greet the winner and his jockey, John Reid.

INDEX

The pictures that introduce this book

Front endpaper *Alan Munro punches the air as Generous passes the winning post five lengths clear of his nearest rival in the 1991 Derby.*

Frontispiece *When Salsabil won the 1,000 Guineas in 1990, such was Willie Carson's delight he could not resist a playful tug of the triumphant filly's ears.*

Title spread *In the winter of 1989-90 a new concept was brought to British racing with the arrival of all-weather competition at Lingfield, pictured here, and Southwell.*

Back endpaper *Brigadier Gerard, who died in 1989, rarely missed a day's exercise after his retirement in 1972. The legend is captured in a memorable early-morning shot.*

PICTURE, ILLUSTRATION AND GRAPHICS CREDITS

Front endpaper
Edward Whitaker

Frontispiece
Mark Cranham

Title spread Trevor Jones

6 Gerry Cranham

8-9 Chris Smith

10-11 Dan Abraham

13 Richard Willson

14 Gerry Cranham

17 George Selwyn

18 George Selwyn

20 Press Association [Sir Gordon Richards], Tony Edenden [Peter Scudamore]

22-23 Trevor Jones

25 Trevor Jones

26 Malky McCormick

29 Gerry Cranham

30-31 Alec Russell

37 Manni Mason's Pictures

41 Richard Willson

45 Trevor Jones

46 Sport & General

49 Chris Smith

52-53 Central Press Photos

54 Malky McCormick

56-57 Laurie Morton

58-59 Ed Byrne

61 Richard Willson

64 The Drummer Boy

69 Sport & General

70 Lesley Sampson

72 Roger Coleman

76 W. W. Rouch & Co

78-79 Chris Smith

81 Malky McCormick

82-85 Richard Cole

88-89 Stephen Lee

91 Gerry Cranham

94-95 Edward Whitaker

97 Richard Willson

100-101 Malky McCormick

102 Stephen Johnson

104-105 Mark Cranham

106-107 Phil Green

109 Gerry Cranham

110 Neil Randon

112 Tony Duffy, ALLSPORT

113 Ed Byrne

114-115 Neil Randon

117 Phil Green

118-119 Gerry Cranham

121 Gerry Cranham

122-123 Sue Montgomery

124-125 Gerry Cranham

126 Edward Whitaker

128-129 Ed Byrne

130-131 Topham

132-133 Gerry Cranham

134-135 Chris Smith

136-137 Marc Hill, Devon & Exeter Press Service

138 Marc Hill, Devon & Exeter Press Service

140 Richard Willson

143 Stuart D. Franklin, Associated Sports Photography

144-145 Sport & General

147 Neil Randon

150-151 Trevor Jones

152-153 Alec Russell

154 Alec Russell

155 Photo: Press Association; Graphic: Neil Randon

156-157 Ed Byrne

158 Gerry Cranham

159 Edward Whitaker

162-163 Neil Randon

164-165 Edward Whitaker

166-167 Edward Whitaker

168 Gerry Cranham

171 John Thirsk

173 Edward Whitaker (top); Gerry Cranham

175 Gerry Cranham

177 Trevor Jones

178-179 Edward Whitaker

180 Caroline Norris

181 Dan Abraham

Back endpaper
Gerry Cranham

TEXT CREDIT

Dudley Doust's account of Bonanza Boy's Racing Post Chase win, starting on page 146, first appeared as a chapter in his book, 221 Peter Scudamore's Record Season, published by Hodder and Stoughton